Pocket PC For Dum...
2nd Edition

C000008239

Troubleshooting Your Pocket PC's Internet Connection

Problem	Probable Solution
Digital Phone Card won't dial	Make certain the "Wait for dial tone" option is not selected
Digital Phone Card won't connect	Be sure your cell phone has a digital signal
Pocket PC won't dial phone number	Make certain the dialing pattern for local numbers includes the letter *G*
Long distance calls won't connect	Check that the long distance dialing pattern is set to "1FG"
Pocket PC reports the connection is in use	Remove your Pocket PC from the synchronization cradle before attempting to use your Internet connection

Using Your Pocket PC's Stylus

Stylus Action	Result
Tap	Opens the item that was tapped
Tap-and-hold	Selects the item and opens a context menu
Drag	Selects the items you dragged across

Pocket PC Quick Tips

To Do . . .	Do This . . .
Use your Pocket PC as an alarm clock	Tap the date on the Today screen and then tap the Alarms tab
Turn off the speaker	Tap the Speaker icon in the title bar of the Today screen and select Off
Change the input option	While in an application tap the up arrow at the lower-right corner of the Pocket PC's screen and make your selection
Switch to another open application	Tap the Start button and choose the icon in the row above the Start menu
Listen to music in stereo	Plug the earphones into the earphone jack
Choose a different Today screen	Tap the Start button, choose Settings, choose Today, select the theme you want, and then tap OK

For Dummies: Bestselling Book Series for Beginners

Pocket PC For Dummies, 2nd Edition

Personalizing Your Pocket PC

Option	Settings Tab	What It Does
About	System	Enables you to specify a unique name for your Pocket PC
AvantGo Connect	Connections	Configures AvantGo channels
Beam	Connections	Controls your infrared port settings
Buttons	Personal	Sets up the actions performed by the front panel buttons
Clock	System	Sets time zones and alarms
Connections	Connections	Configures your Internet and network connections
Front Light (may be Backlight on some systems)	System	Sets the power-saving feature of screen light
Input	Personal	Configures the onscreen keyboard and other input options
Memory	System	Enables you to adjust memory allocation and stop running programs
Menus	Personal	Enables you to control the Start menu
Network Adapters	Connections	Allows configuration of network cards
Owner Information	Personal	Stores your contact information
Password	Personal	Configures your Pocket PC to use a password for access
Power	System	Adjusts power-conservation settings
Regional Settings	System	Sets all of the international settings such as currency, number formats, and time displays
Remove Programs	System	Enables you to free memory by removing programs you've installed
Screen	System	Corrects input errors caused by misalignment of the touch screen
Sounds & Notifications	Personal	Sets up the sounds made by your Pocket PC to signal actions or reminders
Today	Personal	Configures the Today screen

For Dummies: Bestselling Book Series for Beginners

Pocket PC
FOR
DUMMIES®
2ND EDITION

by Brian Underdahl

Wiley Publishing, Inc.

Best-Selling Books • Digital Downloads • e-Books • Answer Networks • e-Newsletters • Branded Web Sites • e-Learning

Pocket PC For Dummies; 2nd Edition

Copyright © 2002 by Wiley Publishing, Inc., Indianapolis, Indiana

Published by Wiley Publishing, Inc., Indianapolis, Indiana

Published simultaneously in Canada

For general information on our other products and services or to obtain technical support please contact our Customer Care Department within the U.S. at 800-762-2974, outside the U.S. at 317-572-3993 or fax 317-572-4002.

Wiley also publishes its books in a variety of electronic formats. Some content that appears in print may not be available in electronic books.

Library of Congress Control No.: 2002103291

ISBN: 076451640X

Printed in the United States of America

10 9 8 7 6 5 4 3 2 1

2O/QX/QW/QS/IN

Wiley Publishing, Inc. is a trademark of Wiley Publishing, Inc.

About the Author

Brian Underdahl is the best-selling author of over 60 books, numerous magazine articles, and dozens of Web pieces. He has appeared on a number of TV shows as an expert on computing and has taught many different computer courses.

Brian loves to play with the newest gadgets, and he gets a lot of enjoyment out of making computers easier to understand and use for people who don't have the time to wade through all the gory details on their own. When he isn't at the keyboard typing, you'll often find Brian preparing a gourmet meal at his home in the mountains above Reno, Nevada. His wife enjoys that part, too.

Dedication

This book is dedicated to the dreamers who keep coming up with neat toys for me to play with. I hope you never run out of interesting ideas.

Author's Acknowledgments

This book owes its existence to so many different people that it is hard to know just where to begin, but I'll try anyway. I'd like to offer my thanks to the following:

Tiffany Franklin and Andy Cummings at Wiley for giving me the chance to do this book.

Freelance Production Editor Colleen Esterline for making certain the book was up to the high standards you expect from Wiley's books. John Tidwell and Robin Kalvan for their excellent technical review.

Angela Child, James Oyang, Cheryl Balbach, Alison Jung, Cherie Britt, Pat Pekary, John Psuik, Henry Y, Aaron Roth, Alison Merifield, Julie Likman, Jennifer Weland, Christine Fullerton, Christophe Narpinian, Christopher Chennault, Dawn Benton, Dianne Escude, Joanne Macdonald, Eddy Hahn, Jamil Moledina, Jason Patterson, Jennifer Ryan, Marie Labrie, Jeff Wheeler, Michael Hess, Michael D. Flom, Mike Wong, Morreale Agostino, Jaja Lin, Nicole Pham, Patrick Minotti, Kelly Poffenberger, Richie Pacheco, Roxanne Pascente, Samir Saxena, Sarah Znerold, Tim Field, Tomas Gerborg, and the dozens of other people whose names I may have misplaced.

Publisher's Acknowledgments

We're proud of this book; please send us your comments through our Online Registration Form located at www.dummies.com.

Some of the people who helped bring this book to market include the following:

Acquisitions, Editorial, and Media Development

Project Editor: Colleen Williams Esterline

(Previous Edition: Andrea C. Boucher)

Acquisitions Editor: Tiffany Franklin

Technical Editors: John Tidwell, Robin Kalvan

Editorial Manager: Constance Carlisle

Media Development Supervisor: Richard Graves

Editorial Assistant: Amanda Foxworth

Production

Project Coordinator: Jennifer Bingham

Layout and Graphics: Beth Brooks, Joyce Haughey, LeAndra Johnson, Stephanie D. Jumper, Barry Offringa, Heather Pope, Laurie Petrone, Betty Schulte, Julie Trippetti, Jeremey Unger

Proofreader: Laura Albert, John Greenough, Andy Hollandbeck, Carl Pierce

Indexer: TECHBOOKS Production Services

General and Administrative

Wiley Publishing Technology Publishing Group: Richard Swadley, Vice President and Executive Group Publisher; Bob Ipsen, Vice President and Group Publisher; Joseph Wikert, Vice President and Publisher; Barry Pruett, Vice President and Publisher; Mary Bednarek, Editorial Director; Mary C. Corder, Editorial Director; Andy Cummings, Editorial Director

Wiley Publishing Manufacturing: Ivor Parker, Vice President, Manufacturing

Wiley Publishing Marketing: John Helmus, Assistant Vice President, Director of Marketing

Wiley Publishing Production for Branded Press: Debbie Stailey, Production Director

Wiley Publishing Sales: Michael Violano, Vice President, International Sales and Sub Rights

Table of Contents

Introduction

*W*ho would have thought that so much computing power could fit into a package that easily fits into your pocket? The Pocket PC is an extremely capable and easy-to-use computer that is, quite honestly, amazing. In a package that weighs just a few ounces, you've got computing power that rivals the huge filing cabinet–sized systems of a decade ago.

The Pocket PC itself may be relatively new, but that wonderful little package you hold in your hand is the result of years of evolutionary progress. Along the way there have been a number of interesting developments, and your Pocket PC has benefited from what has been learned along the way.

In writing this book I've discovered hundreds of neat and fun ways to make use of a Pocket PC. In reading this book I hope you'll get lots of enjoyment and see just how much you really can do with your Pocket PC!

About This Book

Pocket PC For Dummies, 2nd Edition, is your road map to using your Pocket PC. This is a hands-on guide that uses real-world examples to show you just what you need to know about Pocket PCs and why you want to know it. You won't find a lot of hype or jargon. You will find useful information presented clearly and concisely.

Pocket PC For Dummies, 2nd Edition, is a reference that you can use according to your own style. If you are already somewhat familiar with your Pocket PC, you can skip around to find out about things you are a little unsure of. If you are new to Pocket PCs, you may want to read the entire book. Either way, you are bound to find out lots of little things — and some very important and useful ones.

Finally, *Pocket PC For Dummies,* 2nd Edition, is about the new Pocket PC 2002 systems. It has been fully updated to cover the new ways of doing things on the Pocket PC 2002 units, and you will find all sorts of new products covered that simply didn't exist a short time ago.

Conventions Used in This Book

We've used a few conventions in this book to make it easier for you to spot special information. Here are those conventions:

- New terms are identified by using *italic*.

- Web site addresses (URLs) are designated by using a `monospace font`.

- Any command you enter at a command prompt is shown in bold and usually set on a separate line. Set-off text in italic represents a placeholder. For example, the text might read:

  At the command prompt, enter the command in the following format:

  ping *IPaddress*

  where *IPaddress* is the IP address of the remote computer that you want to query.

- Command arrows, which are typeset as ⇨, are used in a list of menus and options. For example, Tools⇨Options means to choose the Tools menu and then choose the Options command.

- Key combinations are shown with a plus sign, such as Ctrl+F2. This means you should hold down the Ctrl key while you press the F2 key.

What You're Not to Read

If you were really looking for a book about how to miniaturize your desktop PC so you can stuff it into your pocket, you can probably skip this entire book. Otherwise you may want to read most of it — especially if you are interested in knowing why and not just how things work on your Pocket PC. Still, I recognize that you may not want to waste any time on technical explanations. If so, you can skip the text next to the Technical Stuff icons. You will probably find a few other things you can skip, too, if you really want to. For example, you can certainly skip the chapter on playing games if you are one of those people who never wants to have any fun.

Foolish Assumptions

It's always a gamble to make assumptions because they can quickly come back to haunt you. In writing this book I made some assumptions about you. This book is for you if:

✔ You have a Pocket PC and want to know how to get the most from it.

✔ You don't have a Pocket PC yet, but you are wondering whether you should get one.

✔ You have a different type of portable computer and are thinking of upgrading to a Pocket PC.

✔ You have one of the original Pocket PC 2000 systems, and you want to learn what is new and improved in the Pocket PC 2002 systems.

✔ You want to give someone other than Palm a chance to survive.

✔ You realize that you really could make use of your commute time if only you had the right tools.

✔ You want to find out whether it really is possible to surf the Internet while you're sitting on the beach.

✔ You'd like to be able to take a trip and still be able to handle your e-mail so you don't come back to find 648 messages in your inbox.

✔ You want to complete your framed set of *The 5th Wave* cartoons.

How This Book Is Organized

Pocket PC For Dummies, 2nd Edition, has seven parts. Each part is self-contained, but you'll also find that the parts are somewhat interconnected. That way you'll see the most useful information without a lot of boring repetition.

Part I: What You Can Do with a Pocket PC

Part I lays the foundation for getting to know your Pocket PC. You discover how your Pocket PC compares with other computers you may have used in the past and you learn how to take advantage of the Pocket PC's unique features. You find out how to use all of the basic features of your Pocket PC quickly and efficiently. Finally, you learn how to interact with your Pocket PC, including how to make use of the great handwriting recognition that's built into your system.

Part II: Personal Organization with Your Pocket PC

Part II shows you how to use your Pocket PC to help keep your personal life in order. You see how your Pocket PC can keep track of your address book, act as your personal note taker, and help you manage your schedule no matter how hectic your life may seem. Finally, you see how to establish a partnership between your Pocket PC and your desktop PC so that you never have to enter the same information twice.

Part III: Putting Your Pocket PC Tools to Work

Part III shows you how to use the powerful yet easy-to-use applications that are built into your Pocket PC, and that set it apart from those other, less powerful palm-sized devices some people use. You'll see how to use Pocket Word to read, edit, and create Word documents. You'll learn how Pocket Excel gives you most of the power of your desktop PC's Excel program right in the palm of your hand. You'll see how Pocket Money makes it easy for you to track your expenses on the go. Finally, you'll see that your Pocket PC is also a handy little calculator.

Part IV: The Pocket PC and the Internet

Part IV describes how you can use your Pocket PC to access the Internet as well as how to connect directly to your network. Here you'll see just how convenient it can be to be able to surf the Internet and handle your e-mail from wherever you happen to be. You'll see how you can make use of the exciting new wireless Internet options as well as the more familiar wired connections. You haven't surfed until you've done it on a Pocket PC miles away from your desktop.

Part V: Multimedia Time

Part V shows you how to have some fun with your Pocket PC. In this part you'll see why a Pocket PC can be a great musical companion, how you can read all sorts of the new electronic books on your Pocket PC, how to make your Pocket PC into the perfect partner for your digital camera, and why your Pocket PC is the ultimate handheld game machine. In addition, you will see that your Pocket PC can even show your favorite TV show and even become a great tool for presentations with the right accessories.

Part VI: Working with Pocket PC Add-ons

Part VI shows you some of the many great ways to add even more utility to your Pocket PC by adding new programs, and how your Pocket PC can be a great traveling companion. You'll see where to find Pocket PC programs, how to install them, and how to make the ones you want fit into the available space. You'll learn the essential information you need to make traveling with your Pocket PC a truly enjoyable experience.

Part VII: The Part of Tens

The Part of Tens provides information on some great ways to enhance your Pocket PC by showing you the best Pocket PC accessories. You'll also find that I include a chapter that shows you some of the best Pocket PC business-related programs. You'll see some great ways to get even more productivity from your Pocket PC.

Icons in This Book

Pocket PC For Dummies, 2nd Edition, includes icons that point out special information. Here are the icons I use and what they mean:

Technical Stuff is information for folks who want to know all the gory details. You can probably skip this stuff unless you really find it interesting.

This icon is the one that will make you seem like a real Pocket PC expert in no time. It highlights special tricks and shortcuts that make using a Pocket PC even easier. Don't miss any of these!

Be careful when you see this icon. It points out an area where you'll want to be extra cautious so that you don't cause yourself problems. It also tells you how to avoid the problems.

The Note icon will steer you to additional, informative information about Pocket PCs.

Where to Go from Here

You are about to find out just how much fun a Pocket PC really can be. As you read through *Pocket PC For Dummies,* 2nd Edition, you'll notice that I've emphasized ways to really enjoy using your Pocket PC. Along the way you'll become more efficient and comfortable using your Pocket PC, but I guarantee you'll have fun doing so. Feel free to jump around, but I'd suggest you start with Chapter 1 for a good introduction to your Pocket PC.

Part I

What You Can Do with a Pocket PC

The 5th Wave   By Rich Tennant

It's an e-mail from my mother. She wants me to know how happy she is for us.

In this part . . .

Y ou will find out how to get started with your Pocket PC. In just three short chapters you will see how to take advantage of the Pocket PC's unique features. You find out basics of using your Pocket PC. Finally, you learn how to input information into your Pocket PC, including how to use handwriting recognition so you can write directly on your screen.

Chapter 1

Getting to Know the Pocket PC

*H*ave you ever noticed that some of the coolest gadgets turn out to be a lot more useful and fun than you first thought they were? That's one of the neat things about Pocket PCs — you may pick one up because it looks like an interesting little toy, but after you start using one, you find out that the thing is really useful. But just because a Pocket PC is useful doesn't mean that it's boring — Pocket PCs can be a lot of fun, too. Before long, you're going to wonder how you ever got along without it!

If you have a Pocket PC, this chapter shows you some of the neat things you can do with it. And if you don't have a Pocket PC yet, this chapter is a good place to start because you get a chance to see just how much fun you can have with something that really can fit into your pocket. If you have an older Pocket PC, this chapter will show you some of the reasons why you may want to upgrade to one of the newer Pocket PC 2002 units. Of course, Chapter 1 is really just a teaser — later chapters show you a whole lot more about really using your Pocket PC.

Understanding Your Pocket PC

So just what is a Pocket PC, anyway? Is it a real PC, and does it really fit into a pocket? Do you look like a propeller-head as soon as you pull it out and start using it? Here are some basics about the Pocket PC to answer some of these types of questions:

- A Pocket PC is a real computer that's shrunk down into a very small package — typically a little less than five inches high, three inches wide, and three-quarters of an inch deep. So, yes, a Pocket PC actually does fit into a pocket as long as the pocket is average-sized.

- Although a Pocket PC fits into a pocket, stuffing one into your jeans pocket isn't a good idea. Pocket PCs are, after all, electronic devices that aren't well suited to being sat upon.

- Pocket PCs are referred to as *palm-sized PCs*. But because someone else already makes similar-sized PDAs using the Palm brand name, Pocket PCs use the name "Pocket PC" to avoid confusion.

- Pocket PCs and Palm PCs use completely different *operating systems* (OS), meaning that they can't run each other's programs. Make certain any programs you buy specifically state that they are designed for the Pocket PC.

- The Pocket PC OS is technically a version of Windows, but this doesn't mean that you can run your favorite Windows-based programs on your Pocket PC. You need special Pocket PC versions of any programs you want to run. But because the Pocket PC OS is based on Windows, at least you won't have to learn new ways of doing things because most of what you know about using Windows-based programs still applies on your Pocket PC. Figure 1-1 shows an example of the Pocket PC screen when Pocket Word has a document open.

Finding some real power in your pocket

Sure, a Pocket PC may seem like a cool toy, but can something that size *really* be a powerful computer? Actually, yes, it not only can but it is. Consider for just a moment how far PCs have advanced in just a few short years. Comparing a Pocket PC to a desktop PC, here are some interesting points:

- The brain inside the Pocket PC (okay, the *processor* for all you technical types) is functionally as powerful as the fastest desktop processors of two to three years ago.

- Your Pocket PC has as much memory as most desktop systems of just a few years ago.

- A Pocket PC is typically able to run for an entire workday on a single charge — all the more amazing when you consider that the battery is inside that pocket-sized package along with the processor, the memory, the display, and all the other components!

- Pocket PCs are ready to use immediately. Touch a button and you can instantly pick up right where you were without waiting for the system to boot up.

- The Pocket PC runs special versions of programs you're already familiar with such as Word and Excel. You can even share your document files between your Pocket PC and your desktop PC.

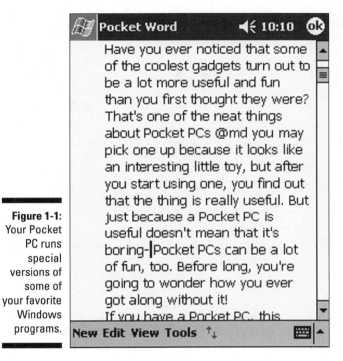

Figure 1-1:
Your Pocket
PC runs
special
versions of
some of
your favorite
Windows
programs.

> ✔ As for the question about whether you look like a propeller-head when you pull out your Pocket PC, I don't really know. But maybe there are worse things in the world than having the coolest toy on the block!

What's New in Pocket PC 2002

As great as the first Pocket PCs were, the new Pocket PC 2002 systems represent a big step forward in putting real computing power into your pocket. Here are the changes in the Pocket PC 2002 compared to the Pocket PC 2000 systems:

> ✔ You have many more choices when buying a Pocket PC 2002. In addition to Casio, Compaq, HP, and Symbol, you can now buy Pocket PC 2002 systems from Audiovox, Intermec, NEC, and Toshiba. With more manufacturers building Pocket PC 2002 systems, you have a better chance of finding exactly the one you want when you go shopping.

> ✔ All Pocket PC 2002 systems have upgradeable flash memory. This means that both the Pocket PC operating system and the built-in applications can be upgraded so there is less chance of your Pocket PC becoming obsolete. In addition, both the Pocket PC operating system and the built-in applications have been updated for the Pocket PC 2002.

- Every Pocket PC 2002 system now uses the same processor — the 206 MHz Intel StrongARM, which only appeared in the Compaq Pocket PC 2000 units. As a result, every Pocket PC 2002 can now run exactly the same version of any Pocket PC application. You no longer have to try to remember which processor you have. (Not all Pocket PC software manufacturers have tumbled to this yet, so if you have a Pocket PC 2002 system and want to buy some new software, simply ask for the Compaq iPAQ version.)

- All of the new Pocket PC 2002 systems now use a *reflective* display that can show 65,536 colors. This is a huge improvement over the displays on the Pocket PC 2000 systems since you can now view pictures in full color, and more importantly, you can now see the display quite well in bright sunlight! If you add a GPS receiver to your Pocket PC, you can easily see the display in your car or when you are out hiking.

- Many of the Pocket PC 2002 systems now have a second memory expansion slot for SD (Secure Digital) memory cards in addition to the standard CF (Compact Flash) expansion slot. This second memory slot opens up a whole new world of possibilities since you can have the advantage of expanded memory capabilities and still use a device such as a GPS receiver, a digital camera attachment, a Bluetooth card, a wireless network adapter, or whatever else you might want to add to the CF expansion slot. For example, by adding a 128MB SD memory card, you can store detailed maps for your GPS receiver that cover a large part of the country or you can store a full-length movie that you can watch during a cross-country flight.

- The Pocket PC 2002 systems also come equipped with more base memory than their Pocket PC 2000 counterparts. In fact, all of the new systems have at least 32MB of memory and 64MB is not uncommon in many of the units.

- You can also personalize your Pocket PC 2002 system as I've done in Figure 1-2. In this case, I've created my own *theme* so that my system shows a photo in the background. I'll show you how to use themes in Chapter 2.

One problem you may encounter is deciding which Pocket PC 2002 system is the right one for you. Since all of the systems are now so similar, it's a lot harder making that choice. Now your choice is more likely to come down to some of the extras that a particular model offers rather than simply which one has the best basic design. For example,

- If you happen to have an Audiovox CDM-9000 cell phone, you may want to look closely at the Audiovox Maestro since it includes a digital phone cable so you can surf the Web on your Pocket PC through your cell phone.

- Or, if you are interested in a free owner's site on the Web, you may want to seriously consider the Casio E-200 so that you can take advantage of the myCasio Web site.

Figure 1-2:
You can personalize your Pocket PC using themes you create or download.

✔ Maybe you would like to talk to your Pocket PC and have it respond by speaking back to you with the date, time, and any upcoming appointments you might have. If so, the HP Jornada 568 may be your cup of tea.

These are just a few examples of the differences you will find in different Pocket PC 2002 models. Some offer more expansion possibilities than others, while some just seem to fit into an ordinary pocket a little better. Regardless of their differences, you'll find that it's hard to go wrong no matter which Pocket PC 2002 you choose.

Your Desktop PC's Partner

Even though your Pocket PC is a powerful computer on its own, thinking of your desktop PC and your Pocket PC as partners is probably the better way to go. The two of them make a great team, and each has features that comple-ment the other. It's just a fact that there are some things you simply wouldn't want to do with one or the other. For example:

✔ Even though you can type on the onscreen keyboard or even use the handwriting recognition feature to enter data into your Pocket PC, you aren't likely to use either one when you type in your great novel.

Your desktop keyboard simply works better when you need to enter a lot of text.

✔ On the other hand, your desktop PC or even your notebook PC simply won't fit into a shirt pocket — no matter how big your shirts may be. When you're on the go, your Pocket PC gives you access to your files in a package that is easy to carry along.

Figure 1-3 shows how you can write notes directly on your Pocket PC's screen. Of course, if your handwriting is as bad as mine, you may end up with some interesting results after you click the Recognize button.

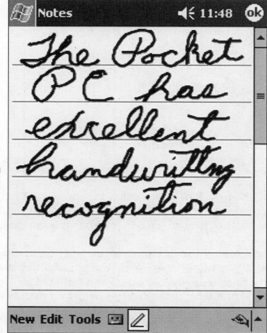

Figure 1-3:
You can enter information using the character recognition feature on your Pocket PC.

What really makes the partnership between your desktop PC and your Pocket PC work is that you can easily share files between the two. In fact, it's very easy to designate certain files or even complete folders that you want to *synchronize* between your Pocket PC and your desktop PC. Then, whenever the two of them connect, those files are automatically updated. So, if you add a new person to your Pocket PC address list, that person can be added to your desktop's address list without any further effort on your part. Of course, your address list is just one example. You can also synchronize your calendar, your résumé, or even your Pokémon collection database. The possibilities are endless.

You can set up partnerships between your Pocket PC and two different desktop PCs, making your Pocket PC a great way to work on the same document on the PC in your office and the one in your home. Having said that, read the following paragraph.

Even though you can partner your Pocket PC with two desktop PCs, you can synchronize your e-mail only with one desktop PC. If you need to have the same e-mail messages on two different desktop PCs, you may want to configure the e-mail program on one of them to leave messages on the server, and then later download those messages on the second PC. Or maybe it would simply be easier to set up a Web-based e-mail account at `www.hotmail.com` or `www.operamail.com` and forward important messages to your second desktop system using the Web-based mail account. If you need more information on Web-based e-mail accounts, you may want to refer to the *Internet Bible,* 2nd Edition, by Brian Underdahl and Keith Underdahl (Hungry Minds, Inc.). Alternatively, you can connect directly to your mail server through your Pocket PC without even bothering with your desktop system.

If you're a real Pocket PC fanatic like me, it's possible to set up partnerships between any number of Pocket PCs and a single desktop system. You need to be aware of a few caveats, however. First, each Pocket PC needs a unique name (you'll see more on this topic in Chapter 2), and second, only one Pocket PC can connect at a time. Most Pocket PC owners won't have to worry about this, of course, but it can get interesting connecting five different Pocket PCs to a single desktop system!

Putting Some Multimedia in Your Pocket

The next time you want to make those Palm PC owners jealous, just whip out your Pocket PC and start using some of its *multimedia* capabilities. Because your Pocket PC is a real computer that has both fantastic sound and video capabilities built in, it's really great at playing music and displaying color images. You won't find any other devices that can do all that, let you read your e-mail, and still fit into your pocket!

Putting music in your pocket

You've probably seen those little pocket-sized gadgets that people use to download music from the Internet or audio CDs so they can carry their favorite music with them. What you may not realize is that your Pocket PC can not only serve the same function, but offers plenty of advantages over those single-purpose music players, too.

Music you download is usually stored in either an MP3 (MPEG version 3) or a WMA (Windows Media Audio) file. These are simply two different ways of *compressing* audio files so they don't take so much storage room. After you load either type of file into your Pocket PC (or standalone music player), you can play back the music almost as if you were playing an audio CD. See Chapter 16 for more about using your Pocket PC as a portable music player.

MP3 and WMA files don't sound quite as good as the originals because both types of compression are *lossy* — some of the audio signal data is tossed out, or lost, to make the files smaller. You probably won't notice much difference, though, because you probably play the music back through the tiny set of earphones that came with your Pocket PC or music player. Unless you're a musician, you may not even detect the lower quality if you play the music back through a high-end stereo system. The quality difference between the original and the compressed file isn't likely to be very significant in most listening environments.

When choosing the format for audio files for your Pocket PC, choose WMA rather than MP3. WMA files can be as small as one-half the size of similar sounding MP3 files.

Putting images in your pocket

In addition to playing back your favorite music, you can also view images on the Pocket PC screen. Of course, at 240 pixels wide by 320 pixels high, the Pocket PC screen has just one-fourth the display capability of a plain old VGA monitor, but the Pocket PC does have to fit in your pocket, after all. (*Pixels* are picture elements — the number of dots that can appear on the screen per line.)

A lot has changed since the Pocket PC was first introduced. At that time there wasn't a PowerPoint viewer available, and you couldn't show PowerPoint slide shows using your Pocket PC. Now there are several different ways to show PowerPoint slide shows using a Pocket PC. In fact, as you'll see in Chapter 21, you can even connect your Pocket PC to a video projector, a large screen TV, or a standard computer monitor so that the slide show can easily be seen by whatever size crowd you have assembled (and you are no longer limited to the 240 x 320 Pocket PC screen resolution, either). It would be hard to imagine a more convenient way to bring along a PowerPoint presentation than in your Pocket PC.

The Pocket PC as Your Personal Assistant

Let's face it — most of us probably need some help keeping track of our schedules, our contacts, and our to-do list. The first *PDAs* (Personal Digital Assistants) were created primarily to fulfill just this set of functions.

The Pocket PC can serve as a superb personal assistant. It's got a built-in calendar so you can maintain your schedule. It's got a great contact manager so you can always remember those important details — like someone's birthday. And it's got a task manager that helps you get your to-do list in order (even if it's still up to you to actually do the tasks sometime).

Oh sure, you're probably saying something like "I can do all that stuff with this little paper notebook I carry." But have you considered how much more convenient the Pocket PC makes these tasks? Here are just a few ways the Pocket PC beats out the little paper note method:

- ✔ The Pocket PC always has a correct calendar for any date — no matter if it's next week, next year, or two years from now. You can easily schedule an appointment for any date and time you choose.

- ✔ Adding a new contact or changing someone's information is always easy in the Pocket PC Contact list. You don't have to worry about finding room on the right page as you can add as many new contacts as necessary and they always appear in just the right place.

- ✔ You can set a reminder so that your Pocket PC automatically lets you know when you're supposed to do something. Your paper notebook is perfectly happy to just sit there and let you forget about that important dinner date.

- ✔ With the right software, you can even have your Pocket PC read your appointments aloud so you can hear your schedule. Try getting your paper notebook to match that!

Figure 1-4 shows an example of how you can keep your schedule using your Pocket PC.

Figure 1-4:
You can use your Pocket PC to make certain you never miss an important date.

Keeping in Touch While on the Go

Do you ever experience e-mail withdrawal if you have to go without access to your messages for a few days (or even just a few hours if you're a *really* connected person)? With a Pocket PC, you no longer have to do without e-mail, instant messaging, the Internet, or even the latest beach-cam shot. Your Pocket PC has the Pocket Internet Explorer and Pocket Inbox built right in, so you can access all of that from almost anywhere and at just about any time you like.

Because you have a lot of options for connecting on the go, Pocket PCs don't generally include the necessary hardware bits and pieces you need — you purchase the necessary hardware after you know which connection option you want to use. For example, here are a few of the methods you may use to connect your Pocket PC to the Internet:

 ✔ If you have access to a telephone line, you may use a modem that fits into the expansion slot on your Pocket PC. This type of connection typically requires a Compact Flash-type of modem, such as the Pretec Compact Modem (www.pretec.com) or the Socket 56K Modem CF Card (www.socketcom.com). Using this type of modem, you can access your regular Internet service provider (ISP) and unless you are making a toll call, you typically won't pay any extra for the service because you can use the same Internet account that you use on your desktop.

✔ If you live in selected areas, you may be able to access the Web using a wireless modem such as one of the Sierra Wireless units (www.SierraWireless.com). Wireless Internet access is generally available in larger metropolitan areas but not in most rural areas. Wireless access is generally more expensive and slower than wired access through a phone line, but you can't beat the convenience of being able to access your e-mail or browse the Web without having to look for a telephone jack.

✔ If you have a cell phone, you may be able to get an adapter that connects your Pocket PC to your phone. If so, you can access the Internet either through your wireless phone service provider or by dialing in to your regular ISP. Of course, you use some of your airtime minutes whenever you connect. You also need to make certain you get the correct adapter specific to the exact make and model of your cell phone.

✔ Finally, some cell phones can communicate with a Pocket PC using a beam of infrared light. Using infrared light works just about the same way as a cell phone adapter cable does, except that there's no need to physically connect the Pocket PC and the cell phone. But you do have to keep the two fairly close together and make certain nothing blocks the line-of-sight path between them.

If you're buying a cell phone with the idea of connecting it to your Pocket PC, make certain that the correct adapter is currently available before you sign on the bottom line. Some cell phone manufacturers have sold phones with "data connectors" and then later decided not to make the necessary data cable available. If you go ahead and buy a phone based on the promise that the necessary data connection equipment will be released at some future date, you may be left with a phone that can't be used with your Pocket PC.

As always, there are a couple downsides to browsing the Web on the relatively small Pocket PC screen. For one thing, you have to spend so much time scrolling the display that browsing isn't always a lot of fun. For another, typing in Web site URLs on that tiny onscreen keyboard gets old pretty fast, too. Still, it is pretty cool to be able to whip out your Pocket PC and get on the Web. And being able to send and receive e-mail wherever you are is pretty slick, too.

Reading eBooks

Just owning a Pocket PC is a good indication that you are the type of person who likes to make the best use of your time. The Pocket PC adds one more element that helps you to do even more — eBooks.

eBooks are electronic books that you can download into your Pocket PC and read on the screen. At first glance you may wonder just how readable a book on the Pocket PC screen can be — even a small paperback book has larger pages. Surprisingly, though, the Pocket PC makes eBooks quite easy and enjoyable to read. For example, I have found that the downloadable *Rough Guides,* which are available for a number of major travel destinations, can make you a real expert on having a great time when you're traveling. You'll find the *Rough Guides* at www.roughguides.com.

Among the things that make eBooks easy to read, none is quite as important as something called *ClearType Technology,* a new method of making even small-sized text extremely easy to read. For now, this technology is available only on the Pocket PC (and even there, only in the eBook Reader). ClearType Technology works its magic by making very subtle changes in the way characters are displayed. In a sense, ClearType makes it seem like your Pocket PC's screen has higher resolution than it really does — at least while it is displaying ClearType characters. Of course, the *backlighting* on the Pocket PC screen also contributes to improved readability, too. Backlighting is the light that makes the screen on your Pocket PC bright — it's light that comes from behind the images on the screen. With backlighting, you don't need to hold a flashlight next to your ear as you read under the covers late at night (or whatever other dark place you prefer for reading scary stories).

A number of publishers and booksellers, including Amazon.com and Barnes & Noble, offer eBooks. Often you can download an eBook for free, but even when you have to pay for one, the cost is surprisingly low. With no printing, warehousing, or stocking costs to jack up the price, eBooks can be a real bargain.

To download some eBooks you need to supply the serial number from your Pocket PC certificate of authenticity. If you intend to download a lot of eBooks, you may want to store that serial number in a document file so it's always handy when you need it. You see how to create document files in Chapter 8.

In addition to downloading eBooks, your Pocket PC includes quite a few sample books on the ActiveSync CD-ROM. You can copy the books that interest you to your Pocket PC, and then read them when you have a few minutes to spare. For example, if you want to catch up on some of the fantastic tales you missed as a child, check out *Around the World in 80 Days* as shown in Figure 1-5.

Figure 1-5:
The Micro-
soft Reader
program
enables
you to read
eBooks
on your
Pocket PC.

Why a Pocket PC Beats a Palm

If you're still trying to decide whether to buy a Pocket PC or if you should go with one of those Palm-brand devices, you're probably looking for some good, unbiased advice. I'm afraid you won't find it here. Quite simply, I can't think of a good reason why anyone should even consider a Palm when they can get a Pocket PC. Take a look at the following:

✔ The Pocket PC is a far more versatile device than a Palm, meaning that you simply can do a whole lot more with your Pocket PC than you could with a Palm — things like send and receive e-mail on the go, surf your favorite Web sites, work on your novel, and create the great spreadsheet that will convince your boss that you deserve a raise.

✔ The Pocket PC is also far more powerful and expandable than any Palm device. You can easily add more memory, a modem, or other great toys like a digital camera card.

✔ With just a few exceptions, the Palm devices all have those boring, monochrome screens. Pocket PCs have color displays that are far cooler.

✔ Pocket PCs have far clearer screens, too. In fact, the Pocket PC screen has over three times the resolution of the Palm screen.

✔ Palm devices don't really have much in the way of multimedia capabilities. If you like the idea of carrying along your own music selections or viewing images onscreen, Pocket PC is the way to go.

The Bottom Line

In this chapter I show just a few of the neat things you can do with a Pocket PC. The Pocket PC is really a cool piece of equipment that you're going to have a lot of fun using. And as for the rest of this book, hang on — it's going to be an exciting ride!

Chapter 2

Understanding the Basics

*E*ven though the Pocket PC is "Windows-powered," you find a lot of obvious differences between using a Pocket PC and a desktop PC (I use the term "Windows-powered" here because your Pocket PC uses a version of Microsoft Windows — but probably not the version you've used in the past). One of the most glaring differences probably strikes most Pocket PC users the first time they want to enter some information: "Where's my keyboard?" After you get over the fact that your Pocket PC doesn't have some standard PC features (like a keyboard), you most likely start to wonder just how you actually use the darn thing. Well, never fear, for when you complete this chapter, you'll be quite comfortable using a Pocket PC.

(Although this chapter does cover the basics of using a Pocket PC, I'm going to hold off on most of the details about the onscreen keyboard and hand-writing recognition until Chapter 3. Those topics really do deserve a chapter all to themselves.)

Using the Touch Screen

Okay, since the typical Pocket PC doesn't have a keyboard, just how do you interact with it? Those four or five buttons certainly don't seem to hold much promise, do they? The answer is right in front of you — the Pocket PC's screen. Every Pocket PC uses a *touch screen* — a screen that recognizes when and where you touch the screen. Figure 2-1 shows several different items to give you a better idea how this works.

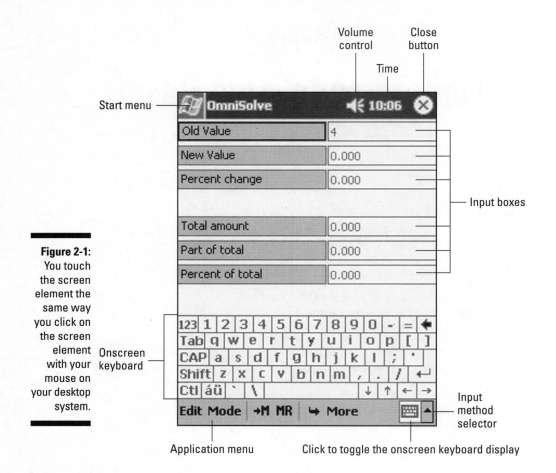

Figure 2-1:
You touch
the screen
element the
same way
you click on
the screen
element
with your
mouse on
your desktop
system.

The figure shows several different areas where you touch the screen in order to use your Pocket PC. Following are some typical things you may find.

The Pocket PC Start button

The Windows flag emblem in the upper-left corner of the Pocket PC screen is the Start button. Clicking this button works very much like the Start button on a desktop PC — it displays the Start menu — but there are some important differences:

✔ The Pocket PC Start button drops down the Start menu from the top rather than zooming up from the bottom, which is intended to keep you from covering up the Start menu with your hand. In truth, though, your Start menu probably fills up most of the screen's height anyway, so the location doesn't really matter.

✔ The top row of the Start menu displays the Pocket PC equivalent of the Quick Launch toolbar, which normally appears next to your desktop Start button. The Pocket PC Quick Launch toolbar is a little different, though, as it changes to show the programs you use the most.

✔ Unlike your desktop Start menu, many of your Pocket PC applications appear on the main Start menu, which can be a little confusing if a program you want to run doesn't appear on the Pocket PC Start menu. The solution is simple — select the Programs item in the lower half of the Start menu to open the Programs folder. You can start your program from that folder by clicking on the program's icon.

The Pocket PC program menus

Because the Pocket PC Start button is at the top, the program menus are now at the bottom of the screen. I guess that means it's okay for your hand to cover up a program menu but not to cover up the Start menu. Pocket PC program menus work just like the menus on your desktop PC. You tap — the Pocket PC way of saying "click" — on a menu to open the menu, and then tap the menu selection you want to open. In Figure 2-2 I've tapped on the Pocket Excel Edit menu to open that menu.

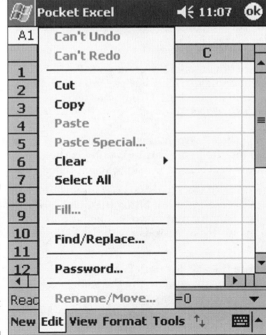

Figure 2-2:
Tap on a program menu to open the menu so you can select commands.

Items that are grayed-out on the Pocket PC program menus are currently unavailable — just like on your desktop PC.

If you accidentally open the wrong menu, you can close the menu by tapping outside the menu. This first tap outside the menu closes only the menu that's open, so you need to tap again if you want to open a different menu.

Using your stylus

By now you've probably figured out that the Pocket PC screen is too small to tap accurately using your fingers. Sure, sometimes you may get away with pointing your finger in just the right place, but you quickly learn the meaning of frustration in doing so — especially when you start trying to type on the onscreen keyboard.

Every Pocket PC comes with a *stylus* — a small plastic pen-like device that you use to tap on or to write on your screen. Unlike a pen, though, the stylus doesn't contain any ink, so it won't leave permanent marks on your screen.

You'll likely find that your Pocket PC manufacturer offers a package containing replacement styli. You won't, of course, give too much thought to buying these until you've already lost the stylus that came with your Pocket PC (or, if you absent-mindedly used it as a toothpick, chewed the end off of it). Now would be a great time to go to the manufacturer's Web site and place your order (or be happy that you bought a Pocket PC like the Audiovox Maestro, which comes with three extras).

Never use a pen or any sort of metal pointer on your Pocket PC screen. You will quickly do permanent damage to the screen, and it's virtually certain that this type of damage is explicitly excluded from your warrantee. The three basic stylus actions you use are as follows:

✔ **Tap:** To lightly touch the onscreen item you want to select or open. Lift the stylus after you tap the item. This tap action is the equivalent of clicking an item on your desktop PC using the left mouse button.

✔ **Drag:** To place the point of the stylus on an item onscreen and then drag the stylus across the screen without lifting the pointer until you have completed the selection. This action works like holding down the Shift key while you drag your desktop mouse with the left mouse button held down.

✔ **Tap-and-hold:** To hold the stylus pointer on an item for a short time until a context menu pops up, essentially the same as right-clicking your desktop mouse. When you tap-and-hold, a series of red dots will appear around the stylus pointer to let you know that the context menu will soon pop up.

Practice using your stylus to make certain you understand just how long a difference in time there is between the tap and tap-and-hold actions.

Protecting your screen

No, this section isn't about keeping your Pocket PC safe from diseases. But it is about keeping your Pocket PC healthy and in good condition.

If the idea of tapping and dragging a stylus across your Pocket PC screen doesn't bother you, go ahead and pull out your pen and have at it. If you'd rather protect the screen from damage, I've got another tip for you — buy the screen protectors offered by your Pocket PC's manufacturer when you go online to buy that set of spare styli. Screen protectors are simply plastic overlays that fit on top of your Pocket PC screen to protect it from scratches. If you don't use screen protectors you have a 100% chance of scratching your screen — and probably a lot faster than you can imagine. Better safe than sorry!

If the manufacturer of your Pocket PC doesn't offer screen protectors, you can still protect your screen from scratching if you're willing to be a little sneaky about it. All you need to do is go to the Casio Web site (www.casio.com) and buy the screen protectors that are sold for the Casio E-200 Pocket PC. The part number you want is JK834PS5. This trick works because all of the Pocket PC 2002 systems have the same screen size. Just don't tell them that I sent you!

Navigating on Your Pocket PC

I don't tell you about finding your way on the high seas (nor the low plains) using your Pocket PC in this section. For that information, you need to turn to Chapter 20, "Traveling with Your Pocket PC." Rather, here I show you how to find your way around the screen and file system inside your Pocket PC.

Without a keyboard or a mouse, navigating on a Pocket PC seems difficult at best. The reality is far better, though. After you get used to using the stylus and the buttons on the front of your Pocket PC, you'll be able to easily go anywhere you want.

Opening your Start menu

The Start menu is the one item that ultimately gives you access to everything on your Pocket PC. Through this menu you can open any program, access any file, or adjust any of the settings that control how your Pocket PC functions.

Because the Start menu is so vital, it's also easy to find. Just look for that Windows flag in the upper-left corner and give it a click to open the Start menu.

Do you notice how the positions of the Start button and the menu bar sometimes seem to swap places? This swapping can happen when you run an older Windows CE-based program — one designed for Windows CE 2.*x*. (*Windows CE* is the official name of the Pocket PC's operating system.) If the button and the bar switch on your Pocket PC, don't worry. The change is temporary and things move back where they belong when you run a newer Pocket PC program.

Figure 2-3 shows a typical example of a Pocket PC Start menu. Your Start menu may be a little different, especially if you have installed additional programs on your Pocket PC.

Click here to open Start menu

Click one of these icons to open a recently used application

Click to open any Start menu program

Figure 2-3: Open the Start menu to access your programs and files.

Click here to open the Programs folder to start any application

Click here to open the New menu to create a new item such as an appointment or Word document

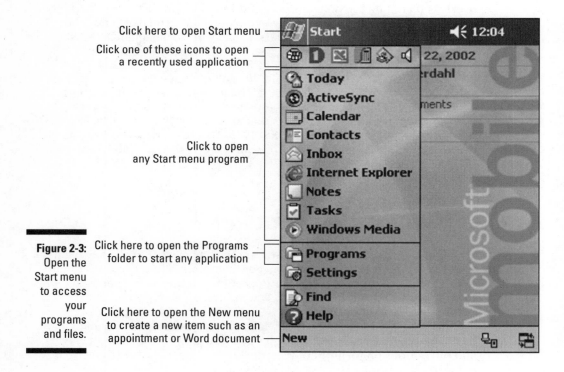

If you don't see the Start button when you first turn on your Pocket PC, you may need to press one of the buttons on the front of the unit to display the Today screen. By default, many Pocket PCs are set up to show the owner's information screen when they are first powered on, and this screen may not show the Start button. And because the buttons are programmable, you may have to experiment to see which button displays the home menu screen on your system.

When the Start menu is open, you can click one of the icons in the top row of the menu to quickly open one of the six applications you used most recently. You can also click one of the items further down on the menu, or you can click the Programs folder to gain access to any of your installed programs. "Adjusting Your Settings" and "Finding your stuff" later in this chapter show you how to use the Settings and Find options.

If you click the New menu, you can quickly create a new item such as an appointment, an e-mail message, a contact record, and so on. This can be much faster than first opening the correct application and then selecting the correct command to begin a new item.

Exploring your Pocket PC

One of the most useful items on the Start menu is the Programs folder. Opening this folder is the key to running any installed program or locating any file. Figure 2-4 shows the Programs folder on a Pocket PC where I've installed a number of third-party programs.

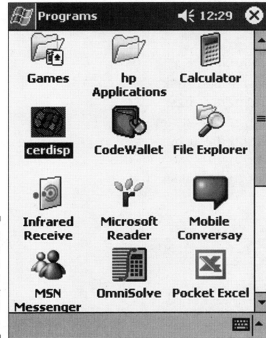

Figure 2-4: Open the Programs folder to run any of your installed programs.

As Figure 2-4 shows, there are additional program icons that aren't currently visible. Some are sitting below the visible icons and some are contained in folders, for example, the hp Applications and Games folders. To view these additional icons, use the scrollbar along the right edge of the screen or click the folder to open the folder.

Using scrollbars on the Pocket PC screen can be a little tricky. Make certain you place the stylus pointer tip just to the left of the right edge of the screen and somewhere near the middle of the scrollbar slider. Then drag the slider up or down as needed. You can also click the up or down arrows at the ends of the scrollbar, but it's really easy to select an icon instead of hitting the arrow in the right place.

Opening the File Explorer

You open a program or folder by simply clicking on it with the stylus. To open the File Explorer, click the File Explorer icon (shown in Figure 2-5).

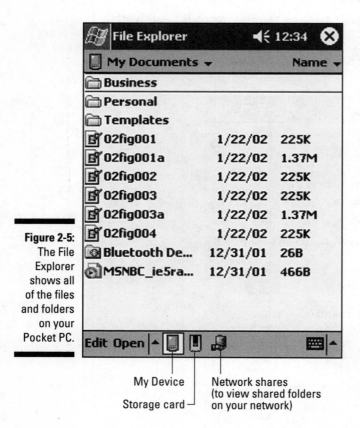

Figure 2-5: The File Explorer shows all of the files and folders on your Pocket PC.

Just as in recent versions of desktop Windows, the File Explorer on a Pocket PC first displays the My Documents folder (more than a mere coincidence). The My Documents folder is one of the most important folders on your

Pocket PC. Many Pocket PC applications find only documents that are in the My Documents folder. If you place document files anywhere else, you have to navigate with the File Explorer, find the document file, and then click to open it in the application.

If you add a memory card — such as a CompactFlash card or a Secure Digital card — to your Pocket PC so you can store additional files, make certain you create a My Documents folder on the memory card. If you store your documents, music, pictures, and so on in this folder, your Pocket PC applications can locate those files without additional fuss and bother on your part.

Navigating your files and folders

Click a file or folder to open it. If you click a file, your Pocket PC first tries to open the application that is *associated* with the type of file you clicked. For example, if you click a Word document, the document opens in Pocket Word (the Word application is associated with the Word document). Sometimes, though, no application has been associated with a file type and your Pocket PC isn't able to open the file. Usually this happens if you click a file other than one of the document file types. You can simply ignore files that aren't associated with applications — they may actually be necessary to the operation of various programs on your Pocket PC but may not be intended to be opened by you. Whatever you do, don't delete or move files you can't open because this could prevent you from using some of the applications that are installed on your Pocket PC.

When you open a folder, you can then view any files or subfolders that the folder contains. In some cases, you may end up several levels deep into the file system before you realize that you wish you'd left a trail of breadcrumbs to help you find your way back. Fortunately, there is an easy way to navigate back up the folder tree even if it doesn't seem obvious at first. Figure 2-6 shows you the clue.

Just below the Start button is a row that normally shows the name of the current folder and the sort method used to display the items in the folder. In Figure 2-6, I clicked on Personal to drop down the navigation list. Click one of the items in the list to move back up the folder tree to the folder you clicked.

When you click the folder name to drop down the navigation list, the folder name drops down to the bottom of the list, and the word *Show* appears where the folder name was, which tells you that clicking one of the folder names in the navigation list shows you the contents of that folder.

You can also use the My Device, Storage Card, or Network Shares icons in the menu bar to quickly navigate through the file system. You may need to set up a special user account to access shared network folders.

To create a new folder, select Edit⇨New Folder from the menu bar at the bottom of the File Explorer window. Use the onscreen keyboard to type in a new name for the folder and then press the Enter key. (The Enter key is indicated by a bent arrow that looks like the one on your desktop's Enter key.)

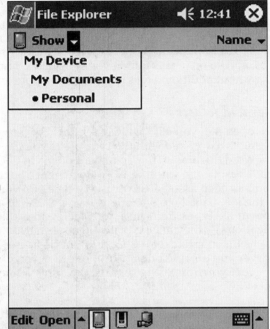

Figure 2-6:
Click the
folder name
in the
second row
to display
the
navigation
list.

Working with your files

In addition to simply opening a file on your Pocket PC, you also can perform many of the same file management functions you do on your desktop PC. The key is knowing how to access these functions rather than automatically opening the file. On your desktop PC you can open a context-sensitive menu by right-clicking on a file. On the Pocket PC you do the same by using the tap-and-hold method. That is, rather than a quick tap, you press lightly with the stylus but don't let up until the menu pops up, as Figure 2-7 shows.

Before deleting files from your Pocket PC, you may want to back them up on your desktop system. You find out more about backing up (and synchronizing) files in Chapter 7, but for now it's important to remember that backing up and synchronizing aren't the same thing. Synchronizing does copy certain files between your Pocket PC and your desktop PC, but doesn't protect those files from being lost if they are accidentally deleted in either place. If you delete a synchronized file from your Pocket PC, that file is also deleted from your desktop system the next time you synchronize files — unless you move the file out of the Pocket_PC My Documents folder on your desktop system *before* you allow the files to synchronize. In reality, synchronizing simply makes certain that the same versions of certain files you've selected are on your Pocket PC and your desktop PC, and that anything you do to those files on either PC will also be done to the same files on the other PC.

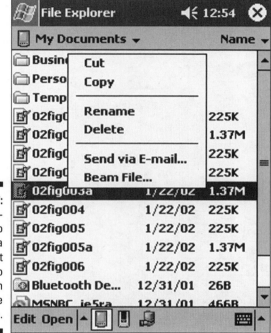

Figure 2-7:
Use tap-
and-hold to
display a
context
menu so
you can
manage
your files.

Finding your stuff

As small as your Pocket PC is, it's still large enough to have plenty of hiding places for your files. And just like on your desktop PC, the files you need the most are the ones you probably won't be able to find when you really need them. But those files can't hide forever — especially when you know the secret to finding them.

To find those errant files, click the Start button and choose Find to display the Find program. If you know the name of the file, click the down arrow to the right of the Find box and use the onscreen keyboard to enter the name. If you want to look for files by type rather than by name, make certain the Find box contains < ... > so that any file name can be found. <...> simply means that you aren't specifying a specific file name — it's the equivalent of *.* on your desktop PC. Be sure to delete any name that is currently showing in the Find box so that <...> appears if you want to find all files of a specific type.

To specify the type of file you want to find, click the down arrow next to the Type box, as shown in Figure 2-8. Click the type of file you want and then click Go to begin the search.

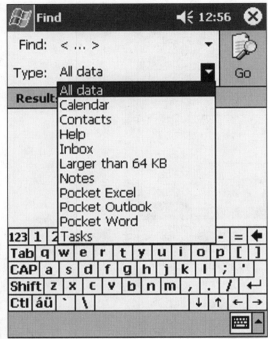

Figure 2-8:
Choose the
type of file
before you
click Go.

Switching between programs

Your Pocket PC can do quite a few different things at the same time. You don't have to close Pocket Word in order to work on a Pocket Excel worksheet, nor do you have to close the eBook you're reading in order to read your e-mail. But you do need to be able to switch between different programs easily if you want to make effective use of several different Pocket PC capabilities this way.

If you're accustomed to using Windows on your desktop PC, you know that you can keep several programs open and switch between them using a variety of techniques. Two of the most common ways to switch are clicking on a program's Taskbar button or pressing Alt+Tab to use the Task Switcher. If you decide to try these techniques on your Pocket PC, though, you're immediately faced with a couple of problems:

✔ To save precious screen real estate, the Pocket PC doesn't have a Taskbar running along the bottom of the screen. This pretty much cuts out clicking on a program's Taskbar button, doesn't it?

✔ Pressing Alt+Tab is also kind of hard when you don't have a keyboard. (And don't even think about trying to do this using the onscreen keyboard — it simply won't work.)

Looks like you'll need a different method to switch between running programs on your Pocket PC. Your Pocket PC probably does have a Task Switcher, but finding it can be a real challenge until you know where to look. Here's how you find it on a few of the more popular Pocket PCs:

✔ On the HP Jornada Pocket PC, click the Start button and choose Today from the Start menu. Then click the icon shown in Figure 2-9 to open the Task Switcher menu.

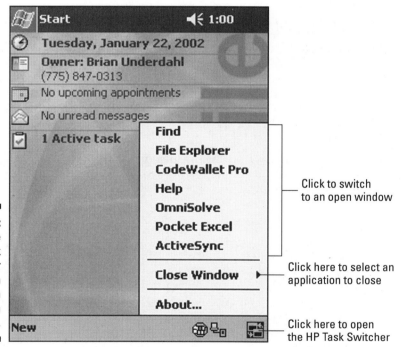

Figure 2-9: Open the HP Task Switcher to switch between open programs.

Click to switch to an open window

Click here to select an application to close

Click here to open the HP Task Switcher

✔ On the Audiovox and Toshiba Pocket PCs, click the Start button and choose Programs from the Start menu. Then click the Home icon to open the Home program. When this program is running, you can click the Running tab to switch between programs. You can also use the tap-and-hold method to stop any running program.

No matter which Pocket PC you use, you can select a different Task Switcher to control your applications. For example, another great Task Switcher option is Developer One TaskPro (`www.developerone.com`).

When the Task Switcher list is open, click the program you want to use, and your Pocket PC brings that program to the front.

You can also switch to a different program by selecting it from the Start menu or, if your Pocket PC has a Home menu, by selecting it from the Home menu. Because the Home menu can generally be displayed by pressing one of the buttons on the front of your Pocket PC, you may find that this method is your favorite option. In addition, the Home menu usually displays a much larger Task Switcher icon next to the icons for settings such as screen brightness and memory.

Although you may expect that selecting a program from the Start menu or the Home menu runs the risk of starting a second copy of a program that's already running, the Pocket PC's operating system prevents this. Only one copy of any particular program can be running at any time, and only one document can be open in a program. You cannot, for example, have two different documents open in Pocket Word at the same time — although you can have a Pocket Word document open and a Note document open at the same time.

Closing programs

By now you're probably getting the idea that you have to do a few things a little differently on your Pocket PC than what you're used to on your desktop system. It should come as no surprise, then, that closing Pocket PC programs is just a little different, too.

On a desktop PC you have several ways to close a program you no longer need. You can usually select File➪Exit (or something similar) from the program's main menu. You can click the Close button in the upper-right corner of the program's window. Or you can press Alt+F4 when the program is in the active window. Well, guess what? None of these options really work in most Pocket PC programs (it's almost as though you're never supposed to close a program once you've opened it).

As I show you in the preceding section, you can have several Pocket PC programs open at the same time, which reduces the need to close programs. It doesn't, however, eliminate this need. Depending on the programs that are running and the amount of memory in your Pocket PC, you may need to close some programs simply so you can run other ones.

Okay, if you *really* want to get picky about it, your Pocket PC is supposed to be able to unload programs from memory if necessary, which is the real reason why it's often so difficult to close Pocket PC programs. Your Pocket PC is supposed to do it automatically without your intervention. You know what? I still like to be able to control that myself.

So how do you close a Pocket PC program? You use a Task Switcher — that's how. You may notice the Close Window item listed on the Task Switcher list shown in Figure 2-9. If you select this option, you see the same list of items shown in the top section of the Task Switcher list. Selecting the item in the Close Window area closes the program you selected. If you use a different Task Switcher on your Pocket PC, you'll probably see slightly different wording. You might see something like Close Active or Close All But Active as options. If so, choosing Close Active shuts down whatever application is listed at the top of the menu, and choosing Close All But Active leaves that program open and closes everything else. If you choose a different option — Close All — you'll stop all of the applications that are currently running.

Okay, so there is another way to close programs, which I'll show you now. You click the Start button and choose Settings. Click the System tab and then the Memory icon. Then you click the Running Programs tab, as shown in Figure 2-10, and choose the programs you want to close. Click Stop to close the selected programs or Stop All to shut down all running programs. Click OK to close the Memory Configuration utility.

Figure 2-10: You can close programs using the Running Programs tab of the Memory Configuration utility.

Using the Home menu

In addition to the Start menu, most Pocket PC manufacturers install some variation of the Home menu on their systems. The Home menu is really a whole lot closer to the desktop on your desktop PC than it is to a menu (see Figure 2-11), but if they want to call it a menu, who am I to argue?

Figure 2-11:
Use the Home menu to easily open programs, adjust settings, and access the Task Switcher.

Here are some of the useful things you can do with the Home menu:

- ✔ Press the Home menu button on the front of your Pocket PC to display the Home menu.

- ✔ Tap a button to open the associated program.

- ✔ Often you will find that you can click one of the icons below the program buttons to view or adjust the battery, memory, or screen settings, or to open the Task Switcher.

- ✔ Click the 1 / 2 icon, the up or down arrow icons, or use the page selection box to switch between the Home menu pages.

Starting with Today

Your Pocket PC is the perfect assistant. Not only does it perfectly keep track of your schedule, but also quite happily gives you timely reminders without nagging. If only humans were as easy to get along with!

The Today screen on your Pocket PC shows all of your essential daily information in one place. You see the current date and time, who owns the Pocket PC (handy when everyone just has to see that neat little gadget), any appointments on your schedule, the status of your incoming and outgoing messages, and all of those tasks you need to get around to doing one of these days.

You can click on any of your Today screen items to open the item for whatever reason — to modify the item, for example. You can also click New on the menu bar and then choose the type of new item to create. Along the right edge of the menu bar, you see several icons. In Figure 2-12, there are icons for currently open connections, Bluetooth, and the Task Switcher. The number of icons varies depending on the current status of your Pocket PC, but you can click on any of the icons to access the associated settings.

Use the Connection icon to close the connection when you are done browsing the Internet.

Make sure that you're closing the correct connection. If you close the USB or serial connection to your desktop PC, your Pocket PC isn't able to synchronize with your desktop PC until the connection is reopened.

To set up your Pocket PC for a different time zone — like when you're traveling — tap-and-hold the date near the top of the Today screen. See the section "Setting the date and time" later in this chapter for more information.

Adjusting Your Settings

Nearly everyone adjusts some of the settings on his desktop PC, so wanting to play around a little with the settings on your Pocket PC is only natural. And, of course, your Pocket PC has a different set of options you can adjust than what you find on your desktop system.

Changing your screen settings

Adjusting the screen settings on your Pocket PC is easy because there really are only two screen-related settings that you can adjust: the brightness of the backlighting and the amount of inactive time before the screen dims. Well, there is one other setting that you *might* consider as screen-related — alignment. But because I consider the alignment setting more closely related to improving the accuracy of character recognition, I'm going to wait and show you more about that one in the following chapter.

If you want to play around with color schemes and background images, see the next section "Using themes" for more information.

You can access the screen settings a couple different ways. You may need to use more than one of the following to get the exact combination that you like:

- ✔ You can adjust the backlight brightness. To do so, click the Screen Settings icon on the Home menu screen (or select Settings from the Start menu, click the System tab, and tap the Backlight or Frontlight icon — depending on your brand of Pocket PC). Drag the slider to adjust the brightness. You may also want to try one of the predefined settings for outdoor, indoor, or low power use if they are available on your Pocket PC.

- ✔ To set the amount of inactive time before the backlight dims, click the Start button and choose Settings. Then click the Backlight icon on the System tab. Choose the time from the drop-down box, and make certain the checkbox is selected. Keeping the time before the backlight dims quite short is usually best because this greatly improves the length of time you can use your Pocket PC between battery charges. If you happen to have an HP Jornada Pocket PC, you may also want to try the Auto on/off according to ambient light option.

The backlight automatically returns to your desired setting as soon as you tap the screen or press one of the buttons on the front of your Pocket PC. If you are going to be using your Pocket PC outdoors in bright sunlight, remember that all of the Pocket PC 2002 systems have a reflective display that is quite visible even with the backlight turned completely off. This setting will help you to extend your Pocket PC's battery life to the maximum.

Using themes

If you are one of those people who really wants your Pocket PC to reflect your own personality, you're going to love the way that you can use *themes* on your Pocket PC 2002 system. Themes enable you to display background images on the Today screen, to choose which items appear on the Today screen, and even to choose different colors for the various screen elements.

Applying new themes

Your Pocket PC 2002 comes with at least one theme that you can use in place of the standard theme. It's really easy to apply a different theme. All you need to do is to tap the Start button, select Settings, and then tap the Today icon on the Personal tab. You can then select a theme from the list, tap OK, and the theme is applied.

Downloading themes

Because custom themes can be so much fun to use, a lot of people have created themes that you can download and use on your Pocket PC. Most of these themes are free, so you can try out a bunch of them to find the one you like the best.

There are quite a few different sites where you can find themes to download. Probably the best place to start is the Club Pocket PC Related Links site (www.microsoft.com/MOBILE/pocketpc/club/links.asp). Look for the links listed under the Pocket PC 2002 Themes heading.

Once you have downloaded some themes you want to try out, copy them to the Pocket_PC My Documents folder. Once you synchronize your Pocket PC, the new themes will appear in the Themes list.

Creating your own themes

Even though there are all sorts of custom themes you can download, sometimes it's simply more fun to create your own themes. There are a few ways you can do so:

- ✔ You can select the Use this picture as the background checkbox on the Appearance tab when you are choosing a theme. Then tap the Browse button and choose the picture you want to use.

- ✔ You can click the Items tab and then choose the items you want to appear on the Today screen. Deselect any items you don't want. You can also use the Move Up, Move Down, and Options buttons to make some additional modifications.

- ✔ The most fun of all is to download the Theme Generator (www.microsoft. com/MOBILE/pocketpc/downloads/ThemeGenerator.asp) and create your own custom themes. Not only does this enable you to use any image file you want, but you can also choose the colors for a number of screen elements. Figure 2-12 shows a custom theme I created using a digital image of Slide Mountain near Reno, Nevada.

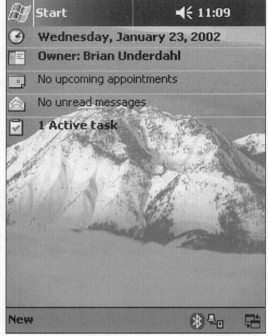

Figure 2-12:
You can use the free Theme Generator to create your own custom themes like this one.

Adjusting your security

One of the great things about a Pocket PC is that it is small enough to fit into a pocket. Unfortunately, this also makes a Pocket PC an attractive target for thieves or even people who simply can't resist playing around with that neat-looking gadget.

Although I can't do much about preventing theft except warn you to be careful about leaving your Pocket PC where someone could grab it, I can, at least, show you how to prevent some bozo from accessing your data. If nothing else, at least you have the satisfaction of knowing that no one can make use of your personal information or files.

Enabling a password

Setting up security on your Pocket PC means creating a password that must be entered whenever the unit is turned on. Without the correct password, no one can access your files or use your Pocket PC.

It's not a good idea to depend too heavily on the Simple 4 digit password option — especially if you tend to keep very sensitive files on your Pocket PC. These passwords consist of just four numeric digits, and someone who really wants in could discover your password just by being quite persistent. Sure, it may take a person several hours, but if your information is valuable enough, a thief or a snoop may decide it is worth the effort. To set a password, click the Start button and choose Settings. On the Personal tab click the Password icon. Next, choose the type of password you want to use and then use the onscreen keypad (if you selected the Simple 4 digit password option) or the onscreen keyboard (if you selected the Strong alphanumeric password option) to enter a password code, as shown in Figure 2-13. To activate the password, select the Enable password protection checkbox. On some Pocket PCs this checkbox is labeled Require password when device is turned on.

Figure 2-13:
Enable password protection to make it harder for people to snoop on your Pocket PC.

If you don't want to have to enter the password every time you turn on your Pocket PC, select the Prompt if device unused for option. Then enter the length of time you want to wait before a password is required. For example, in Figure 2-14, the time interval is 1 hour. If you turn on your Pocket PC when it has been suspended for less than 1 hour, you won't need to enter the password.

What to do when you forget your password

If you set a password and then forget what it was (or if someone else sets a password on your Pocket PC just to be mean), you'd better hope that you can guess the correct password. If this doesn't work, you're in big trouble!

Yes, there is an easy way to bypass (and remove) the password, but you pay a heavy price if you use it. To forcibly remove the password so you can again use your Pocket PC, you must restore your Pocket PC to the factory default settings. In doing so you remove all of your data, any files you've created, and any special settings you've applied. In other words, your Pocket PC is wiped clean of anything you've done.

If you've tried everything else and are so desperate that you feel you *must* start fresh, here is the procedure you use to remove the password:

1. **Remove your Pocket PC from the cradle, making sure that it's running on the internal battery power.**

2. **Use the stylus to press down the recessed reset button on the back of the Pocket PC.**

3. **While the reset button is being held down, press the On/Off button.**

4. **Release the reset button.**

When you press the On/Off button again, your Pocket PC turns on and all of your files are gone. To avoid repeating this major disaster in the future, you may want to refer to Chapter 7 to see how to back up your Pocket PC files on your desktop PC.

If the preceding steps don't work on your Pocket PC, check your owner's manual for a topic entitled "Complete System Reset" or something similar to find the correct procedure for your unit.

Setting the date and time

What good would an assistant be if it didn't know the correct date and time? If you want to be on time to your meetings and appointments, knowing the date and time is certainly important.

In most cases you don't really need to adjust the date and time on your Pocket PC because every time your Pocket PC and your desktop PC synchronize, your Pocket PC asks your desktop system for the correct time. Synchronizing the date and time makes it possible for the two of them to always know which files are newer, and to make certain they don't overwrite newer data with older information.

Still, you can set the date and time on your Pocket PC if necessary. More importantly, you can choose a different time zone so that you're always on schedule even when you're traveling.

Even if you don't travel with your Pocket PC, you can make good use of the time zone feature. Set the visiting time zone for the location of a business partner or relative in a city in another time zone and you can quickly see the current time at their location simply by opening the Clock Settings screen.

To access the Clock Settings screen, tap-and-hold on the date in the Today screen. You can also display this screen by clicking the Start button, choosing Settings, and then clicking the Clock icon on the System tab. Figure 2-14 shows the Clock Settings screen.

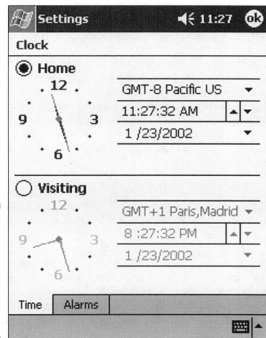

Figure 2-14:
Set your location and time zone using the Clock Settings screen.

After the Clock Settings screen is open, choose your selections using the drop-down boxes. You can also click the Alarms tab if you want your Pocket PC to chirp at you at some specified time.

If you choose a time zone that is different from the one set on your desktop PC, your Pocket PC still synchronizes the time with your desktop system, but the times are offset by the differences between the selected time zones.

Changing memory settings

Mark Twain once said, "This memory of ours stores up a perfect record of the most useless facts and anecdotes and experiences." In the case of the Pocket PC, the memory stores even more than that — there's no other place to store anything when you don't have disk drives or other offline storage.

Your Pocket PC normally manages its own memory automatically. It shifts the balance between storage and program memory as needed. Sometimes, though, you may want to give your Pocket PC just a bit of extra help.

Storage memory is that portion of the total memory used to store your data and document files. *Program memory* is the portion of memory where your programs are run. If necessary, you can drag the memory slider left or right to change the balance between the available storage and program areas. You may, for example, need to make just a bit more space to temporarily store a document that's too large to fit into the remaining storage memory.

Your Pocket PC has two types of memory. *RAM* (Random Access Memory) is the memory where you can store data or programs that you download. This is also where programs are run. *ROM* (Read-Only Memory) is the memory where your Pocket PC's operating system and built-in programs like Pocket Word are stored. All of the Pocket PC 2002 systems use a special type of ROM known as *Flash ROM,* which can be updated by special programs. Normally you cannot add anything to Flash ROM on your own, but as you will see in Chapter 7, you can make use of Flash ROM to store certain types of backup information.

Aside from making temporary changes to the way memory is allocated between storage and programs, you can make a few other adjustments to free up more memory for other uses:

✔ When you click the Running Programs tab, you can choose to stop one or more of the currently running programs. Doing so frees program memory. Freeing up program memory allows your Pocket PC to shift the balance between the two, and gives you a bit more memory to play around with if you want to manually allocate more memory for storage.

✔ If you click the Remove programs link, you can choose to uninstall some of the extra programs you may have added to your Pocket PC, freeing up storage memory (and maybe some program memory if you remove a program that is currently running). In Chapter 19, I show you how to manage your add-on programs.

✔ The ultimate way to free up memory in your Pocket PC is to add a storage card — such as the SanDisk or Kingston CompactFlash or Secure Digital memory cards. Adding a storage card enables you to place programs, documents, and even music files into your Pocket PC without using up your precious built-in memory. Chapter 19 also tells you more about adding a storage card.

You can always reinstall programs from your desktop PC even if you temporarily remove them from storage memory to free up some space in your Pocket PC. Just make certain that you don't remove them from your desktop system when you remove them from your Pocket PC.

Setting your preferences

In addition to the options already mentioned in this chapter, you can adjust quite a few other settings to suit your own personal preferences. Most of these settings are available through the Settings option on the Start menu. Here is a sampling of some of the ones you may find useful:

- ✔ The **Buttons** option lets you specify what the buttons on the front of your Pocket PC do. You can, for example, specify that one of those buttons opens the Media Player if you like to use your Pocket PC as a personal music player.

- ✔ The **Menus** option enables you to add or remove items from your Start menu, giving you quick access to the programs you use most often and reducing the clutter by removing programs you seldom use.

- ✔ Use the **Owner Information** option to change your personal information — such as your address and phone number if you move.

- ✔ Use **Sounds & Notifications** to control the volume of audio alerts and to choose which sounds are played to signal events.

- ✔ Move to **Regional Settings** on the System tab to configure your Pocket PC for a different country.

Your particular brand of Pocket PC may offer some additional settings, like the number of colors used on the screen and whether tapping on the screen wakes up your Pocket PC. Feel free to play around with the options — you can always change back if you don't like the effect created by one of the settings.

Chapter 3

Entering Information into Your Pocket PC

Soon after you first get your Pocket PC you're probably hit with an interesting revelation — the darn thing doesn't have a keyboard! Looks like tapping out an e-mail message on this thing is going to be a whole lot of fun, doesn't it?

Things aren't always quite what they seem at first glance. Getting information into your Pocket PC is one of those things that's probably somewhat different than what you expect, but in many ways it's a lot easier than you may realize. You just need to adjust your thinking a little before you start having fun.

Handwriting and Your Pocket PC

A Pocket PC is about the same size as a pocket-sized notepad. If you use a notepad, you certainly know that the most natural way to put information down in the notepad is simply to pull out a pen or pencil and start writing. You probably hold the notepad in one hand, and write with the other. It turns out this is also one of the best ways to enter information into your Pocket PC.

Earlier generations of handheld Personal Digital Assistants (PDAs) touted their ability to recognize handwriting, but before the PDA got the raw power that's built into the Pocket PC, this recognition capability was pretty much a joke. One famous cartoonist even did a whole series of comic strips making fun of just how bad handwriting recognition was on devices like the Apple Newton. Fortunately, things have improved tremendously on the Pocket PC.

Understanding the options

Handwriting recognition on a Pocket PC is pretty advanced. Unless you're one of those doctors with handwriting no one can read, you'll probably find that your Pocket PC does a pretty good job of deciphering your chicken scratchings — especially if you choose the correct handwriting option to match your style (and maybe practice just a little).

You can choose from three different methods of writing on your Pocket PC's screen. The *Transcriber* allows you to write pretty much like you would in a paper notebook, while the *Letter Recognizer* provides better accuracy at the expense of input speed. The *Block Recognizer* is a simpler version of the Letter Recognizer, which is intended to make life easier for users who move from a Palm to a Pocket PC. (See the following sections for more detail.)

Using the Transcriber

When you use the Transcriber, you write complete words directly on your Pocket PC's screen. The Transcriber accepts printing, cursive writing, or any combination of the two.

The Transcriber has an easier time figuring out where words begin and end when you use cursive writing because you typically write an entire word in one continuous motion.

Figure 3-1 shows how the Transcriber works. You write a complete word and then when you lift the stylus, the Transcriber does its best to understand what you wrote and to convert it into text. In Figure 3-1, I've written my name and the Transcriber correctly converted it into "Brian."

As you complete each word, the Transcriber does the conversion into text. If you continue to add text, your note scrolls up as necessary.

If the Transcriber stops doing an automatic conversion to turn your handwriting into text, tap the Hand icon just to the left of the input method selector at the lower-right corner of the screen. When this icon has a white background the conversion happens automatically as soon as you complete each word. When this icon has a gray background, you must use the Tools⇨Recognize command to tell the Transcriber to convert the handwriting into text. If you don't want to use automatic text conversion, you must have the Pen icon (in the middle of the menu bar) clicked in order to write on the screen.

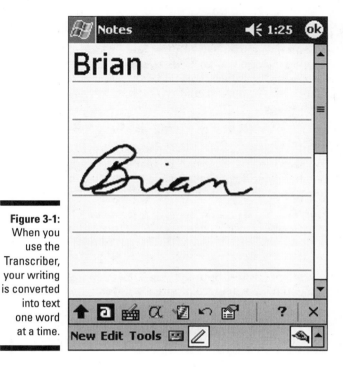

Figure 3-1:
When you
use the
Transcriber,
your writing
is converted
into text
one word
at a time.

Transcriber also uses a series of *gestures* to enable you to enter things like pressing the Enter key or making a quick correction by simply writing a specific character without having to stop and find the key. When you select Transcriber as your input option, the first screen you see as Transcriber opens shows you how to enter these special gestures. The Transcriber Help file shows a bunch more special gestures — most of which you probably won't use often enough to remember.

To choose the Transcriber, click the up arrow in the lower-right corner of the screen and select Transcriber. You can also click Options at the top of the pop-up menu to adjust the Transcriber's settings. When the Settings screen opens, click the Options button to choose from several settings:

✔ On the General tab, select Sound on to enable sound effects. You may want to turn this one off if you need to work silently.

✔ Select Show intro screen to redisplay the introductory screen so you can once again see the hints about how to create the special gestures. This will only be necessary if you clicked off the option to show that screen when it was displayed.

- ✔ Choose Show iconbar to display a set of tools that works with the Transcriber. For example, one tool pops up a small keyboard that makes it easier to enter symbols such as parentheses and brackets. Another tool adjusts the angle at which you write on the screen so you can write diagonally or even vertically if that's more comfortable for you. These tools make it easier to enter unusual characters, but they also eat up some of your screen space.

- ✔ If you have trouble seeing what you're writing, use the color and width options to select a choice that is easier to see.

- ✔ Move to the Recognizer tab and choose Add space after to have the Transcriber automatically add spaces between words. In this mode, you don't have to enter a special gesture whenever you finish a word.

- ✔ If you want to enter individual characters rather than complete words, choose the Separate letters mode checkbox. Using this option may help if you have really sloppy handwriting and the Transcriber is making a lot of mistakes reading your writing.

  Don't choose the Add space after option if you select separate letters mode — otherwise you'll have a space after each letter.

- ✔ Use the Speed vs. Quality slider to improve either the speed or the accuracy of handwriting recognition. This is one of those delicate balancing acts where you have to decide the best setting based on how accurately the Transcriber is understanding your handwriting.

- ✔ Finally, use the Recognition delay slider to make certain you have enough time to cross your T's and dot your I's. A shorter delay improves the speed of recognition, but may reduce the overall accuracy.

When the Transcriber's iconbar is showing, you can click the fourth icon from the left to display the Letter Shapes screen. On this screen you can specify how you tend to write each character. If you say you never use a certain shape when writing a character, the Transcriber won't waste time trying to translate that shape into the specified character. This can improve handwriting recognition speed, but may also lead to the Transcriber making more errors. You just have to experiment to see what works best for you.

The Transcriber is supposed to respond to a series of gestures that indicate certain keystrokes and actions such as the Enter key, the Tab key, Undo, Copy, Paste, and so on. For example, a motion that first moves down and then left is supposed to be recognized as pressing the Enter key. Whether the Transcriber actually recognizes each gesture depends pretty heavily on how accurate you are at remembering and executing the correct stylus motions. If you really want to learn the set of gestures you can make on your Pocket PC, tap the Question Mark icon on the iconbar to open the Transcriber Help file. Then, tap Microsoft Transcriber Gestures. Remember, though, that you must use the stylus to enter any gestures — not one of your fingers.

If you want to adjust the angle you can write on the screen, tap the arrow at the left end of the iconbar. Continue tapping the arrow until it points upwards at the angle you prefer. You will probably have to play around with this setting to find the one that works the best for you.

Using character recognition

If you happen to be one of those people whose handwriting is really bad — you're often not even sure what you wrote — the Transcriber may not be such a hot idea. Spending half of your time correcting transcription mistakes probably isn't the best way to get much done.

Just because the Transcriber doesn't work too well for you doesn't mean you have to give up on handwriting recognition, though. Your Pocket PC has two other options for understanding your handwriting — the Letter Recognizer and the Block Recognizer.

Using the Letter Recognizer

The Letter Recognizer can be a better choice than the Transcriber when it comes to understanding your handwriting because it works one character at a time. It also uses specific areas near the bottom of the screen for different types of characters, so Letter Recognizer has a bit less guessing to do than the Transcriber might. With no ambiguity about where one character ends and the next one begins, it can be far easier to translate even sloppy handwriting into text. Figure 3-2 shows the Letter Recognizer in action.

Another thing that helps the Letter Recognizer work is that it uses three distinct areas to separate your input of capital letters, lowercase letters, and numbers (plus one special area where you can select special characters). Sure, it's more work for you because you have to select the correct area to enter different types of characters. But because this cuts down the number of possibilities that the Letter Recognizer has to consider, it tends to improve the accuracy. Of course, if your handwriting is *really* bad, even this may not be enough. (But in that case you're probably one of those people who gets a lot of calls from pharmacists asking what that prescription says, so you're used to no one being able to read your writing, anyway.)

The Letter Recognizer takes over the bottom third of your Pocket PC's screen and is divided into four areas:

 ✔ The left section (under ABC) is the area where you enter letters when you want to enter capital letters. You can enter letters as upper- or lowercase — they appear as uppercase in the document.

✔ The second section (under abc) is the area for entering lowercase letters. Here, too, you can use upper- or lowercase, and the letters appear as lowercase in the document.

✔ The third section (under 123) is where you enter numbers and symbols.

✔ You can also enter spaces or delete characters using the area below the solid line.

✔ The right-most section has seven blocks you can tap for special purposes. The fat left arrow at the top is the one you use the most — it's the back-space that wipes out characters that weren't recognized correctly. Below it are arrows to move one place left or right, then the Enter key and the spacebar, and in the bottom row, a Help button and one to make entering special characters easier.

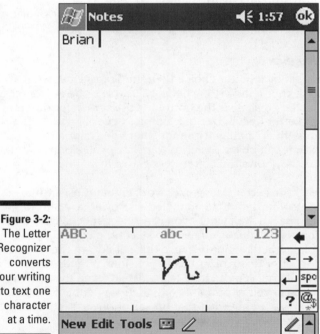

Figure 3-2:
The Letter
Recognizer
converts
your writing
into text one
character
at a time.

Learning how to write

Do you want to feel like a kid again? If so, learning how to write on your Pocket PC may be just the ticket. Remember how frustrating it was when you drew a picture and your kindergarten teacher didn't see what you knew was in the picture? At first it may seem like you've gone back to those days, but with just a little practice, your Pocket PC will understand what you're trying to say. Unfortunately, learning to write on a Pocket PC won't make you into a better artist, but hey, you can't have everything!

You've probably noticed that two horizontal lines divide the Letter Recognizer's input area (see Figure 3-2). The upper line is a dashed line and the lower one is solid. Sort of reminds you of that lined paper you had back in grade school, doesn't it? Actually, the lines in the Letter Recognizer do serve the same purpose as those on that lined paper — they're there to show you where to write:

- ✔ The solid line is where the base of all of your characters should rest.

- ✔ The dashed line is where the top of most lowercase characters should end. Uppercase characters should have the dashed line right about in their middle.

- ✔ Descenders and ascenders should go below the solid line or above the dashed line, respectively.

One of the hardest things to learn about writing on your Pocket PC's screen is to create an entire character in a single motion. In most cases lifting the stylus off the screen signals the end of a character — even if you weren't done with it. When you realize the importance of keeping the stylus on the screen until you're done, you find that the character recognition accuracy goes way up.

Don't waste your time trying to go back and add more to a character you've already drawn. Just wait to see whether it's recognized correctly and if not, click the backspace arrow. Try again, but this time use a single motion to enter the entire character.

If you are having a lot of trouble with the Letter Recognizer not understanding certain characters, tap the Help button — the button with the question mark. Then click the Demo button and tap the character on the onscreen keyboard to see a couple of examples of how to write the character. Figure 3-3 shows how the letter *q* appears after the demo finishes drawing it two different ways.

What Figure 3-3 can't show you is that the demo slowly draws the character so you can see the best way to write it. You may find that it helps to watch the demo several times to learn the correct method of drawing some of the more difficult characters.

If the onscreen keyboard disappears after you've seen a demo, tap the Demo button to make it return. The keyboard then remains visible until you click OK.

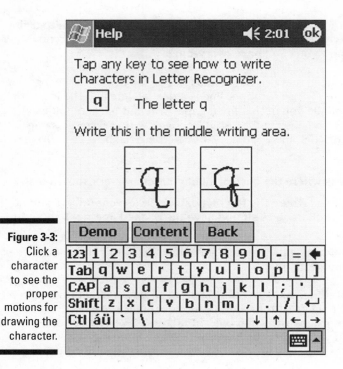

Improving accuracy

Okay, so maybe it isn't just that your handwriting stinks. If you've looked at the character input demos and have practiced until your hand is sore but the Letter Recognizer still doesn't understand your handwriting, it's possible that it really isn't your fault. It might just be that your Pocket PC needs a bit of a tune-up in the form of a screen alignment.

Aligning your Pocket PC's screen can also improve the accuracy of how the unit responds to clicking items on the screen such as characters on the onscreen keyboard.

Aligning your screen takes just a minute or so. To align, follow these steps:

1. **Click the Start button and choose Settings.**

2. **Tap the System tab.**

3. **Next click the Screen icon and then the Align Screen button.**

4. **When the large plus sign (+) appears in the middle of your screen, press the stylus firmly into the middle of the plus sign. You need to press the middle of each new plus sign that appears near the corners of the screen.**

5. **When the alignment is finished, click OK. Too bad you can't align your car's front end so quickly and easily!**

Using the Block Recognizer

The Block Recognizer is somewhat similar to the Letter Recognizer, but unless you are used to using a Palm, you probably won't find the Block Recognizer to be nearly as convenient. The reason for this is simple — the Block Recognizer emulates the Graffiti handwriting recognition found on Palms.

Using the Soft Keyboard

If your handwriting skills are really rusty or if you maybe just prefer typing, your Pocket PC includes an onscreen keyboard that is sometimes referred to as the *soft keyboard* because it's created by software rather than out of various bits and pieces of plastic and metal. The onscreen keyboard is pretty darn small, though, so you can forget any notions about touch-typing on that thing.

Using the onscreen keyboard is pretty easy if rather slow. Poking out your several hundred–page novel by tapping one key at a time with that little stylus isn't likely to win you too many awards for being the world's fastest writer. Still, for short notes and the like, it isn't too much of an ordeal to use the onscreen keyboard.

Typing on your screen

The onscreen keyboard works pretty much like an old-fashioned typewriter. You stab at each key to enter a character and then move on to the next one. If you want to type an uppercase character, tap the Shift key and then the character you want. The keyboard returns to lowercase after you tap the character. To keep the keyboard in uppercase mode, tap the CAP key instead of the Shift key.

To move the insertion point, you can use the movement keys at the right edge of the lower row of the keyboard. You may find it easier to simply tap in the text with your stylus to move the insertion point.

If you need to enter accented characters, tap the second key from the left in the bottom row — the key with áü on the face. This shifts the keyboard so it shows accented characters. You can click the same key again to return to normal characters.

Some shortcuts to speed your typing

With a keyboard as small and awkward to use as the onscreen keyboard, you can probably use some help by way of typing shortcuts. As Figure 3-4 shows, the onscreen keyboard does its best to try to help you out by suggesting words that seem to match what you are typing. If the correct word appears in the pop-up list, tap that word to enter the word into the document without having to finish typing it out. One really cool feature about this is that your Pocket PC learns words you enter often — such as your name — so that they are added to the list of suggestions. Then when you start typing the same word in the future, you'll be able to select the word instead of having to retype it each time.

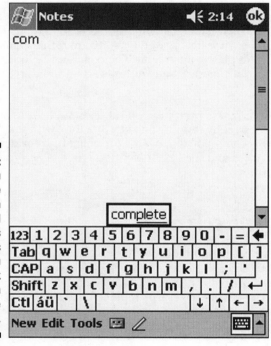

Figure 3-4:
As you type, the onscreen keyboard offers possibilities that you can click rather than typing the entire word.

To control how your Pocket PC suggests words as you type, tap the input selector and select Options at the top of the menu. Then click the Word Completion tab.

TIP

In the drop-down Suggest box, choose 4 as the number of words to suggest; your Pocket PC now offers four alternatives rather than just one possibility, and you're more likely to be able to select the word you want.

If you want to enter a bunch of numbers, don't waste your time with the number keys in the top row of the keyboard. Click the 123 key in the upper-left corner to change the keyboard into a numeric keypad for faster entries. Tap the 123 key again to return to the standard keyboard.

You can also use some of the Control key shortcuts you're used to from your desktop PC. For example:

- ✔ Tap Ctl and then A to select all text.
- ✔ Tap Ctl and then C to copy the text.
- ✔ Tap Ctl and then X to cut the selected text.
- ✔ Tap Ctl and then V to paste the text you copied.
- ✔ Tap Ctl and then Z to undo.
- ✔ Tap Ctl and then Q to close the current application.
- ✔ Tap Ctl and then N to begin a new document.

Using Other Ways to Input Info

Lets face it — if you need to enter a lot of information into a document, there's really no substitute for a real keyboard. But just because your Pocket PC doesn't come with a keyboard doesn't mean that all is lost. There are several ways to add a real keyboard to your Pocket PC, including the following products:

- ✔ iBIZ KeySync portable keyboard
- ✔ Targus folding keyboard
- ✔ Seiko SmartPad

Each offers certain advantages. Let's have a brief look at how they can make your life a little easier.

Using a portable keyboard with your Pocket PC

The iBIZ KeySync keyboard is a real keyboard, but it's far smaller and more portable than a full-sized keyboard. You really can type on the thing, too.

To use the iBIZ KeySync keyboard you'll need to get the correct serial cable that works with your particular Pocket PC. Some Pocket PCs include a serial cable in addition to the USB cable, but for others you'll need to buy the cable from your Pocket PC's manufacturer.

One really cool feature of the iBIZ KeySync keyboard is that it has ten *hotkeys* and six *function* keys you can program. These can be used to run programs or quickly enter text on your Pocket PC. For example, you might program a function key to enter your full name with a single keystroke, or program a hotkey to open your favorite game.

Using a folding keyboard with your Pocket PC

If you can't even stand the idea of carrying around a small, portable keyboard to use with your Pocket PC, you may want to consider another option — a folding keyboard such as the one made by Targus.

Folding keyboards are the ultimate space saver. They fold into a compact package that's just about the same size as your Pocket PC itself. To use a folding keyboard, you unfold it, set it on a hard flat surface, and insert your Pocket PC into the connector. Then you select the folding keyboard input option from the list that appears when you click the up arrow at the lower-right corner of the screen and begin typing.

Each type of Pocket PC requires a folding keyboard model specifically designed for that brand and model of Pocket PC. That's because the folding keyboard attaches using the same connector on the bottom of your Pocket PC that connects to the synchronization cradle, and these connectors are different on different brands and models of Pocket PCs.

Because a folding keyboard folds, it's not very adept at sitting on your lap as you type. You really will need to find a place for the folding keyboard that helps keep the keyboard flat as you type.

Using a Seiko SmartPad with your Pocket PC

The Seiko SmartPad can function as a keyboard, but it is really a whole lot more than just another way to type on your Pocket PC. Unlike a portable keyboard, the Seiko SmartPad lets you draw on a pad of ordinary paper (using a special pen) and then automatically transfers your drawing to your Pocket PC using the infrared port. Figure 3-5 shows an example of a drawing I made using the Seiko SmartPad.

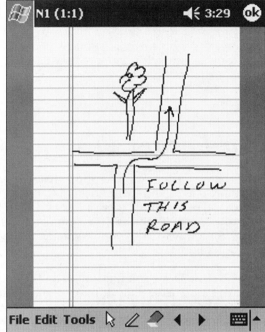

Figure 3-5:
You can draw on ordinary paper and automatically transfer your drawing to your Pocket PC using the Seiko SmartPad.

In addition to being a really cool way to draw on your Pocket PC, the Seiko SmartPad is a leather portfolio with room for your cell phone, business cards, and your Pocket PC. In addition, you'll find a touch-sensitive keyboard under the paper notepad, and you'll find that its larger size makes typing far easier than using the onscreen keyboard.

You use an included program, InkNote Manager, to organize the notes you create with the Seiko SmartPad. You can send notes as e-mail messages, and you can save them in several different formats. To learn more about the Seiko SmartPad, visit the Seiko Instruments Web site (www.seikosmart.com).

Be sure to buy the correct Seiko SmartPad to match your brand of Pocket PC. The original SmartPad has a fixed infrared port, which only works with Pocket PC models whose infrared port is on the top. The SmartPad II has a movable infrared port that can work with any Pocket PC (but you give up the cell phone pocket for this added flexibility).

Using MyScript with your Pocket PC

As if you didn't already have enough input options for your Pocket PC, I'm going to offer yet another one you may want to check out. MyScript, from Vision Objects (www.visionobjects.com) is a very interesting alternative to the built-in handwriting-recognition options you find on your Pocket PC.

MyScript is designed to solve the problems that you may encounter with other handwriting-recognition software. It's not only very fast, but it also seems to be able to read almost anyone's chicken scratching more accurately than any of the other alternatives.

Printing from Your Pocket PC

It's only natural to expect that you might want to print whatever data you've spent so much time and effort putting into your Pocket PC, right? Well, even though this seems like a logical expectation, there's just one little problem — none of the programs on your Pocket PC has a Print command. In fact, no matter how much you look for a way to print your documents directly from your Pocket PC, you just won't find it!

The basic idea behind this lack of native printing ability on the Pocket PC is that you are expected to print stuff using your desktop system. But what if your desktop PC isn't handy and you just have to print out a document? After all, the idea behind having a Pocket PC is so that you can carry your computing power along in your pocket wherever you go.

As you might expect, other people have had the same thought about their Pocket PC. Some of those people were clever programmers who figured out how to add printing capabilities. For example, Field Software (www.fieldsoftware.com) has created several small utilities including PrintPocketCE (for printing Pocket Word documents and e-mails), PocketPixPrint (for printing images), and PocketClipPrint (for printing items from the Clipboard).

Figure 3-6 shows an example where I'm using PrintPocketCE to print a Pocket Word document. In this case I'm printing using the infrared port, but you can print using a wired connection or even a wireless option such as a Bluetooth card.

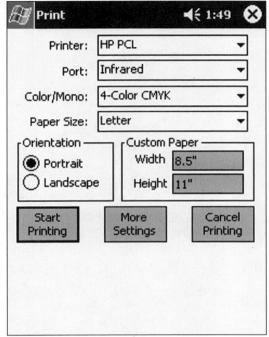

Figure 3-6:
Your Pocket
PC gains
the ability
to print
when
you use
Print-
PocketCE.

Part II

Personal Organization with Your Pocket PC

The 5th Wave   By Rich Tennant

"It's a Weber PocketPit Pro Handheld barbeque with 24 btu, rechargeable battery pack, and applications for roasting, smoking, and open-flame cooking."

In this part . . .

Your Pocket PC can help keep your personal life in order. It can keep track of your address book, help you manage your schedule, and act as your personal note taker. In this part you'll see how to do all of this and how to establish a partnership between your Pocket PC and your desktop PC so they can share important information.

Chapter 4

Keeping Your Address Book

● ●

In This Chapter

▶ Innovative uses for your Pocket PC address book

▶ Managing your contacts

▶ Sharing contact information

▶ Managing your contacts by speaking to your Pocket PC

● ●

*T*he first hand-held computer-like devices filled an interesting niche. They weren't very powerful. They didn't have much memory. They couldn't perform a broad range of tasks. But they did make an excellent replacement for those pocket-sized paper address books that most people kept.

The Pocket PC, of course, is quite powerful, has a lot of memory, and can be called upon to handle many different types of tasks. Yet in spite of all of this, some people don't realize just how great the Pocket PC is at replacing those handwritten address books. Once you start keeping your address book in your Pocket PC, you may never have an excuse for misplacing someone's phone number again.

What You Can Do with Your Address Book

One key to getting the most out of an innovative product like a Pocket PC is to think outside the box. That is, you have to stop thinking about limits and start thinking wildly. It's kind of hard to do that sometimes — especially when you're stuck in the rut of comparing a new product with whatever it replaced. Imagine just how little advancement there might have been in personal transportation if the early automobile manufacturers had thought of cars only in terms of a replacement for a horse. You probably wouldn't have climate control in your new car, for one thing. It's only when you realize that a car can enclose you in a mobile, weather-tight cabin that you can even begin to think about heating and cooling the air around the passengers.

The same thing applies in thinking about how your Pocket PC's address book can replace your little black book. You simply need to remember that the same old limitations that prevented you from doing things with your paper address book don't apply. You need to use your imagination to think about ways your Pocket PC address book can be useful.

Your address book as an address book

Okay, so maybe using your Pocket PC's address book as an address book doesn't sound all that unusual. But consider this — when was the last time you tried to keep up with a little hand-written address book? Comparing the two, the Pocket PC's address book has lots of advantages:

✔ Your Pocket PC address book never runs out of room for another Johnson, Olson, or Smith. Try that with your paper notebook — especially if your family's name happens to be Johnson, Olson, or Smith!

✔ You won't have to worry about old Pocket PC address book entries getting too faded or smudged to read.

✔ If someone you know happens to be like certain relatives of mine, you won't fill up your entire Pocket PC address book changing his address listing every few months. (Yes, so maybe you'd just give up on them if you were using a paper notebook, but with the Pocket PC address book you still need only one record no matter how many times someone moves.)

✔ Because your Pocket PC can easily exchange address book information with your desktop PC, having several copies of your address book that are all up-to-date is far easier. If something happens to one copy, you still have at least one more copy to bail you out. If you lose your little black book, you may lose your only copy (and then how would you get a date for Saturday night?).

✔ Because you can use a password to restrict access to your Pocket PC, you can make certain no one else can snoop through the listings in your Pocket PC address book. Your snoopy boss won't have any way to know that you've been in contact with that executive recruiter. See "Adjusting Your Security" in Chapter 2 for information about using a password to control access to the information you have stored on your Pocket PC.

✔ Because your Pocket PC's screen has a backlight, you can look up phone numbers and make calls late at night without turning on a light — a definite advantage if all you can find is some broken down phone booth when you're lost out in the boondocks. To see how to control the backlight on your Pocket PC, see "Changing Your Screen Settings" in Chapter 2.

✔ Finally, if you add the voice recognition software I introduce near the end of this chapter, you can amaze everyone by simply talking to your Pocket PC to tell it whose record you want to see!

Your address book as an organizer

Some people are *really* well organized. They're the ones whose sock drawer has dividers and a specific place for each pair of socks. Most of us are far less organized, but almost anyone can benefit from a certain amount of neatness and advance planning — as long as you don't get too obsessed with it, that is.

If you've used a paper notebook to keep your address book in the past, you're used to having a certain amount of organization. But the static nature of things written down on paper can also limit your thinking to a rather narrow view of ways to organize your little black book. Consider these options you may not have realized would be practical or even possible:

✔ When you add people to your Pocket PC address book, you can assign them categories. Some people may belong in the Personal category, some in Business, and some may be members of your favorite organization. Because your Pocket PC address book gives you the option of limiting the view to display only people who are in a specific category, your one Pocket PC address book can serve the function of a whole series of different paper notebooks.

✔ You can add people to more than one category in your Pocket PC address book, so you need only to record their information in one place even if they fit several categories. If their address or phone number changes, you have to make the correction just one time to have it correct in every one of the categories they belong to.

✔ Because you can easily create as many new categories as you like, creating special categories for one time use is an easy task. You can, for example, create a category that includes all of the members of your book club. Then you can create a special category for members of the book club who want to be notified about book signings in your area by your favorite author. This enables you to first show just the book club members, and then easily add the author's fans to the special category. When you hear about a last minute local appearance by the author, you won't have to waste time trying to remember who wants to know about it — your Pocket PC address book can tell you in a flash.

Your address book as an electronic business card

I bet you don't have your own contact information listed in your address book — why would you? Well, for one very good reason — so you can easily exchange your information in the form of an electronic business card.

Pocket PCs all have an infrared (or IR) port built in, allowing them to send and receive data with other infrared-equipped devices like Pocket PCs, most laptop PCs, certain printers, and yes, even Palm PCs. One of the coolest ways to exchange business cards with other Pocket PC or Palm PC users is to *beam* your card through the IR port. In Figure 4-1, I've selected my record in the Pocket PC address book and used tap-and-hold to display the context menu. All I need to do now is aim my Pocket PC at the other device and tap Beam Contact.

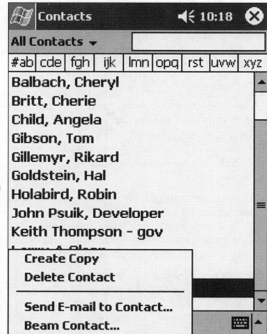

Figure 4-1:
To be really cool, exchange your business card using the infrared beam.

You may want to create more than one business card for different purposes. For example, you may not want everyone to receive all of your home contact information, or you may want to create one card for business use and a different one for use in your position as a club's officer.

You can actually send any contact record via the IR beam. You aren't limited to sending just your own business card. Whichever records you send, you can be certain that the other person gets a complete record without worrying that he or she wrote something down incorrectly.

To exchange data with a laptop PC, you may need to activate the IR port on the laptop. You may also need to install ActiveSync on the laptop if it isn't already installed. Some laptops use special applications to control infrared file transfers, so consult your laptop's user manual if you're unable to exchange information with your Pocket PC. (See also Chapter 7 for more information on using ActiveSync.)

Entering New Contacts

Even the New York City phone book is just a bunch of blank paper until it has all of the names and phone numbers printed into its pages. Your Pocket PC address book is almost as useful as that blank paper before you start adding some contact information to it — although the blank paper may be more useful in some instances (making paper airplanes, for example).

Doing it the old-fashioned way: Adding records manually

Of all of the methods of adding people to your Pocket PC address book, you'll probably spend the most time adding records manually, which isn't the easiest way to add records, nor is it the quickest. But adding records manually is the one way that's always available, and the one that gives you the most flexibility.

 You may find that your Pocket PC manufacturer has added its own enhanced version of the address book to your unit. While this enhanced version probably has a bunch of neat features that aren't in the standard version, you may get confused if you try to use the fancy version in place of the plain old vanilla version discussed in here — at least while you're following along so you can see how this all works. You can always switch over to the fancy-pants version later because they both share the same data file, but I recommend starting off with the standard one in the beginning.

You need to begin by opening the Contacts application, which is what the Pocket PC address book is called. You can open Contacts by pressing the appropriate button on the front of your Pocket PC — if you remember which button does this on your unit and you haven't changed the button assignments, that is. You can also open Contacts by clicking the Start button and tapping Contacts on the Start menu.

Now you're ready to add a new record to the list. Begin by tapping New in the lower-left corner of the Pocket PC's screen, which opens a new blank record so you can add information. Figure 4-2 shows how a record looks after you've added information in several of the fields.

Contacts ◀€ 10:30 ok

Name:	Cole Underdahl ▼
Job title:	Security Officer
Department:	
Company:	Underdahl Computing
Work tel:	(775) 122-4455
Work fax:	
Work addr:	▼
E-mail:	toughguy@under.net
Mobile tel:	
Web page:	
Office loc:	
Home tel:	
Home addr:	▼

Details | Notes

Edit

Figure 4-2:
Enter
contact
information
into any of
the fields as
necessary.

Although the entry form shown in Figure 4-2 has so many different fields that you'd need several screens to view all of them, you don't have to use any of the fields that you don't need. In fact, when you later have a look at one of the records in your address book you find that your Pocket PC is smart enough to show a field only if it actually contains information. In most cases, this means that anyone's record can easily read on a single screen.

When you're done adding information, tap OK to close the new record and add it to the address book.

To confirm that the record was added correctly, you can find and view the record. Depending on just how many people you've added to your address book, finding a record can be a bit of a pain unless you understand a few of the tools that are available to help you out.

There are two ways to narrow your search so you don't have to scroll through quite so many records in your Pocket PC address book — using categories or the alphabet bar. Figure 4-3 shows both of them.

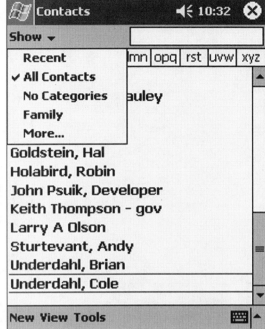

Figure 4-3:
Use
categories
to make
finding
specific
records
easier.

If you selected a category when you entered someone's record, you can narrow your search by clicking on the category list (just below the Start button). This drops down the list so you can choose a category to view. When you select a category, only those records that are in that category appear in your Contact list.

Remember to select All Contacts to make the full list available again.

In addition to selecting a category, you can also click on the alphabet bar (just above the list of records) to jump to a spot someplace in the middle of your address records, which beats using the scrollbar to move the entire distance.

When you've found the record you want, click the record to view it. As Figure 4-4 shows, the information is condensed so that you see only those fields with information filled in.

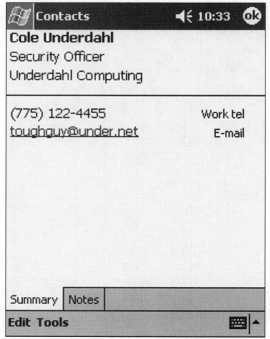

Figure 4-4:
Open the
record
to verify
that the
information
you added is
really there.

To quickly modify the record you're viewing, tap Edit on the menu bar. This opens the record and shows all of the fields — even the ones that don't have any information yet.

Doing it the new-fangled way: Bringing records over from your desktop

As powerful as your Pocket PC may be, it was never really intended to be your only computer. Your Pocket PC makes far more sense as a partner to your desktop PC. One area where this partnership really shines is in sharing information — such as your address book — between your Pocket PC and your desktop PC. This sharing makes it possible for you to enter the information once and then use it anywhere.

To share information between your desktop PC and your Pocket PC, you need to use ActiveSync — a program that comes with your Pocket PC. Chapter 7 covers the use of ActiveSync in detail, but there are some important things to know about sharing your address book information between the two types of PCs.

You need to install Outlook

You need to install Outlook 2000 (or later) on your desktop PC in order to share contact information with your Pocket PC. Outlook 2002 is included on the Pocket PC Companion CD-ROM if you don't already have it installed on your desktop system.

Even if you already have Outlook 2000 installed on your desktop PC, you should give serious consideration to upgrading to Outlook 2002, which is included with your Pocket PC. Outlook 2002 includes a number of very important security enhancements — such as automatic blocking of a number of potentially dangerous types of attachments — which make it a far better choice than Outlook 2000. For the balance of this discussion, I'll assume that you have installed Outlook 2002.

There's no rule that says you have to actually *use* Outlook on your desktop, but Microsoft certainly has made it clear that they would like you to do so. Outlook is the only program that can share contact information with a Pocket PC, so keeping your address book in any application other than Outlook is going to involve a lot of extra steps whenever you want to update the information in your Pocket PC or your desktop PC.

You need the information in Outlook

If your contact information is currently in some program other than Outlook, you need to import that information into Outlook before you can add the information to your Pocket PC. In Outlook you can import information using the File⇨Import and Export command. This starts the Import and Export Wizard, which helps you import your data.

You can import information from many different applications, but Outlook can sometimes be a little picky about which file formats it will accept. I've noticed, for example, that sometimes I have to try three or four different formats before I find one that works. Unfortunately, the Import and Export Wizard allows you to go through almost the entire process before it tells you that it cannot import a particular file. If this happens, going back to the original application and trying to export the data in a different format is usually the best route.

If all else fails, see whether you can export the data in *delimited* text format. Delimited text format simply writes out the data as a text file with each field separated by commas and the values enclosed in quotes. Most programs offer this as an export option, and Outlook can easily import a delimited text file.

You need to set the Contacts option in ActiveSync

After you have the address book information in Outlook, you need to enable sharing of contact information in ActiveSync. Select Tools⇨Options in

ActiveSync for this option. Chapter 7 covers all of the ActiveSync options so you can see what else you may need to do.

Beam It Over, Scotty!

By far the coolest way to add address book information to your Pocket PC is to beam it over from another Pocket PC (or, if you're upgrading, from a Palm PC). After you see how fun this beaming is, you'll probably start looking for other Pocket PC owners just so you can have beaming sessions.

Exchanging information using the infrared beams is pretty easy once you get the hang of it. To make it a bit easier for you, here's a step-by-step approach that works pretty well:

1. **Choose the contacts you want to beam over to the other Pocket PC.**

   You can choose more than one contact to send.

2. **Tap Tools on the menu bar.**

   This displays the pop-up menu, shown in Figure 4-5.

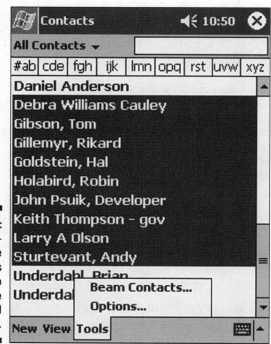

Figure 4-5:
Tap-and-hold the contacts you want to send on the infrared beam.

3. **Tap Beam Contacts to begin the transfer.**

   Aim the infrared ports of the two Pocket PCs at each other, keeping the two within a few inches of each other. While your Pocket PC is looking for the other Pocket PC, you see the `Align ports` and `Searching` messages shown in Figure 4-6.

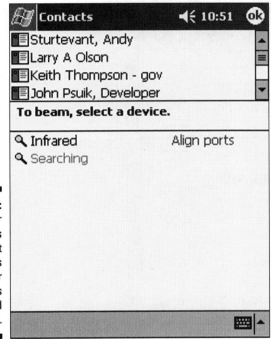

Figure 4-6: Aim your Pocket PC's infrared port towards the other Pocket PC's infrared port.

4. **Tell the other Pocket PC to save the records.**

   Select Yes or Save All, depending on the number of records you sent. When the receiving Pocket PC has received the transmission, you see the `Receiving Data` message shown in Figure 4-7.

If you find that the transfer didn't work, here are some things to try:

- First simply try starting the transfer again. This usually resolves the problem.

- If you can't get the transfer working after a couple of tries, make sure the two infrared ports are really pointing at each other. Different brands of Pocket PCs hide their infrared ports in different locations.

- Make certain there is nothing between the two Pocket PCs that could be blocking the infrared light beam. Really bright sunlight can be a problem. You may also be holding your Pocket PC with your hand over the infrared port — but try to blame it on something else if you realize this is the problem before anyone else does.

✔ Blame it on some secret encryption software that prevents anyone from stealing your data. It's not true, but how are they going to know?

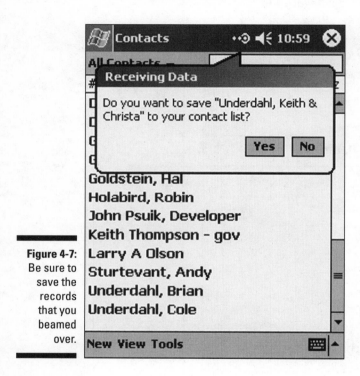

Figure 4-7:
Be sure to save the records that you beamed over.

Using Voice Recognition to Manage Your Contacts

Your Pocket PC is pretty cool all by itself, but this next program I'm going to show you could be called the iceberg of cool! In fact, this is the program I use when I want to impress someone by showing them how useful and advanced the Pocket PC has become.

The software I'm talking about (and talking to) is *Voice LookUp* from HandHeld Speech (www.handheldspeech.com). This amazing application enables your Pocket PC to recognize your voice so that you can look up contact records simply by speaking the name you want into the microphone. Once you have someone's record onscreen, placing a call to them or sending an e-mail message is just another simple voice command away. You can even use voice commands to switch to different applications on your Pocket PC. You can download a trial copy of the program from the HandHeld Speech Web site, and register it once you see how well it works.

Voice LookUp is a very easy program to use. Once you have downloaded and installed it, you will probably want to set up your Pocket PC so that pressing the Record button on the side of your Pocket PC starts the program (the readme file that accompanies Voice LookUp tells you exactly how to do this). This will make it even easier for you to use Voice LookUp since you can do so just by pressing that Record button.

Before you can use Voice LookUp for the first time, you'll need to spend just a few minutes training it to recognize your voice. To do so, you tap the Enroll icon in the Programs folder, and then spend about five minutes reading some text. At the end of the enrollment you can begin using the program (although you'll want to continue training it as you use the program to improve the accuracy — see the user documentation included with the program for more details).

Once the enrollment is completed and you start the program, you will see the LookUp screen. This is your starting point for using Voice LookUp.

When the LookUp screen is displayed, you see a message in the lower left of the screen telling you that the microphone is off. Now it's time to have some fun. Press the Record button so that the microphone turns on, hold the microphone on your Pocket PC close to your mouth, and say "look up" and the name of someone in your Contact list. Figure 4-8 shows the result.

Once a contact record is displayed, you can easily send an e-mail or place a phone call to that person. For example, I can press the Record button and say "call work" to tell Voice LookUp to dial my office number. Once I enter my command, a countdown timer appears on the screen, and at the end of the countdown Voice LookUp plays the proper touchtone dialing notes from the Pocket PC's speaker. By holding the Pocket PC's speaker next to the telephone receiver, this automatically dials the call for me.

As I mentioned a bit earlier, you do need to train Voice LookUp a bit in order to improve the accuracy. If you find that the program has displayed the wrong record, choose the correct record from the list above the Adapt button and then tap the Adapt button. As you continue to do this, you will find that Voice LookUp finds the correct record far more often. You'll want to do a bit of training before you start bragging to other people about how smart your Pocket PC is, but you'll find that it is time well spent — especially once you see the reactions on people's faces when they see your Pocket PC respond to voice commands!

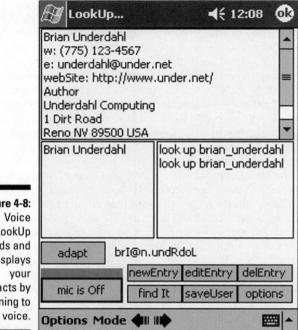

Figure 4-8:
Voice
LookUp
finds and
displays
your
contacts by
listening to
your voice.

Chapter 5

Taking Some Notes

In This Chapter

▶ Discovering some great uses for notes

▶ Creating notes

▶ Recording notes by speaking

As I go over in Chapter 4, your Pocket PC makes old-fashioned paper address books seem pretty lame. Well, get ready to throw out your paper notepads, too. Your Pocket PC is going to make writing notes on a pad of paper seem like the equivalent of scratching a letter out on a piece of bark you've peeled off a tree.

If you aren't in the habit of writing yourself notes, you may wonder why anyone would need to use a Pocket PC for note taking. If so, go ahead and skip this chapter — but write yourself a note to remind you to come back later when you discover you've forgotten something important.

Finding Uses for Your Pocket PC Notes

Notes are probably the most free-form type of document that exists. There's really nothing formal about all those sticky notes that people paste all over the side of their monitors, and there are no rules about what you can or can't do with a note. Notes simply are the Swiss Army knife style of documents. (Why, even using the word "document" to describe a note seems kind of pretentious, doesn't it?)

Still, there are a lot of things you can do with notes on your Pocket PC:

 ✔ You can use a note to quickly write down a Web address you see in a TV commercial.

 ✔ You can use a note to create your weekly grocery list — although you may get some funny looks in the frozen food aisle.

✔ You can whip out a quick note to remind yourself of the punch line of that great joke you just heard. Just don't try to tell people the joke by reading it off your Pocket PC's screen — they may laugh, but it won't be at the joke!

✔ When you wake up in the middle of the night with that idea for a new product that's going to make you rich, write it down in a Pocket PC note. You won't have to turn on a light to see the Pocket PC's screen, and that way, no one will ever know about the dumb idea when you read the note the next day.

✔ If you use the Transcriber, your Pocket PC may be able to read your handwriting better than almost anyone else. So even if your handwriting is pretty sloppy, you'll still be able to create notes that someone can actually read. Don't forget to proofread it, though — the Transcriber can't produce miracles! See Chapter 3 for information on how to use the Transcriber.

Of course, there are some things you shouldn't try to do with notes on your Pocket PC:

✔ Leaving your Pocket PC taped to a friend's door with a note telling him you dropped by when he wasn't home probably isn't a good idea.

✔ Ransom notes on your Pocket PC is another bad idea.

✔ Finally, don't try to use a Pocket PC note to tell a bank teller that "this is a stickup." This situation could be especially bad if you run out with the money but forget your Pocket PC — especially if you entered your real name and address in the owner information screen.

Writing Yourself a Note

The Pocket PC Notes application seems like a very simple program, but you may be a little surprised to find out just how much it can really do. In addition to being a quick way to jot down a thought, this program offers some really cool options like voice notes and an electronic drawing pad where you can literally draw a picture right on your screen. You'll probably miss many of the neatest options if I don't point them out before you begin, so here is a quick look at the note options.

Choosing your note options

You can just go ahead and begin using the Notes program, but why not start with a little detour to see whether some of the available options are better suited for your needs? Open the Notes program by clicking the Start button and choosing Notes from the Start menu. When you see the list of existing notes (or a blank list if you haven't used Notes before), click Tools⇨Options to display the Notes Options. Then follow along through the following four sections to see what these options do and which settings will work best for you.

Selecting your entry mode

The first optional setting is the Default mode setting. You can choose to start new notes in Writing mode or Typing mode. As you can easily guess, these modes refer to using handwriting or the onscreen keyboard to enter text into your notes.

Choosing a default input mode for notes may seem odd when you can easily select your input method using the SIP (Secondary Input Panel) selector in the lower-right corner of your screen. In reality, though, this Notes option is pretty cool because it enables you to select a different input mode for notes than the one you typically use in other types of applications.

You could, for example, choose Writing as your Notes default, and leave the onscreen keyboard selected for all other input. When you want to write out a quick note, you don't have to remember to first switch the input method (or worry about losing your train of thought when you have to first attend to such details).

Using the Writing mode in Notes is not quite the same thing as using the Transcriber. When you use the Transcriber, your notes are automatically converted into text a short time after you finish writing. When you use the Notes Writing mode, you need to select Tools⇨Recognize to convert your handwriting into text.

Picking a template

You'll probably be pleasantly surprised by the next optional setting — the Default template option. You may not even realize that the Notes application uses templates.

In addition to the Blank Note template, you can choose from meeting notes, memos, phone memos, and to-do templates. Each template is set up specifically to make taking certain types of notes easier, so choosing the correct template can help you produce better notes with less work. Indeed, choosing the right template can save you a lot of trouble by making certain that you don't forget to write down an important piece of information — such as the phone number so you can return a call.

In addition to adding fields for important information you won't want to forget, the templates also use quite large text in the field names so you can more easily see where and what you need to enter.

After you select a default template, any new notes you create use that template until you choose a different template option. Remember to use the Tools⇨ Options command to select a different template when you want to create a different type of note.

Deciding where to save it

When you close a note that you've created, your Pocket PC saves the note into the storage memory area. If you have a storage card installed in your Pocket PC, you can use the Save to option to choose to save the note on the memory card rather than in the main storage memory.

Your Pocket PC uses a very efficient file storage system, which minimizes the amount of memory that is used to store your files. Even so, the built-in storage memory is limited, and using an extra memory card can greatly enhance your ability to save files.

Saving your notes to a storage card rather than to main memory can be especially important if you create a lot of voice notes. These types of notes can really eat up memory, especially if you choose one of the higher-quality recording settings.

The Save to setting won't have any effect if you don't have a storage card inserted into your Pocket PC. If you choose the storage card option rather than main memory and then swap out your storage memory card for a different type of device that fits into the expansion slot, any new notes you create are stored in main memory. If you reinsert the storage card, it's used again to store new notes, but existing notes in main memory won't automatically be moved.

Programming the Record button

Your Pocket PC has a button that you can press to begin recording a voice note (see "Recording a Note" later in this chapter for more information). Use the Record button action setting to choose what you want to happen when you press the button.

This option controls whether your Pocket PC automatically opens the Notes application when you press the Record button. Either way, your Pocket PC records your voice note, but because other applications may not know how to deal with the voice note, keeping the default action set to Switch to Notes is usually best.

Starting a new note

After you know what the Notes application can do and have selected the settings you prefer, you can begin using the program with a new note. If you haven't started the Notes program yet, click the Start button and choose Notes from the Start menu.

If you've used Notes to create other notes, you see a list of the existing notes. Tap one of them to open it so you can read it, edit it, or simply add more to it. To begin a new note, click New.

What you do next depends on the input method you selected. In most cases, using handwriting is probably the easiest, but you have to decide what works best for you.

Editing your note

As good as the handwriting recognition may be, you may encounter errors from time to time. That's when you need to get out the red pen and begin some serious editing (I'm not *really* advocating using a red pen — it's just that human editors traditionally used red pens to mark their corrections in a manuscript).

Editing a note on your Pocket PC seems very familiar as you use the same commands you're used to from your desktop PC. Figure 5-1 shows the Edit menu in the Pocket PC Notes program.

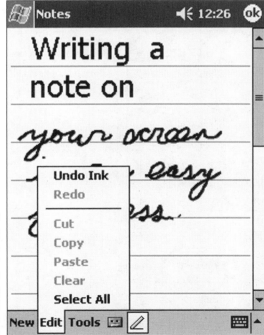

Figure 5-1: Use the familiar Edit menu commands to edit your notes.

Editing a note using the onscreen keyboard is often easier than handwriting recognition. If, however, you are using the Transcriber, you can teach your Pocket PC to do a better job of recognizing your handwriting by training it when it makes an error. *Training* consists of selecting the letter that was incorrectly recognized and then rewriting the letter. How successful this training is depends heavily on how patient you are as you may need to repeat the process a number of times before the recognition improves.

To edit your note, tap where you want to make the correction. If you want to replace a word, drag the stylus across the word to select the word. Then type in your correction or use the Edit menu commands as necessary. If you want to delete the last handwriting, select Edit⇨Undo Ink.

If you're using handwriting recognition and discover that some words are incorrect after you select Tools⇨Recognize, try the Tools⇨Alternates command. First select the misspelled word and then select the command. As Figure 5-2 shows, using the Alternates command often saves you the trouble of a lot of manual editing. If the correct word is one of the alternates, choose the correction from the list. If the correct word is not shown, edit the word manually.

Figure 5-2:
Use Tools⇨
Alternates
as a quick
method
to correct
incorrectly
recognized
words.

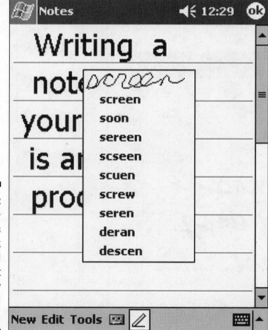

A picture is worth a thousand words

Sometimes showing something in a quick drawing is far easier than writing out a whole long description. Even a crude map can be more understandable than someone's list of directions. And you don't have to give up the ability to make a quick drawing just because you're taking notes on a Pocket PC rather than on a pad of paper.

Figure 5-3 shows an example of a quick map I drew to show how to find a campground where a bunch of friends were going to be gathering. I could have added a lot more detail and even included some written directions, but even this crude map got me to the campground.

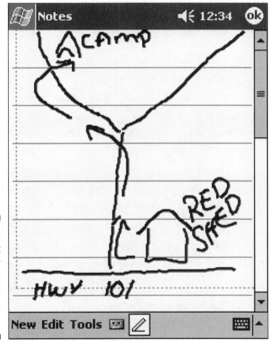

Figure 5-3:
Draw right on your screen to include a drawing in your note.

You may be wondering how your Pocket PC knows when you've made a drawing rather than some really odd handwriting. The answer is simple: When you cross three of the horizontal gridlines in a single motion, your Pocket PC knows that you are using *digital ink* to make a drawing. When you complete your drawing it becomes a *bitmap* image within your note (a bitmap is simply a graphic image where each dot in the image can be modified on its own without affecting the rest of the image). You can tell this because tapping within the drawing displays a dotted line that indicates the borders of the drawing. Don't tap within the drawing if it's already selected, though. That will add a dot to the drawing. You can tell that the drawing is selected because the dotted line appears around a drawing when it is selected. To see more information about the Transcriber and the horizontal guidelines it uses, see Chapter 3.

You can expand a drawing by starting a new line within the current boundaries of the drawing and simply continuing outside those boundaries. You can change the size of the drawing by tapping it to select it, and then using the handles that appear along the borders to stretch or contract it.

To edit your drawing, use the Edit➪Undo Ink command to remove elements from the drawing in the order they were added. But you aren't limited to this sequential editing mode. You can also tap an element within the drawing to select it, and then use the Edit menu commands or drag and drop to modify it.

Recording a Note

In addition to typing, handwriting, and drawing, you've got another interesting option for creating a note. You can record a note in your own voice — or someone else's if you can get her to talk into your Pocket PC.

Voice notes are often the most convenient way to create a note because you can record a note while you're doing something else. You can even create a voice note when writing is pretty much impossible, such as while riding in a crowded bus on a very bumpy road.

Although recording voice notes on your Pocket PC while you're driving seems mighty tempting, I don't recommend it. Even talking into your Pocket PC takes too much concentration for this to be safe. If you absolutely have to record a voice note while driving, try to find a safe place to pull over so you don't endanger everyone else (and yourself) on the road.

How good do you want it to sound?

Remember those commercials for audio recording tape that asked "Is it live or is it Memorex?" Well, no one is going to mistake a recording you make on your Pocket PC with a live voice. Quite honestly, if you really want high fidelity recordings, you need to look somewhere else.

The voice-recording feature on your Pocket PC is somewhat lacking in audio quality for one very good reason: Storing high quality digital sound recordings takes up a lot of space. By choosing a lower quality level, you greatly reduce the amount of memory needed for your recording.

Choosing the best recording format can be a bit of a pain. Your Pocket PC offers quite a few options that range all the way from one setting that uses about 2 kilobytes for each second of recording to another option that uses about 172 kilobytes per second — a ratio of 86 to 1!

Unfortunately, the choices aren't quite as simple as they may seem. The smallest-sized voice setting certainly gives you the longest recording time on a given amount of memory, but you may not be able to understand your own voice recordings if you select that option. The largest-sized files certainly sound better, but they waste half of the space they use because they're in stereo format — even though you're recording from a monaural microphone on your Pocket PC (both channels of the stereo recording have exactly the same signal).

To make matters worse, if you want to share your recording with your desktop system or perhaps to e-mail a voice note to someone, only some of the recording formats are likely to be usable, depending on exactly where the recording is played back. For example, the GSM 6.10 format — the one that happens to produce the smallest files — won't be playable on most desktop PCs. And it figures that the format that produces the largest files is the one that pretty much anyone is able to play. You'll probably find that it takes some trial and error testing to see which recording formats are usable for other people since any particular desktop PC may not have the ability to use the format you select. (For details on selecting the recording format, see the following section, "Choosing your recording format.")

So experiment a little before you decide on the recording format. Create a few sample files using different formats, and then try listening to those recordings on the different PCs and in the different applications you're using. That way, you won't have any unpleasant surprises when you actually need to make an important recording.

Choosing your recording format

In order to select the format that will work the best you may want to try out several different ones. To select the recording format, follow these steps:

1. Click the Start button and choose Notes from the Start menu.

Make certain you are viewing the list of notes rather than creating a new note. If you're in a note, you have to close the note in order to access the recording settings.

2. **Next, choose Tools⇨Options and then tap Global Input Options to display the Settings screen.**

3. **Click the down arrow on the Voice Recording Format list and choose the option you prefer from the list.**

4. **Click OK when you have made your selection.**

Don't waste memory choosing a stereo recording format. In most cases, the equivalent mono format works just as well and takes half as much space.

When you select a recording format, the frequency that is listed is the number of *samples* — little bits of data that define the sound you're recording — per second that are used to record the sound. But this number generally represents a figure that is about double the highest audio frequency that's included in the recording. As a result, choosing a format that is listed as 8,000 Hz effectively limits the recording to sounds below 4,000 Hz. This isn't as bad as it sounds. Sure, a musical recording that cuts off everything above 4,000 Hz would sound terrible, but the human voice typically doesn't use many sounds above about 3,000 Hz. So for a voice-only recording, you don't gain much by including higher frequencies.

Recording your note

The easiest way to record a note is to simply hold down the Record button on the side of your Pocket PC and begin speaking into the microphone. Continue holding down the button until you're done. You can also click the Record button on the Recording controls toolbar to begin a recording and click the Stop button to end the recording. You can display this toolbar by clicking the icon that looks like a miniature cassette tape on the Notes menu bar.

If possible, try to make your recording in one pass. Each time you press and release the Record button on the side of your Pocket PC, you create a new recording. So if you want all of your thoughts to be included in a single recording, be sure to hold the button down continuously while speaking.

Using your recording

After you've made a recording, you'll want to play it back, especially if you selected a new recording format — you want to make sure you can actually understand what you've recorded.

To play back your recording, tap the recording in the list of notes. If you can't hear the recording, click the Speaker icon on the right side of the Recording toolbar to display the volume control (see Figure 5-4). Drag the slider up or down as necessary.

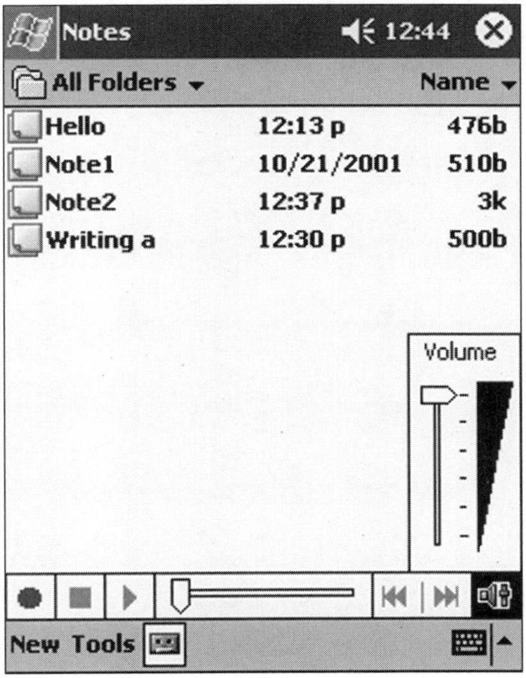

![Notes screen showing a list of notes: Hello 12:13 p 476b, Note1 10/21/2001 510b, Note2 12:37 p 3k, Writing a 12:30 p 500b, with a Volume slider control and recording toolbar at the bottom.]

Figure 5-4:
Use the
Recording
toolbar to
control
playback
and volume.

Understanding a recording is much easier if you listen to it using headphones rather than trying to use the built-in speaker (especially if you've selected one of the smaller recording formats). Any standard stereo headphones should work, although the small ear bud type may be the most convenient to carry along with your Pocket PC.

After you check your recording and find that it's okay, you can use that recording many different ways. Here are just a few ideas:

- ✔ If someone is giving you directions to someplace, ask him to record the directions on your Pocket PC so you can play them back if you get confused or turned around. You may want to have them record each leg as a separate voice note so that you can repeat a single note without listening to directions you have already completed.

- ✔ You can send a recording to someone as an e-mail attachment, which is a great way to send someone birthday greetings — especially if you sing "Happy Birthday" in the recording. What better way to get someone to stop complaining that you always forget his birthday?

✔ A voice note can be included in a spreadsheet or other document. When someone is viewing the document, she can click on the Recording icon in the document to hear your explanation justifying the cost of your latest business dinner.

✔ Finally, if you have a recording of your buddy telling you he'll eat his hat if you get that promotion, you'll probably work extra hard to make certain you actually do get the new job. And won't it be fun passing the salt and pepper?

Chapter 6

Keeping Your Mobile Calendar

● ●

In This Chapter

▶ Setting up your calendar options

▶ Creating your pocket calendar

▶ Putting your to-do list in your pocket

● ●

I bet that you're just too darn busy and that managing your time seems a lot harder than it should be. Even if there were eight days in a week, you still wouldn't have enough time for everything you want to do, would you?

Your Pocket PC can't create more time, but it can help you make better use of the time you have. Not only does the Pocket PC help you organize your schedule, but it keeps track of your to-do list — all of those things that need to get done sometime, but don't fit neatly into a schedule. And, as an added bonus, your Pocket PC can keep you out of the doghouse by making sure you never forget an important personal event like a birthday or anniversary. (That alone could be worth whatever you have to pay for a Pocket PC!)

As with a number of the other applications of your Pocket PC, you may find that the manufacturer offers an alternative to the standard Calendar program I discuss in this chapter. For example, HP includes an application called *Conversay Mobile Conversay,* which enhances the Pocket PC's Calendar program by adding certain voice-recognition functions. You may want to check the Pocket PC Companion CD that accompanies your Pocket PC to see whether your system offers similar enhancements. I will not be covering these types of enhancements because they are specific to certain brands and models of the Pocket PC — rather, I will concentrate on the basics, which I am sure will be available to you.

Setting Up Your Options

When you're dealing with something as personal as your calendar, you certainly want it to reflect your way of looking at things. You can make a bunch of changes to the calendar using the calendar options, so you're sure to enjoy using it.

To begin setting the calendar options the way you want them, first open the Calendar by clicking the Start button and choosing Calendar from the Start menu. Or you can press the appropriate button on the front of your Pocket PC (whichever button is set up to open the calendar on your brand and model of Pocket PC). Next, click Tools⇨Options on the menu bar, which displays the Calendar Options screen. Read on for details on each option.

Defining your week

Your first choice in the calendar options is defining your week — at least in terms of how you'll be using the calendar.

Depending on your needs, you can have the calendar begin each week by showing either Sunday or Monday as the first day of the week. And you're stuck with choosing either Sunday or Monday, so if you've got one of those strange work schedules that rotate starting days or if you always begin work on a day other than Sunday or Monday, you're out of luck.

Next, you can choose the number of days in your week. Okay, so we all know that there are seven days in a week, but you can set your calendar to five, six, or seven days. The intent is to allow you to show only workdays if you want. Setting the number of days is really a matter of personal choice; you're on your own in deciding what to use.

Controlling the clutter

Now get ready to decide just how cluttered you'd like your calendar to appear. Choose from the following options:

- **Show half hour slots:** Choose this option if you want to be able to easily tap the exact time slot for appointments that begin at half past the hour in addition to those beginning right on the hour. Choosing to show half hour slots makes the daily schedule take up a lot more room on the Pocket PC's screen, so I prefer to skip this option. You can easily set the correct time for an appointment no matter how this option is set.

- **Show week numbers:** Select this to include the week number — the number of weeks since the first of the year — in the calendar header when you choose the week view. Unless you really need to know the week number for some odd reason, this option seems to serve no important purpose other than adding more clutter to the screen.

- **Use large font:** Choose this option if your calendar display is just too hard to read. Of course, pulling out your reading glasses is another viable option. The larger the font, the less information the small Pocket PC screen can show and the more you need to scroll.

✔ **Set reminders for new items:** This option automatically creates an *aide memoire* to make certain you don't forget your appointments. You can always set reminders for individual calendar items, but this option makes certain you don't forget to do so.

If you select the Set reminders for new items option, you can use the two boxes immediately below the option to determine how far in advance you want to be notified. I prefer more notice than the default settings of 15 minutes, but you can choose whatever works best for you.

✔ **Show icons:** Tap any of the icons to choose the ones you want to see on your calendar. The icons (left to right) indicate reminders, recurring appointments, notes, location, attendees, and private. Select only those icons that really mean something important to you to keep your calendar listings from being crowded out by all sorts of unnecessary icons.

Sending meeting requests

The final calendar option is the choice of how to send meeting requests. Your choices here would generally be to use ActiveSync or to send the requests via e-mail. If you access your e-mail directly from your Pocket PC by dialing in to your mail server, you may want to choose the e-mail option so that the requests go out sooner. If you regularly synchronize your Pocket PC with your desktop PC, and you handle most of your e-mail messages through your desktop system, choose ActiveSync.

Click OK when you have finished setting your calendar options.

Setting Up Your Schedule

The Pocket PC calendar is more than a pretty display of dates. What makes the calendar really useful is adding the items that are on your schedule so you can plan ahead. After your Pocket PC calendar has your schedule included in the listings, you can easily see when you're going to be busy, when you'll have some free time, and when you can arrange for new appointments.

Because you probably use your Pocket PC as a partner to your desktop PC, you'll almost certainly want to have the same list of events and appointments on both systems. Fortunately, the software that comes with your Pocket PC — specifically ActiveSync — makes keeping your two calendars up to date a simple automated process. When you've set up the items you want to share between your Pocket PC and your desktop PC, you'll be able to synchronize your calendars by simply popping your Pocket PC into the cradle on your desk. Chapter 7 shows you how to set up ActiveSync so you won't even have to think about it.

In the following sections I cover how to set up and manage your appointments on your Pocket PC. If you sometimes manage your schedule using your desktop PC, you'll find that the process is very similar no matter which PC you use.

Adding an appointment

Adding a new appointment to your schedule is very easy. At least it's easy in terms of what you need to do on your Pocket PC. Finding the time to accommodate the items you've added is your problem.

Just because your Pocket PC's calendar uses the fancy term "appointment" for things you add to your schedule doesn't mean that you can only add business-related items to the list. Birthdays, anniversaries, dates, or anything else that happens on a specific date or time are also fair game. Someone had to pick a name for the items you add to your calendar, and it just so happens that the person chose appointment. If you'd prefer to think of these things as rendezvous, prior engagements, or something else, feel free.

To add a new appointment, open your calendar and then tap New on the menu bar. You can also tap-and-hold on a specific date and time for the appointment, and select New Appointment from the pop-up menu. Selecting the date and time first offers a couple of advantages and some disadvantages:

- **Advantage:** Starting by selecting the date and time enables you to quickly see whether the new item is in conflict with existing items.

- **Advantage:** If you select a specific date and time, the New Appointment form automatically uses that date and time as the starting point for the item. You can easily change the date and time, but you won't have to if the date and time are already correct when you begin creating the schedule item.

- **Disadvantage:** If you're setting up an event that's far off in the future, navigating to the correct date may be a bit of a pain.

- **Disadvantage:** If the new item *conflicts* with an existing item, tapping the time of the new item opens the existing item rather than opening a new appointment form. Events conflict with each other if they share some of the same dates and times on your calendar. For example, an all-day event like a birthday would conflict with a dental appointment at 10 a.m. on the same day.

Choosing a subject

Begin by entering a subject for the item. You can select a subject from the drop-down list, as shown in Figure 6-1, or you can enter a new subject.

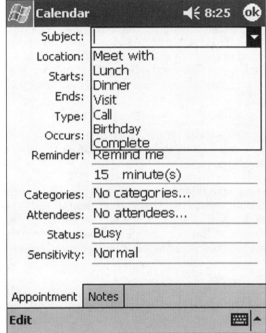

Generally you see only the event's subject in the calendar, so picking a subject that's clear enables you to understand your schedule with a quick glance, even after you've added a bunch of things to your calendar. If you can't figure out an event from looking at the calendar, you have to open the individual items to see what they contain. So make the subject as clear as possible for your own sake.

Even if you pick one of the items from the drop-down list, you can personalize it by adding your own text. For example, if you select "Meet with" from the list, add the name of the person you're meeting to the Subject line.

Setting the location

After you've specified the subject, you can add a location for the event. Including a location isn't always necessary because some events simply don't require you to be in some particular place. A good example is if the event you're adding is someone's birthday. In that case, the location doesn't matter (unless you happen to be going to her birthday party, of course). You also don't need a location if you're listing something like a phone call you need to make. The point is, you can leave this field blank.

For an event like a scheduled phone call, use the location field for the phone number you'll need to call (especially if you're calling someone who isn't included in your list of contacts).

The drop-down location list starts out empty. As you set up appointments, the locations you've used in the past are added to the list. Eventually you find that you can select locations from the list rather than always having to enter them manually.

Setting the times

Now it's time to set the times for most events. You don't have to worry about times for some all-day events like birthdays, but in most cases you want both a starting and an ending time.

Each item you add to your calendar is considered as running continuously from the specified starting time to the specified ending time. If you need to add an event that runs during the same hours — but not all day — on several consecutive days, you can use the Occurs field to specify a recurrence pattern. See "Setting the pattern" section later in this chapter for details on how to do this.

To set the dates and times, tap on the date or time you want to change and either type in the correct information or select what you want from the item that drops down. As Figure 6-2 shows, if you tap one of the date fields, a calendar drops down. If you tap a time field, a list of times appears.

When you're viewing the drop-down calendar, shown in Figure 6-2, you can click a date in the calendar to place that date in the field. If the date you want isn't visible, use the arrows at the top of the drop-down calendar to scroll to the correct month so you can choose the date you want.

You aren't limited to the times shown in the drop-down time lists. If you need to set an event for 4:11 a.m., go ahead and type in the correct time. Remember, though, that your Pocket PC automatically assumes that all events run for exactly an hour so you may need to specify both the starting and ending times.

Picking an event type

The Pocket PC calendar recognizes two types of events: Normal and All Day. Choose Normal for events that have a beginning and ending time; choose All Day for events like birthdays that don't have specified beginning and ending times. You make this choice in the Type field.

Figure 6-2:
Choose the correct beginning and ending dates and times.

Your definition of an all-day event may differ from your Pocket PC's definition. In the Pocket PC's definition, an event that is all day begins at midnight and ends at the next midnight. Don't try to use All Day as the event type for things that really do have a beginning and ending time — such as a training class that lasts your entire workday. If you do use All Day, your Pocket PC doesn't warn you if the scheduled event conflicts with other items on your schedule.

Setting the pattern

The next appointment field is the Occurs field. Use this item to specify events that happen more than once. For example, if you have a regular staff meeting every Monday morning at 9 a.m., you need to set up only one occurrence of the meeting and then specify when it repeats. Your Pocket PC offers several common types of patterns to make it easy to set up recurring events.

In addition to the options presented in the drop-down list, you can set your own unique schedule. Just tap on <Edit pattern...> and use the screens that follow to set up the recurrence schedule. You can, for example, schedule a meeting to run at the same time for three consecutive days or schedule a club meeting on the second Saturday of each month.

Use the fourth recurrence option — the one that specifies the same date each year — as a reminder for annual events like birthdays and anniversaries.

Choosing a category

If you keep different types of events in your Pocket PC calendar, you may want to select categories for those events. Just tap the Categories box and choose the appropriate categories for the event. These are the same categories that you use to organize your list of contacts. In case you missed it or just decided to skip around, I cover categories in Chapter 4. I'll also show you more about using them with your calendar entries later in this chapter in the section "Using categories to simplify your life."

Creating a meeting

Your Pocket PC helps you set up a meeting that you're scheduling by sending a message inviting each of the proposed attendees. But you're still responsible for keeping everyone awake during the meeting — your Pocket PC can't handle *all* the details!

To select attendees, tap the Attendees box and then select each of the people you want to notify. Your Pocket PC sends an e-mail message to each person with all the details you've included while setting up the event in your calendar.

You may be a little surprised when you try to select the potential attendees because only those people in your list of contacts who have an e-mail address can be selected. (Which actually makes total sense because your Pocket PC can't send an e-mail message unless it knows the correct e-mail address.)

Specifying the status

Not all appointments are set in stone. Sometimes you may want to set aside a period of time without making an absolute commitment. This situation certainly applies in the case where someone else is trying to set up a meeting and has asked you to set aside a couple of different blocks of time while he or she tries to see what works best for everyone else.

The Status drop-down box offers four different choices to handle a range of possibilities: Free, Tentative, Busy, and Out of office. You can probably figure out quite easily which one fits any event you're scheduling.

Marking it sensitive

You can specify that an appointment is a private event by selecting Private rather than Normal in the Sensitivity box. On your Pocket PC the only real effect of this change is that if you choose to, you can flag private events with a little key icon.

If you share your Pocket PC calendar with Outlook on your desktop PC, you can choose to prevent private events from appearing in a printed schedule. Use the printing options in Outlook to control just what appears in printed versions of your calendar.

Adding some notes

Preparation is one of the keys to success. When you're scheduling events in your calendar, why not take an extra step to make certain you're prepared for your appointments?

You may notice that in addition to the Appointment tab, the form you use to create a new calendar item also has a Notes tab. You can use this tab to create a note that is tied to the appointment.

You can use handwriting or voice recording to create notes attached to events exactly the same way you use these features to create standalone notes. If you need more help with these options, see Chapter 5.

Rescheduling an appointment

Appointments get rescheduled; it's an irrefutable fact of life. Another meeting may cause a conflict, someone may get sick, or you may just decide that the day is too nice to spend stuck inside with a bunch of boring executives. Whatever the reason, events do get moved from one time or date to another.

There are two basic ways to move an event from one place to another on your Pocket PC's calendar:

✔ When viewing your calendar, tap-and-hold the event you wish to move. Choose Cut from the pop-up menu to move the item to the Clipboard. Then tap-and-hold the new date and time, and choose Paste. This method is simple and straightforward, but you do have to be careful to make certain you tap-and-hold the correct time slot when you paste the event. But if you have to move the event very far off in the future — say a month or so — this isn't your best choice because you'll have to navigate to the correct date and hope you don't get distracted before you're done moving the event. If you do have to move an event quite a distance, try this next method. . . .

✔ Open an appointment by tapping it, and then open the item for editing by tapping Edit in the menu bar. Use the drop-down boxes to specify new starting and ending dates and times. This method ensures that you can specify the precise times you want without error.

Changing your view

Designing a single way of looking at a calendar that fits every need is a nearly impossible task — especially on the small screen of a Pocket PC. A view that makes it easy to select a date six months in the future isn't a lot of help if you're also trying to juggle six different appointments for next Monday. So rather than trying to make you use one method of looking at your calendar, your Pocket PC offers five different views. Figure 6-3 shows the Year view — you can choose any of these by clicking the icons on the menu bar.

Figure 6-3:
Use the view icons to decide how your calendar appears.

Here's a quick look at the view options (as they appear left to right in the menu bar):

- **Agenda:** Shows your upcoming appointments in a condensed list. In this view, your appointments are shown in chronological order, two lines per appointment.

- **Day:** Shows your schedule for one complete day, with time slots for each hour of the day (or each half hour if you enabled that option). This view is generally the most useful — especially when you need to add new items to your schedule.

✔ **Week:** Similar to the day view, but includes a column for each day of the week in addition to a row for each hour. This view makes it easy to see when things are scheduled for an entire week, but doesn't show any details. Still, this view is useful if you need to move an appointment because you can see an entire week's worth of time slots.

✔ **Month:** Shows the entire month and uses a small triangle in the lower-right corner to indicate which days have items scheduled. Use this view when planning your schedule a couple of weeks in advance.

✔ **Year:** Shows the whole year. Use this view if you're a real long-range planner!

Tap a date in the month or year view to open a day view of the selected date.

Using categories to simplify your life

If you assigned categories to the events on your calendar, you can choose to view only those items that fit into specified categories, letting you place business, personal, family, organization, or any other category of events on your calendar and still be able to keep them separate. For example:

✔ Mark birthdays as personal or family so you don't forget them, but reduce the clutter by excluding this category when you're setting up business appointments.

✔ Mark your club events in their own special category. Then switch to the agenda view and select just this one category. In this mode, you see only the club's activities, and you can beam them to another club member without including the rest of your schedule.

✔ Choose to show only the business category when participating in a meeting in the office. (Certainly exclude your private meetings with the headhunter from displaying — especially when your boss wants to play around with "that neat little toy you've got there.")

Setting reminders

Adding things to your busy schedule is only half the battle. You've also got to remember to send that anniversary card, make that important phone call, or meet that potential backer for lunch. And, to make matters worse, you've got to do those things on time!

One way to make certain you don't forget the important details is to have your Pocket PC give you a reminder of an upcoming event. By default your Pocket PC does this, but only 15 minutes ahead of the actual appointment.

When setting up reminders, you have three options you can select:

✔ In the Reminder box, choose Remind me or None. If you choose to be reminded of an event, your Pocket PC sounds an audible alarm and pops up a message box at the specified time. If your Pocket PC is off when the reminder is due, it automatically wakes up and gives you the reminder anyway.

✔ Use the Number box in the next row down to set the number of minutes (or other time increment) in advance of the event to set off the reminder.

✔ Use the Interval box to specify whether the reminder should come minutes, hours, days, or weeks in advance. One really neat feature of your Pocket PC's reminder feature is that you don't even have to remember to turn your Pocket PC on to get the reminder. When the reminder time comes along, your Pocket PC wakes up and chirps at you. After you get over your annoyance at this rude interruption and take a look at the Pocket PC's screen, you see a reminder similar to the one in Figure 6-4.

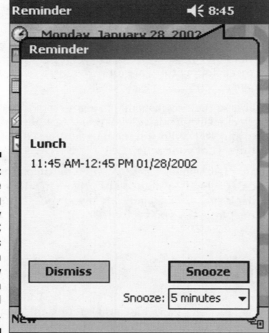

Figure 6-4:
I may be
running
late, but my
Pocket PC
makes
certain
I know
where I'm
supposed
to be.

When you're creating an appointment or other item on your schedule, be sure you set the reminder far enough in advance to be useful. The default 15-minute reminder probably won't help a lot for most items on your calendar. For those annual events, especially ones where you may need to send a gift or a card, give yourself at least a week of advance notice. When the reminder does go off, you can always reset it for a later time.

Tracking Your Tasks List

Scheduling a specific time for tasks can be a real chore. How do you schedule something that doesn't really have a date associated with it? Still, a few tasks have at least some relationship to your calendar.

Taking out the trash is a good example of how tasks can relate to your schedule. You probably don't want to waste time by taking out the garbage when there's only a little bit in the basket, but you probably do want to take it out before the trash haulers arrive at 8 a.m. Monday morning.

Setting Tasks options

In the spirit of keeping things as simple as they deserve to be, your Pocket PC keeps the Tasks options to a minimum. To set the few Tasks options that do exist, first open the Tasks application by clicking the Start button and choosing Tasks from the Start menu. Then tap Tools⇨Options to display the list.

It's pretty easy to guess what the three task options do:

- ✔ **Set reminders for new items:** Makes certain that your Pocket PC will nag you about any new tasks you add to your list until you mark them as completed.

- ✔ **Show start and due date:** Ties tasks more closely to your schedule by adding in a date when you should start the task and a date when the task must be completed.

- ✔ **Use large font:** Displays your tasks in large characters so they're harder to ignore.

Pick the blend of options that works the best for you and then click OK to return to the Tasks list.

 If you don't need to know the starting and due dates for your tasks, leave the Show start and due date option unchecked. When this option is selected, each task requires an extra row on your screen — even if these dates aren't filled in.

Adding tasks

To add yet another job to your electronic job jar, tap New on the Tasks menu. You can also display the Entry Bar above your list of tasks by selecting Tools⇨Entry Bar, but this really just takes up an extra row to do something you can do just as well by tapping New.

Figure 6-5 shows a new task being created in my Tasks list. If you compare the new Tasks form to the New Appointment form you use to add items to your calendar (see the section "Adding an appointment" earlier in the chapter), you notice that the two forms are quite similar. In fact, the differences are quite minor:

✔ You cannot set specific times (although you can set dates) for tasks.

✔ Tasks can be set to different priority levels, and your Tasks list can be sorted to show which tasks are most important.

✔ You don't have to set any dates for tasks if you don't want to. Giving the dog a bath can wait until you're darn good and ready!

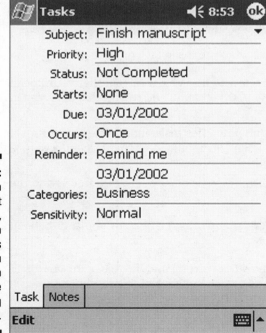

Figure 6-5: When you've got things to do, put them in your Tasks list so you know when you're ignoring them.

Sorting your to-do list

As your list of stuff that needs to be done grows, you'll probably want to figure out which items you can continue to put off and which ones you're just going to have to do. One way to do this is to sort the list. You can choose to sort your task list by Status, Priority, Subject, Start Date, or Due Date — depending on which order is easier for you to ignore.

The drop-down list shows the different sorting options you can choose. When the list is not dropped down, the sorting option you've selected replaces the words Sort By.

You can also use categories to help organize your tasks. Some good choices may be "Yeah, right," "Forget it," and "Geez, do I really have to?" You'll have to add these categories yourself. For some reason they aren't default categories that you can select.

Chapter 7

Keeping It in Sync

In This Chapter

▶ Getting to know synchronization

▶ Exchanging data with your desktop PC

▶ Backing up your Pocket PC

*Y*ou can have just a Pocket PC and no desktop PC, but somehow that seems a bit like Laurel without Hardy, apple pie without ice cream, or maybe even pancakes without syrup. There's just something missing when one of the two partners isn't there.

The Pocket PC is the perfect companion for a desktop PC. The two of them can share information seamlessly, allowing you to work on either one and still be assured of having the most up-to-date data that is available. When you're in the office, you'll probably opt for the large screen and comfortable keyboard on your desktop system. On the go, you'll most likely prefer the small, convenient size of your Pocket PC. There's no reason why you can't enjoy the best features of each system and still be on top of your world.

To make that partnership work, your Pocket PC and your desktop PC must exchange data automatically. The mechanism that makes this work is *synchronization*. In this chapter I show you how to make synchronization work for you.

Understanding Synchronization

Synchronization can be defined many different ways. Among other things, synchronization can be defined as harmonization, organization, management, or bringing together. These are some pretty fancy ways of saying that you want the same information to exist in more than one place, and that you want that information to be the same in all of those places. From a practical standpoint, what this means in terms of your Pocket PC is that you want to share certain files with your desktop PC, and that you want to be able to work on those files on whichever PC happens to be handy.

Why you need to synchronize

For just a moment I'd like you to imagine a scenario that probably isn't too unusual. Suppose that you keep all of your personal address book listings in a small paper notebook. Now, imagine that someone else in your house has her own address book, too. Nothing at all unusual there, right? Okay, so you're talking with Aunt Dee and you find out that your cousin Paige has just moved. You write down the new information in your address book and you're all set. But what about that other address book? Shouldn't it also be updated with the corrected information? Of course it should, and you should probably update your address book with the new information she has about cousin Lynda, too. The problem is, there's probably no formal system set up so that whenever someone gets new information he or she automatically shares it with everyone else in the house.

Okay, so that example was pretty obvious. Here's another example that may not seem quite so apparent. Suppose you write a report on your desktop PC and then copy that report to your Pocket PC so you can easily take the report along to a meeting. Just before you leave for the meeting, someone phones you to tell you that it's Jim Johnson, not Jim Jensen, who's getting that big promotion. You quickly open your word processor and fix the error in your report, but because you're in such a hurry, you forget to copy the corrected report to your Pocket PC. When you arrive at the meeting and begin your presentation, do you remember that whenever the report says Jim Jensen it really should say Jim Johnson? Or do you make the announcement that you're promoting the wrong guy?

These two examples are but a small sampling of the reasons why you need to synchronize information. Fortunately, synchronizing data files between your Pocket PC and your desktop PC is a snap. And when you do synchronize, you won't have to worry about not having the correct information at your fingertips, whether your fingertips are on your Pocket PC or desktop PC.

Setting up partnerships

You use a program called ActiveSync to synchronize the information between your Pocket PC and your desktop PC. ActiveSync synchronizes information by creating a partnership between your Pocket PC and your desktop PC. A partnership has several characteristics:

✔ Whenever your Pocket PC and desktop PC are synchronized, changes to files you've specified are updated in both directions. This simply means that changes on your desktop PC appear on your Pocket PC, and changes on your Pocket PC also appear on your desktop PC.

✔ You can choose the types of items that each partnership synchronizes. If you set up partnerships between your Pocket PC and two different desktop PCs, you synchronize the same set of files with each desktop PC.

If you set up partnerships between your Pocket PC and two different desktop PCs, you can specify only one of those partnerships for sharing e-mail messages.

✔ In most cases, the partnership specifies that the synchronization happens automatically whenever the Pocket PC and desktop PC connect, but you can control exactly how each partnership synchronizes its files.

✔ Your desktop PC can have partnerships with more than one Pocket PC, but the default settings share the same set of files between your desktop PC and all of the Pocket PCs. You can change this by creating unique Pocket PC identities, as I explain shortly in the section "Creating unique Pocket PC identities."

Creating basic partnerships

Creating a basic partnership is one of those tasks that sounds a lot harder than it really is. All you have to do is insert a CD-ROM, click a few buttons, and you're done. Here's the rundown:

1. **Before you connect your Pocket PC to your desktop PC, get out the Pocket PC Companion CD-ROM that came with your Pocket PC and insert it into your desktop PC's CD-ROM drive.**

2. **If the setup program doesn't start automatically, click the Start button on your desktop PC and choose Run.**

   In the Open text box, enter **x:\setup.exe** (where *x* is the drive letter for your CD-ROM drive). Click OK to run the setup program.

3. **Click the Next button that appears in the first screen.**

4. **Click Start Here.**

5. **Select Install Outlook 2002 and then ActiveSync 3.5.**

6. **Connect your Pocket PC to your desktop PC.**

   In most cases, you do this by turning on the Pocket PC and popping it into the cradle (after you've plugged in the cables, of course).

7. **When the setup program asks, tell it you want to establish a partnership between your Pocket PC and your desktop PC.**

   When you get to choose the number of desktop PCs in the partnership, choose two rather than one. There's no rule that says you have to create that second partnership, but you may as well leave the door open so that you *can* create it later if you want to.

8. **Keep on clicking the buttons until the setup program concludes.**

   Basically, you just say OK to everything that remains to accept the default installation options.

Setting up the ActiveSync options

When ActiveSync is first installed, it's set up to synchronize a lot of different types of items. You'll probably find that a number of these are things you don't really want synchronized, if for no better reason than the amount of time it takes for ActiveSync to check the status of items you don't use. Rather than continue to be frustrated every time you pop your Pocket PC into the cradle, you can change the ActiveSync settings.

To configure ActiveSync to work the way you want, follow these steps:

1. **If ActiveSync hasn't popped up into view, click the ActiveSync icon in the system tray and choose Open Microsoft ActiveSync from the pop-up menu.**

2. **Select Tools⇨Options (or click the Options button) to display the Options dialog box (see Figure 7-1).**

   You use this dialog box to control how ActiveSync works.

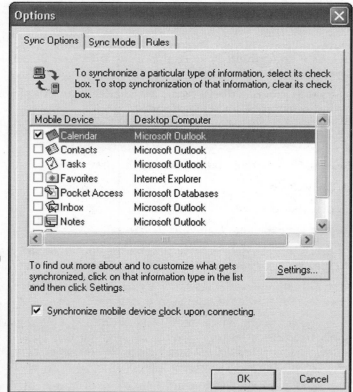

Figure 7-1:
Open the Options dialog box to choose your ActiveSync settings.

3. **Go down the list of items and select those you want to synchronize or deselect those you don't want to synchronize.**

   For example, if you don't intend to browse Web pages on your Pocket PC, deselect both Favorites and AvantGo.

4. **To modify an item for even more precise control, highlight the item and click the Settings button.**

   Figure 7-2 shows the settings you can choose for synchronizing your calendar. Other types of items do, of course, have other options.

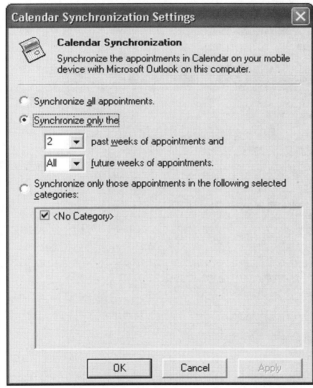

Figure 7-2: Use the Settings button to make it possible to exert even more precise control over an item such as your calendar.

5. **Before you leave the Sync Options tab completely, make certain the Synchronize mobile device clock upon connecting option is selected.**

   This ensures that your Pocket PC and your desktop PC always agree on the correct date and time. That they agree on this is very important; otherwise, an older file may overwrite a newer one because ActiveSync isn't able to determine which file is newer.

6. Click the Sync Mode tab (see Figure 7-3).

Choose the option you prefer. The default setting, Continuously while the device is connected, is the safest option because it ensures that your files are always up to date at the moment you pop the Pocket PC out of the cradle and into your pocket.

7. Click the Rules tab, as shown in Figure 7-4.

Here you can decide the rules for how the synchronization is performed. The best advice here is don't tinker around too much. The default settings shown in the figure really do work the best in most instances. You'll also find that messing around with the conversion settings is just asking for trouble.

8. Click OK to close the dialog box.

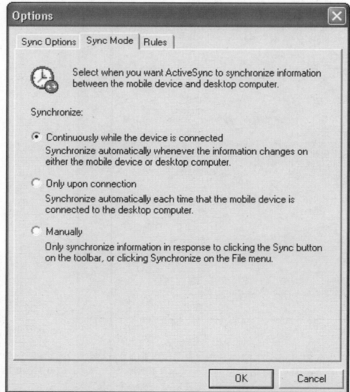

Figure 7-3:
Select when you would like your files to be synchronized.

Creating unique Pocket PC identities

There's one thing about the Pocket PC that happens to almost everyone who spends a few minutes playing around with one — before long you want one of your own. This isn't much of a problem unless several people in your family all decide they want their own Pocket PC, and you all share a desktop PC. If that's the case, you need to create separate identities for each Pocket PC to make sure everyone has his or her own files synchronized rather than everyone else's. Believe me, you'll understand the first time your Pocket PC's storage is filled up with some rap "music" that another family member has loaded onto his Pocket PC.

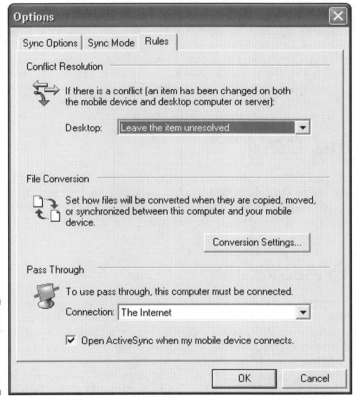

Figure 7-4:
Choose your synchronization rules.

Be sure to create the unique Pocket PC identity *before* you create a partnership with your desktop PC. Otherwise, you end up sharing the same files that are being synchronized with an existing partnership.

To create a unique Pocket PC identity, follow these steps:

1. **On your Pocket PC, click the Start button and choose Settings.**

2. **Tap the System tab in Settings.**

3. **Click the About icon.**

4. **Click the Device ID tab.**

5. **Enter a name for your Pocket PC in the Device name box.**

   Keeping Pocket_PC as a part of the name is best because ActiveSync creates a folder in your desktop PC's My Documents folder using this name, and then places a shortcut to the folder on the desktop.

6. **Click OK when you're finished.**

Because ActiveSync uses the Pocket PC's name when creating the synchronization folder on your desktop PC, only those files that are in the folder associated with a particular Pocket PC are synchronized (if you have selected the ActiveSync option to synchronize files). Because of this, you may need to move files manually from the existing synchronization folder to the new one if you change the device name *after* you've already set up a partnership with your desktop system.

Exchanging Data

If your Pocket PC and your desktop PC are going to be partners, they need to be able to share your data. You wouldn't want to have to retype everything just because you wanted to use it on both computers. Let's see how you share information between these systems.

Using ActiveSync

You've already seen that you use ActiveSync to create a partnership between your Pocket PC and your desktop PC. Earlier in this chapter I also cover how you can control which types of information are shared. But just how does this really work? Here are some important details:

- Pocket PCs lack one of the important pieces of hardware that you find on every modern desktop PC — a hard drive. This is an important difference for reasons you may not realize. In terms of sharing data, the lack of a hard drive is important because your Pocket PC stores data differently than your desktop PC does. In fact, your Pocket PC stores much information in a format that your desktop PC simply cannot use.

- Because of the differences between the ways your Pocket PC and your desktop PC store information, you can't just copy most files between the two systems. Rather, the files must be converted from one format to the other as they are transferred. Likewise, they must be converted in the other direction if you transfer them back.

✔ ActiveSync automatically handles the format conversions as it transfers files, which is one reason it can take a few minutes to move files between your Pocket PC and your desktop PC.

✔ Remember that ActiveSync can convert only *data* files. You can't convert your desktop PC programs to run on your Pocket PC (or the other way around, for that matter).

Synchronizing your contacts with Outlook

Most Pocket PC users probably want to keep their Contact list available on their Pocket PC. Because of this, sharing address book information is one of those tasks that is virtually transparent. If you make any modifications in your Outlook Contacts folder on your desktop PC, those same changes appear in your Pocket PC's Contacts list the next time you synchronize your Pocket PC and your desktop PC — assuming that you've specified that you want your contacts synchronized, of course. And any changes you make in your Pocket PC's Contacts list also appear in your desktop Outlook Contacts folder.

If you don't have Outlook installed on your desktop PC, or if your version of Outlook is an older one, you can install Outlook 2002 from the Pocket PC Companion CD-ROM.

Figure 7-5 shows a contact record that I've entered into Outlook on my desktop PC. When I click Save and Close, this record is added to the Outlook Contacts folder.

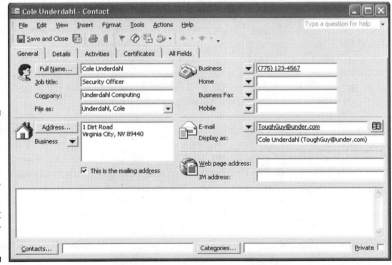

Figure 7-5: Clicking Save and Close adds this new record to my Contact list on my desktop PC.

Next I place my Pocket PC in the cradle and wait for ActiveSync to do its thing. If the only change is in one contact record, the synchronization may even go so fast you won't notice anything happening. But if you open Contacts on your Pocket PC and look for the new record, it will be there.

So ActiveSync handles the synchronization of every Outlook-related item as transparently as it does your Contact list. So transparent, for example, that the same appointments appear both on your Pocket PC and your desktop PC.

Sharing data with other types of applications

You use a slightly different method of sharing other types of data between your Pocket PC and your desktop PC. For this, ActiveSync uses a special folder on your desktop PC and automatically synchronizes the contents of that folder with the My Documents folder on your Pocket PC.

When you create a partnership between your Pocket PC and your desktop PC, ActiveSync creates a new folder on your desktop PC. This folder appears as a subfolder in your My Documents folder. The folder is named with the device ID of your Pocket PC and the words My Documents added on the end. Your Pocket PC uses the device ID "Pocket_PC" by default, so you'll most likely find that the synchronization folder is C:\My Documents\Pocket_PC My Documents. In Figure 7-6 the folder is named Pocket_PC_e570 My Documents since I have more than one Pocket PC and have assigned each of them different names.

If you add a memory storage card to your Pocket PC, you have to create a My Documents folder on the storage card and use it to store your files in order for most Pocket PC applications to find the files on the storage card. This does not mean, however, that ActiveSync synchronizes the files on the storage card with your desktop PC. Indeed, when synchronizing files, ActiveSync simply ignores any files that are stored only on the storage card. As I discuss later in this chapter (the section "Exploring Your Pocket PC Files"), however, you can use ActiveSync to explore the storage card.

If you select the ActiveSync option to synchronize files, any files you place into the Pocket_PC My Documents folder on your desktop PC automatically convert and copy to your Pocket PC. Likewise, any new or changed documents in the My Documents folder on your Pocket PC are converted and copied to your desktop PC. There are limits to this, however. If a file is too large for the storage space on your Pocket PC, it won't be copied to your Pocket PC. Also, if ActiveSync is unable to determine the type of the file, it may be copied without any translation. That is, the file is simply copied without trying to make it compatible with your Pocket PC. You may or may not be able to use the file on your Pocket PC — depending on how lucky you are that day.

Figure 7-6: Place items you want to synchronize into the Pocket_PC My Documents folder.

Backing Up Your Pocket PC Files

Synchronizing your files is a great way to keep your Pocket PC and your desktop PC working together, but there's one big problem with synchronization — it doesn't protect you from losing important data. It's easy to become confused by the process of synchronizing your files and think that somehow having the same files on both your Pocket PC and your desktop PC is the same as having a backup of your Pocket PC files. Unfortunately, synchronization doesn't protect you because:

✔ If you delete a synchronized file on your Pocket PC or on your desktop PC, that file is also deleted from the other PC the next time you synchronize your files. If you somehow think you'll remember to copy the file someplace else before synchronization and thereby protect it, good luck! Old Murphy is sure to step in and make certain you pop that Pocket PC into the cradle without remembering to make your copy.

✔ If you have to do a hard reset (the same thing as a *cold boot* on your desktop PC) on your Pocket PC because of a system problem, any files on your Pocket PC will be lost. Isn't it a good bet that this will happen just *before* you were going to synchronize your files?

✔ If a synchronized file somehow becomes corrupted on either your Pocket PC or on your desktop PC, you won't be able to complete the synchronization until that file is deleted. And of course, the corrupt file will almost certainly be one that you've spent hours on, or one that you can't re-create easily.

Doing a backup

When you back up the files from your Pocket PC, all of your data files, any programs you've installed, and any settings that you've adjusted on your Pocket PC are saved in a file on your desktop PC's hard drive, which essentially protects your entire investment of time that you've placed in your Pocket PC.

You can choose from two different types of backups:

✔ A *full* backup saves everything on your Pocket PC that can be backed up. Full backups take a little longer and use more disk space on your desktop PC, but because everything is backed up in one file, you don't have to worry about where your backed up data may be.

✔ An *incremental* backup saves only items that are new or have been changed since the last backup. Incremental backups are usually somewhat faster than full backups, and they generally take less disk space. Of course, this can vary according to how much you've done with your Pocket PC since the last backup.

Allow plenty of time for a full backup to finish. Depending on the method you use to connect your Pocket PC to your desktop PC and the size of the backup, the entire process can take anywhere from a few minutes to over an hour.

To back up your Pocket PC files on your desktop PC, follow these steps:

1. **Make certain your Pocket PC is connected to your desktop PC.**

   This usually means placing it in the synchronization cradle, but you have to determine the proper method in your case.

2. **Open ActiveSync by clicking the ActiveSync icon and choosing Open Microsoft ActiveSync from the pop-up menu.**

   You can skip this step if the ActiveSync window is already open on your desktop.

3. **Select Tools⇨Backup/Restore from the ActiveSync menu to display the Backup/Restore window (see Figure 7-7).**

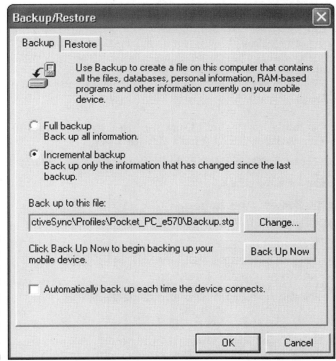

Figure 7-7: Use Backup/ Restore to protect the files on your Pocket PC.

4. **Choose the backup method you prefer.**

   The first time you do a backup both options will function the same way.

5. **If you want to keep more than one full backup, click the Change button and specify the name for the backup file.**

   If you use the default name, new full backups overwrite older ones that use the same name.

6. **Click the Back Up Now button to begin the backup.**

After you click the Back Up Now button, you must leave your Pocket PC alone and connected to your desktop PC until the backup is completed. If you remove your Pocket PC from the cradle before the backup finishes, you run a high risk of corrupting the backup file.

7. **Click OK to complete the backup.**

Restoring from your backup

Restoring your files from an existing backup replaces the files that are currently on your Pocket PC with the files from the backup. If you've made changes on your Pocket PC, those changes will be lost.

Restoring your Pocket PC files is even easier than backing them up. Here's what you do:

1. **Make certain your Pocket PC is connected to your desktop PC, and then open ActiveSync (if it isn't already open).**

2. **Select Tools⇨Backup/Restore from the ActiveSync menu.**

3. **Click the Restore tab.**

4. **Click the Restore Now button.**

5. **Click the Restore button to confirm that you do indeed want to begin the restore.**

   You can't cancel this after the restore has begun, so don't click this button unless you're absolutely sure.

6. **Wait until the restore finishes and click OK.**

When you finish the restore, you're prompted to remove your Pocket PC from the cradle, reset it, and then return it to the cradle. You may then be asked how to resolve a number of items that need synchronization. If so, choose the option that best suits your needs and complete the task.

An alternative to backup and restore

If you don't care for the all-or-nothing approach that a backup and restore offers, there's another "unofficial" way to protect your Pocket PC data files. This alternate method is not a complete replacement for backup and restore because it protects only the files from your Pocket PC's My Documents folder. However, it does offer certain advantages over backup and restore. For one thing, my unofficial method doesn't carry quite the same risk of undoing changes you've made on your Pocket PC.

So what's this unofficial method, you ask? Why it's so simple, you'll probably wonder why you didn't think of it first. When you have important files in your C:\My Documents\Pocket_PC My Documents folder, make a copy of them someplace else. Create a Pocket PC Backups folder somewhere on your hard disk or copy the files to another computer or to removable storage like a CD-R disc or ZIP drive.

If you do use this method, remember that you're responsible for making certain you don't accidentally overwrite newer files in your C:\My Documents\ Pocket_PC My Documents folder with ones from your backup folder. Your desktop PC warns you if you try to do this, but you're the one who is clicking that mouse!

Using storage cards or Flash memory for backup

Depending on the brand of Pocket PC you have and the options you have added, you may have another backup alternative that doesn't depend on your desktop PC. This option is especially attractive since you can use it at any time to protect your important document files from accidental deletion, even if you don't have immediate access to your desktop system.

Since each brand of Pocket PC takes a slightly different approach to this type of backup, the best I can do is to give you some general information about this type of backup.

- ✔ You will find the Backup program either in the Programs folder on your Pocket PC, or in a subfolder contained in the Programs folder. For example, on an HP Jornada 568, you need to open the HP Applications folder to locate the backup program.

- ✔ If Flash ROM is offered as a destination for the backup, you can make your backup without using any of the space on your removable storage card. Files stored in Flash ROM are protected against accidental deletion and will survive even if you have to do a full reset of your Pocket PC.

- ✔ If you select a storage card as the backup destination, you can remove the storage card and store it safely away from your Pocket PC. This will protect your files even if your Pocket PC is stolen or destroyed.

- ✔ You have the option of using a password to protect your backups. If you select this option, make certain you remember the password because without it you won't be able to restore any files from the backup.

- ✔ Once you have backed up your files, you can delete the originals if you feel pretty brave. Personally, I would rather have several copies of any files I feel are important enough to back up.

Exploring Your Pocket PC Files

Even though your Pocket PC includes File Explorer, a program that works much like Windows Explorer on your desktop PC, managing the files on your Pocket PC can be a little difficult. Somehow it just seems a little difficult exploring with a stylus. Wouldn't you like to be able to root around in the Pocket PC files the same way you do on your desktop PC?

Well, I've got good news for you. ActiveSync enables you to explore your Pocket PC using your old familiar Windows Explorer on your desktop PC. Figure 7-8 shows an example of browsing the files and folders on a typical Pocket PC.

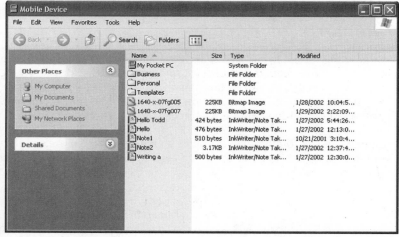

Figure 7-8:
Browse your Pocket PC files the easy way by doing it from your desktop PC.

To explore your Pocket PC's files and folders, click the Explore button in ActiveSync. This opens a Windows Explorer view of your Pocket PC.

Although you can explore your Pocket PC's files and folders from your desktop PC, there are some differences you need to remember:

✔ If you delete files from your Pocket PC, they are completely erased. There is no Recycle Bin on the Pocket PC. If you aren't sure you'll need a file, make a backup on your desktop PC before you erase the file from your Pocket PC.

✔ You can't open files or run applications from your desktop PC. If you try to open a file, a message box appears and tells you the file's properties.

✔ If you copy a file between your desktop PC and your Pocket PC in either direction, ActiveSync checks to see whether the file must be converted to a different format. If ActiveSync offers to make a conversion, allow it to do so — otherwise, the file may not be usable on the system to where it was copied.

✔ To see the contents of a storage card, you must first open the My Pocket PC folder. You then see the card listed as a folder named Storage Card under the My Pocket PC folder.

✔ One of the easiest ways to create new folders — like the My Documents folder on a storage card — is through ActiveSync and Windows Explorer.

Part III

Putting Your Pocket PC Tools to Work

The 5th Wave   By Rich Tennant

Of course it doesn't make any sense, but it's our only chance! Now hook the Pocket PC into the override and see if you can bring this baby in!!

In this part . . .

Your Pocket PC includes several powerful yet easy-to-use applications that are closely related to the Microsoft Office program you probably already use on your desktop PC. In this part you'll see how to use Pocket Word to work with your Word documents. You'll learn how to use Pocket Excel to create and edit Excel spreadsheets. You'll see how to use Pocket Money to keep track of your expenses. Finally, you'll see how to use the calculator on your Pocket PC.

Chapter 8

Working with Pocket Word

In This Chapter

▶ Things you can do with Pocket Word

▶ Creating a document in Pocket Word

▶ Sharing your Pocket Word documents

*O*ne of the things that separate the Pocket PC from all those other palm-sized devices is the high level of utility built into each Pocket PC. Sure, the others can keep your address book and make sure you don't miss your appointments just like the Pocket PC does, but only your Pocket PC is a real computer powerful enough to run Pocket Word.

But is Pocket Word for real? How much word processing can you really do on something that fits so neatly into your pocket, anyway? Well, you can do quite a bit with Pocket Word when it comes right down to it. In this chapter, I give you a taste of just how much fun you can have using Pocket Word.

Uses for Pocket Word

Okay, I'll be the first to admit that there aren't too many people who are going to write a novel on their Pocket PC. Tapping out a long document character by character on the onscreen keyboard isn't likely to fit anyone's definition of a good time. Still, Pocket Word is a very useful addition to your Pocket PC.

Comparing Pocket Word to desktop Word

One of the most important features of Pocket Word is that it can share files directly with the desktop versions of Word. Pocket Word can open and save files as both Word documents and as Word templates, which means that you can work on a document on your desktop PC, transfer it to your Pocket PC, and continue to work with that document while you're away from your desk.

Pocket Word does have its own Pocket Word file format, but ActiveSync automatically converts between Pocket Word format and desktop Word format, so you won't see any difference no matter how you save your files.

Even though Pocket Word works well with most of your documents, there are some important things you need to watch out for. If a Word document contains table formatting, numbered lists, or columns, those items are lost when the document is converted to Pocket Word format. The safest way to avoid any problems is to make certain you do not include these items in documents you intend to share between your desktop PC and your Pocket PC. If you must make documents that include these features available on your Pocket PC, don't save any changes to the file on your Pocket PC.

So, because Pocket Word can use desktop Word documents, how can you use Pocket Word? Here are some ideas:

✔ If someone sends you a report in a Word document, you can transfer the file to your Pocket PC and read the report while you're sitting out in the local park during your lunch break. You may still be working, but at least you'll get a bit of fresh air for a few minutes.

✔ If you've been working on a proposal for some potential new customers, you can keep a current copy of the proposal on your Pocket PC so you can make last-minute changes when you find out something that could give you an advantage over your competitors.

✔ You can use Pocket Word to put the finishing touches on your novel during your daily commute to the office. Of course, this wouldn't be a good idea if you're the driver (unless you happen to sit in stopped traffic for long periods of time).

✔ If necessary, you can finish working on a last-minute project at the airport or on the plane when you're going on vacation. Then you can e-mail the completed document back to the office. This may be the perfect solution if you have one of those bosses who always finds a way to ruin your vacation by insisting that you delay your departure to clean up the mess he or she created.

What you can do in Pocket Word

Pocket Word has many of the features you've come to expect in your word processing software. While it doesn't have everything that you'll find in desktop Word, here are some of the important things that you can do with Pocket Word:

✔ You can open, view, edit, and save documents in a format that retains most of the formatting of a standard Word document — just be certain you note the earlier warning about certain formatting items that cannot be saved on your Pocket PC.

✔ You can cut, copy, and paste just as you do on your desktop.

✔ You can use any standard Windows fonts in your documents.

✔ You can apply formatting to text.

✔ You can use paragraph formatting to control the appearance of documents.

✔ You can create bulleted lists.

✔ You can search for and replace specific text in a document.

✔ If your Pocket PC is a Pocket PC 2002 unit, you can spell check your documents just as you do in Word on your desktop PC.

What you can't do in Pocket Word

As powerful as Pocket Word may be, there are some features that were left out of the program in order to keep it small enough to fit the available memory. Some of the most important of these include:

✔ Pocket Word lacks a grammar checker. Many people would argue that the grammar checker in desktop Word does such a poor job that this may actually be a blessing in disguise.

✔ There is no thesaurus in Pocket Word. If you install the Encarta Pocket Dictionary from the Pocket PC Companion CD-ROM, you can look up words in the Microsoft Reader program, but you aren't likely to find this a very good substitute, replacement, or surrogate for the real thing. The Encarta Pocket Dictionary is available once you install the Microsoft Reader program on your desktop PC.

✔ Pocket Word doesn't support certain types of table formatting, numbered lists, or columns. If you save a document with these features into the Pocket Word format, the features will be lost.

✔ Finally, the one thing that you'll probably miss the most in Pocket Word is that you can't print documents from your Pocket PC unless you install a third-party program such as PrintPocketCE (discussed in Chapter 3). Not being able to print isn't unique to Pocket Word; it's just a limitation of the Pocket PC that probably comes as a big surprise.

Writing in Pocket Word

Creating a document in Pocket Word is really very similar to creating one in desktop Word. Sure, there are the obvious physical differences between a

Pocket PC and a desktop PC, and the few features that are lacking in Pocket Word, but after you get past those differences, the process is remarkably similar.

In the following sections I show you how to use Pocket Word to create a document and to use the editing and formatting options to improve the document's appearance. I've used the opening of a story I wrote to give you a better idea what you can really do in Pocket Word.

Reviewing your input options

To create a document in Pocket Word, you have many of the same options that are available in other Pocket PC applications. In case you've been skipping around and missed discovering those options earlier, here's quick look at them.

Selecting an input method

Your first and possibly most important choice in Pocket Word may be in selecting the way you input text. You choose the input method using the Pocket Word View menu. Your choices include the following options:

- **Writing** enables you to write or print directly on the Pocket PC's screen. To change your writing into text, choose Tools⇨Recognize. See Chapter 3 for more information on using handwriting to input information into your Pocket PC.

- **Drawing** enables you to draw directly on the screen. Drawings are never converted into text; instead the drawing is saved as a bitmap image in your document. For more about adding a drawing to a document, you may want to refer to Chapter 5.

- **Typing** allows you to use the onscreen keyboard to enter text one character at a time. If you have the Word Completion option enabled, your Pocket PC can help speed your text entry by suggesting possible words you may be entering (see Chapter 3 for more information on the text entry options).

- **Recording** turns your Pocket PC into a voice recorder. The recording is added to your document as a sound file as opposed to text. If you need a refresher, Chapter 5 covers recording voice notes to include with your documents.

If you've added an alternate input device to your Pocket PC (see Chapter 3), you can make your input selection using the SIP (Secondary Input Panel) in the lower-right corner of the screen.

Choosing your document view

Almost as important as your choice of input method may be your document view option choices. These choices also appear on the View menu. Here are your options:

- ✔ **Wrap to Window** makes the text fit within the width of the Pocket PC's screen. Choosing this option removes the horizontal scrollbar from the bottom of the screen and wraps the lines of text so you don't have to move side to side to read the document. Choosing this option doesn't make any permanent changes to your document, so it still appears normally when you transfer it back to your desktop PC.

- ✔ **Zoom** enables you to view the text at 75%, 100%, 150%, 200%, or 300% of normal size. Lower zoom percentages let you see more of the document at one time, but can make the text harder to read. Higher zoom percentages can make it far easier to input text using handwriting.

- ✔ **Toolbar** toggles the display of the Pocket Word formatting toolbar. You can use this toolbar to apply formatting to your text. You can also click the icon just to the right of Tools on the menu bar (the icon has an up and a down arrow) to toggle the display of the toolbar.

Editing in Pocket Word

Even though you *can* write entire documents with your Pocket PC and Pocket Word, you're far more likely to use Pocket Word to do some editing of existing documents. Editing typically doesn't involve nearly as much text entry as creating a new document, so the chances are pretty good that you'll use your Pocket PC to review and correct more often than you'll use it to create.

But it really doesn't matter if you're creating new documents or editing existing ones — you still want good editing tools. The next sections offer a look at the ones available in Pocket Word.

Selecting, copying, cutting, and pasting

Figure 8-1 shows the Edit menu in Pocket Word. Here you find many of your old favorites from the Edit menu in desktop Word.

Just as on your desktop PC, commands that are gray rather than black on a Pocket PC menu are currently unavailable. For example, the Cut and Copy commands can be used only after you've selected something.

Notice that the Edit menu has a Select All command but no other commands for selecting text or other objects in your document. You have to use the stylus if you want to select only part of a document. You may need to practice a little to get the hang of selecting text with the stylus. To select text, point to the beginning of the selection and then drag the stylus across the entire set of text you want to select. If you begin your selection on one line and move to another line, all of the text between the beginning of the selection and the current stylus position become part of the selection.

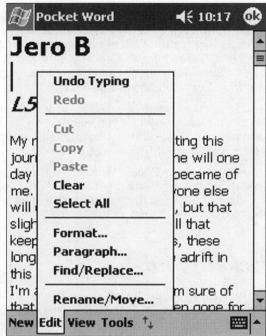

Figure 8-1:
Use the
Edit menu
commands
to select,
cut, copy,
or paste
in your
Pocket Word
documents.

To make selecting text a bit faster, tap twice on a word to select the entire word. Tap three times to select the entire paragraph.

After you've selected some of the text, use the Edit menu commands to work with the selection. Unfortunately, you can't use the drag-and-drop technique you may be used to on your desktop PC — drag-and-drop isn't supported on the Pocket PC.

Finding and replacing text

If you never had to type out a letter on a typewriter in the olden days before word processors became popular, you may not realize just how lucky you really are. In those ancient times people actually had to find their own errors by reading through their documents word by word. To correct mistakes you had two basic options: You could retype the page (or pages, depending on how lucky you were), or you could apply correction fluid (or tape) to the error and then type over it.

Modern PCs (and this includes your Pocket PC) make the whole process a lot easier by allowing you to electronically search for and replace text within your document. There's no more getting any of that white paint all over your fingers, either!

In Pocket Word, you can search for and replace (if necessary) text within your documents using the Edit⇨Find/Replace command. When you select this command, Pocket Word displays the screen shown in Figure 8-2.

Figure 8-2: Quickly find and correct words using the Edit⇨ Find/Replace command.

If you want to replace instances of a word or phrase, tap the Replace button to display a second text box labeled Replace with. Use the Match case and Match whole words only checkboxes to further refine the find and replace operation.

After you've entered the search phrase (and the replacement phrase if appropriate), tap Find to locate the next instance of the phrase. Tapping Find also displays the Find/Replace toolbar, shown just above the menu bar in Figure 8-3. Use this toolbar to control the find or replace process.

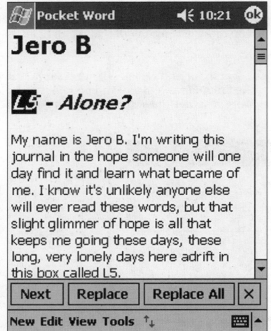

Figure 8-3:
Use the
Find/Replace
toolbar to
continue
searching or
to replace
items in
the text.

The Find/Replace toolbar includes the following commands:

✔ **Next** moves on through the text to the next occurrence of the search phrase. The currently selected item is not changed.

✔ **Replace** first replaces the highlighted text with the replacement text and then moves on to the next place where the search phrase is found in the text. Replace and Replace All are active only if you selected the Replace option.

✔ **Replace All** replaces all instances of the search phrase with the replacement text and closes the Find/Replace toolbar.

✔ **X** closes the Find/Replace toolbar without making any further changes to the text.

Be careful if you use the Replace All option. It's very easy to make a mistake that could be very embarrassing. For example, if you were to decide that you had misspelled "meat" as "meet" throughout your document and used the Replace All command to change all instances of "meet" with "meat," someone may be very surprised to find out that you would like to "meat him for lunch."

Checking your spelling

Speaking of embarrassment, sending out a document that is filled with spelling errors may be near the top of the list — especially if that document is going to an important customer, to your boss, or as a cover letter along with your résumé. That is why spell checkers were invented, and why a Spell Checker was finally added to Pocket Word when the Pocket PC 2002 systems were released.

To make certain your Pocket Word documents use the correct spellings, open the Spell Checker using the Tools⇨Spell Check command. Then choose an option from the pop-up menu, as shown in Figure 8-4. The items in the upper section of the menu are the Spell Checker's suggestions. Just tap one to replace the highlighted word with that selection. You can also choose to ignore the word or add it to your personal dictionary.

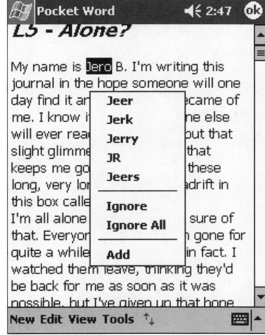

Figure 8-4: Spell check your Pocket Word documents to make certain they do not contain spelling errors.

Adding the date

Your Pocket PC offers a lot of timesaving shortcuts. In Pocket Word, for example, you can enter the current date into a document with just a couple of quick taps, which can be very useful if you want to add the date to a letter or if you're creating a log of something and need the correct date to appear in the log.

To add the date to a Pocket Word document, first make certain that the insertion point is in the correct location. The best way to do this is to tap where you want the date to appear. Next, tap-and-hold and select Insert Date from the pop-up menu. You can also use the Tools⇨Insert Date command if you don't like tap-and-hold.

To change the format of the dates that Pocket Word inserts into documents, click the Start button and choose Settings. Tap the System tab and choose Regional Settings. Tap the Date tab and choose the format you prefer from the drop-down Short date list. Click OK to make the change.

Counting your words

Sometimes it can be important to know exactly how many words a document contains. For example, if you are entering a "50 words or less" contest for a trip to Hawaii, you wouldn't want to lose the contest simply because your entry totaled 51 words, would you?

To determine the exact number of words in your document, simply use the Tools⇨Word Count command. When you do, Pocket Word pops up a message box giving you the current count. Don't forget to send a postcard from Hawaii!

Formatting your text

One thing that separates Pocket Word from a simple text-editing program like the Pocket PC Notes program is the ability to apply formatting to your text. While Pocket Word doesn't include all of the formatting options you find in desktop Word, it does provide the options you're most likely to want.

Take a look at the following sections for the scoop on formatting in Pocket Word.

Using the menus for formatting

To access the fullest set of Pocket Word text-formatting options, first select the text you want to format and then choose Edit⇨Format.

If the font you want to use doesn't appear in the Font list, copy the font from your desktop PC to the \Windows\Fonts folder on your Pocket PC using the ActiveSync Explore function. See "Exploring Your Pocket PC Files" in Chapter 7 for more information on viewing your Pocket PC's files from your desktop PC.

Choose the formatting options you prefer. Any text formatting you apply in Pocket Word remains in the document when you transfer it to your desktop PC.

Note: The Pen Weight option isn't really a text-formatting selection. You use this option to choose how thick lines are that you draw using the stylus. This option is most useful for drawings you may want to add to a Pocket Word document, but it may also help some when you're using handwriting recognition to enter text. Your Pocket PC won't care about the pen weight, but you may have an easier time writing if you choose a pen weight that is closer to the type of pen you normally use for writing on paper.

Using the formatting toolbar

Some of Pocket Word's formatting options are also available on a handy formatting toolbar. The formatting toolbar sits just above the Pocket Word menu bar.

The left side of the formatting toolbar contains buttons to display the formatting options screen as well as three of the text-formatting options. You can choose bold, italics, or underline using these buttons. The middle section of the toolbar has buttons you can tap to select left-aligned, centered, or right-aligned paragraph format. The right side of the toolbar has a button for creating bulleted text.

To display the formatting toolbar, tap the up-and-down-arrow button just to the right of Tools on the Pocket Word menu or select View➪Toolbar. The toolbar setting is a toggle — each time you select it, the toolbar appears or disappears depending on its current state.

Setting paragraph options

You can also choose several paragraph format options (see Figure 8-5). To display this screen, select Edit➪Paragraph.

Don't forget that you can quickly set paragraph alignment and bullets using the formatting toolbar.

The paragraph format options include the following items:

- **Alignment** to align the text in the paragraph to the left, right, or center.

- **Bulleted** to create paragraphs with leading *bullets* — symbols like those that appear in front of the items in this list.

- **Left** to control the distance the text is offset from the left margin.

- **Right** to control the distance the text is offset from the right margin.

- **Special** to control the first line of the paragraph separately from the rest of the paragraph. Choose **First line** to indent the first line, or **Hanging** to outdent (move to the left) the first line of the paragraph.

- **By** controls the distance of the first line's indent or outdent.

When you set the various paragraph options, remember the limitations of the Pocket PC's screen. You may not be able to see exactly how your document will appear when you go to print simply because there isn't enough room on the Pocket PC's screen. Even so, the options you set are saved with the document and transfer with the document to your desktop PC for printing.

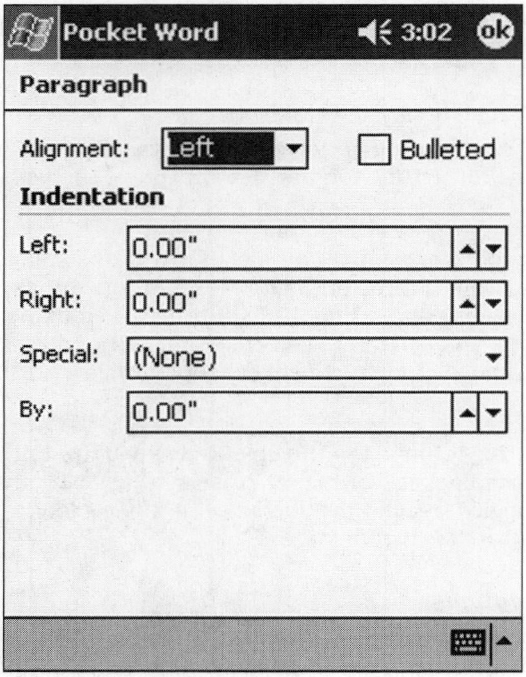

Figure 8-5:
Set para-
graph align-
ment and
margins
using these
options.

Saving your work

There is one very handy difference between a Pocket PC and a desktop PC that may save you from a lot of trouble. The Pocket PC doesn't have a hard drive, so everything is always in memory. As a result, you don't really have to save your Pocket Word documents — they're saved automatically when you click the OK button to close the document. So no more worries about saying no to a Save when you really meant yes.

There are, however, a couple of options that you can use to control how your document is saved.

Selecting the document format

If you want to give your document a specific name, choose the location where it is saved or select the document type; select the Tools⇨Save

Document As command, which displays the Save As screen shown in
Figure 8-6.

Figure 8-6:
Use this
screen to
control
how your
Pocket Word
document
is saved.

By default, Pocket Word uses the first few words in your document as the
name of the document, something that can be really convenient or a big pain
depending on the document. If every document starts out differently, using
the first few words makes it really easy to remember which document you're
dealing with. But if you start a lot of documents the same way — with your
address, for example — you'll probably want to provide your own name for
each new file.

Pocket Word saves all documents in the My Documents folder unless you
specify a different destination. On your desktop PC, you probably use folders
to organize your files into related projects, but this may not be necessary on
your Pocket PC because you aren't likely to keep hundreds of files on your
Pocket PC. It's your call whether you want to get fancy on this.

Use the Type list to select a different format for your file. In most cases just
leaving the type set to Pocket Word Document is best — allow ActiveSync
to handle any necessary conversions. However, you may want to choose a
different format if you intend to send the document file to someone via
e-mail (see "E-mailing your document" later in this chapter).

If you have a storage card inserted into your Pocket PC, you can use the Location list box to choose to store the document file on the storage card rather than in main memory. If you do choose this, remember that you won't be able to access the file if you remove the storage card for any reason — until you reinsert the storage card, of course. This is especially important to remember if you want to e-mail the file to someone and need to replace the storage card with a modem or a digital phone card to send e-mail.

Renaming or moving your document

You can rename or move a Pocket Word file after it has been saved by selecting the Edit⇨Rename/Move command. Why the program's developers thought people would think to look on two different menus to save a file and to rename it is hard to say, but they did.

As you've no doubt noticed, the Rename/Move screen offers the same options as the Save As screen with the exception of the file type selection. The same choices apply when you're renaming or moving a file as when you're saving it in the first place.

Sending Your File

In most cases you'll probably transfer Pocket Word documents to your desktop PC so you can print out whatever copies you need. But because Pocket Word runs on your Pocket PC, you also have additional options for sharing your document.

E-mailing your document

If you have an Internet connection for your Pocket PC, you can send your Pocket Word document via e-mail, which is really handy if you need to get the file to someone quickly.

If you're going to e-mail your Pocket Word document to someone who is not using a Pocket PC, save the file in a format he can open in his desktop PC's word processor. Usually this means one of the versions of Microsoft Word, but you may have to choose Rich Text Document or even Plain Text Document depending on the type of computer and word-processing software he's using.

To send a Pocket Word document via e-mail, select the Tools⇨Send via E-mail command. If you don't already have your e-mail access configured, you may want to refer to Chapter 14 before trying this.

Sending your document on a light beam

For even more fun, you can send a Pocket Word document to another Pocket PC user over a light beam. Just select Tools⇨Beam Document and aim your Pocket PC's IR port at the IR port on the other Pocket PC. The Pocket PC receiving the file will display a message asking whether you want to accept the file. If you haven't beamed documents before, you may want to have a look back at Chapter 4 where I show you some tips on successfully sending information using the IR port.

Okay, so the other PC — the one receiving your file — doesn't *have* to be a Pocket PC. You can send files via infrared to other types of PCs including laptops, handheld PCs, and even Palm PCs, but they do have to be properly equipped with an IR port and the proper software. Sending stuff to Pocket PCs via infrared is far easier than monkeying around with any of those other complications. Try it if you want to, but don't blame me if you end up wasting a lot of time trying to make it work.

Chapter 9

The Pocket Excel Numbers Game

In This Chapter

▶ Finding uses for Pocket Excel

▶ Using your desktop spreadsheet in Pocket Excel

▶ Creating a spreadsheet in Pocket Excel

▶ Sharing your Pocket Excel spreadsheets

*I*t's interesting to think back to the origins of the computer and realize that its original purpose was as a giant numerical calculator. No one had any idea that computers would one day be small enough to fit in your pocket, nor powerful enough to display life-like multimedia productions. But with Excel, the computers of today do hark back to that original purpose.

You don't have to be a mathematical whiz to find uses for Pocket Excel. In fact, that's one of the best things about being able to take Excel along in your pocket — if you can fill in the blanks, Pocket Excel can crank out the numbers you need. (Even with a powerful spreadsheet program like Pocket Excel, the Pocket PC is more often thought of for its other capabilities rather than its numerical calculating ones, but this is one feature you don't want to overlook.)

Uses for Pocket Excel

To get a feel for what you can do with Pocket Excel, you first need to have an idea of just what a spreadsheet really is. Thinking of a spreadsheet as a grid loaded with formulas doesn't really do it justice. I prefer to think of a spreadsheet as this really fancy calculator that already knows how to perform hundreds of super complex calculations on data and then present it so that we simple humans can understand what's going on. Or maybe it's just all magic — you throw in a bunch of numbers at one end, and a bunch of supposedly meaningful numbers fall out of the other end.

So what can you do with Pocket Excel? Here are just a few ideas to get you thinking:

- ✔ If you work in real estate, you can create a Pocket Excel spreadsheet that takes into account the tax implications of mortgage payments, real estate taxes, and so on to "sell up" your customers to help you earn larger commissions.

- ✔ If you're an amateur astronomer, you can use a Pocket Excel spreadsheet to calculate the altitude of satellites that pass overhead. And because your Pocket PC's screen has a backlight that you can easily adjust, you can use the spreadsheet when you're out looking at the sky on a dark night, too.

- ✔ A contractor can use a Pocket Excel spreadsheet to give a customer a preliminary idea of the cost of a project on the spot. A lot of people have no idea what it costs to build things, so being able to name your price may help you weed out the lookers from the doers without going through the entire bid process.

- ✔ A Pocket Excel spreadsheet can help you work on your company's budget while you're commuting between home and the office. You can actually get a chance to play around with some of the numbers without being interrupted by telephones or that lousy background music your employees insist on playing.

- ✔ If you bet on the horses, a Pocket Excel spreadsheet can help you figure out which ones you want to put your money on based on the statistics and records you've entered. Of course, there's no guarantee that you've got the right formula to produce winners, but that's part of the fun of going to the races, isn't it? Remember; just keep telling yourself "It's only money."

- ✔ Of course, anyone who keeps a household budget knows how handy a calculator is. Think of how much handier it would be to use a Pocket Excel spreadsheet so that you'd always be able to look back at your numbers to make certain you didn't mess things up by accidentally entering the wrong number for something.

Transferring Your Desktop Spreadsheet

Your Pocket PC may be a great tool for *using* a Pocket Excel spreadsheet, but no one is going to suggest that it's a great tool for *creating* one. Sure, you can do it, but do you want to do it? Transferring an Excel spreadsheet from your desktop PC is much easier than creating some complex monster from scratch right on your Pocket PC. Entering complex formulas using the Pocket PC's onscreen keyboard just isn't going to rank very high up on your fun things to do list!

Transferring an Excel spreadsheet to your Pocket PC takes just a few moments. As I discuss in Chapter 7, when you copy your Excel spreadsheet file into your Pocket_PC My Documents folder on your desktop PC, ActiveSync takes care of the rest the next time you pop the Pocket PC into the synchronization cradle.

Figure 9-1 shows an Excel spreadsheet that I copied from my desktop PC to my Pocket PC. In this case, the spreadsheet is one I created to help out the local Building Department calculate the cost of a building permit more easily.

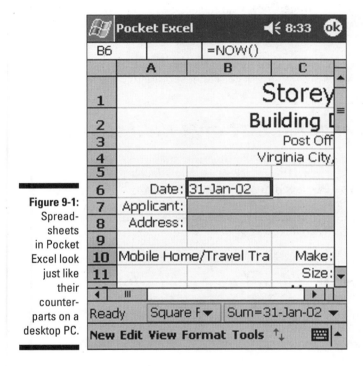

Figure 9-1: Spreadsheets in Pocket Excel look just like their counterparts on a desktop PC.

Things to Forget about in Pocket Excel

Of course, there are some differences between Excel on your desktop PC and Pocket Excel on your Pocket PC. Read on for a look at a few important ones.

Macros need not apply

Many years ago, the user manual for Lotus 1-2-3, the first spreadsheet program that became popular on the PC, asked the readers if they really wanted to become a programmer. This question was the lead-in to a short description of the *macro* commands that one could use to automate certain operations in the spreadsheet (macros are really just a simple programming language built into many different types of application programs). Over the years, macros became almost an institution with some users, and spreadsheet automation was the sign of a true spreadsheet guru.

As popular as macros and other programming languages were, they were also complex and allowed users to create spreadsheets that no one could really understand. You still see some of those monsters on occasion, but macros aren't nearly the rage they once were, which is a good thing if you want to use your spreadsheet in Pocket Excel on your Pocket PC — macros simply don't work in Pocket Excel.

One good thing about macros not running in Pocket Excel: You don't have to worry about macro viruses in your Pocket Excel spreadsheets.

Forget the graphs, just give me the facts

Graphs are another of those spreadsheet features that don't make it across the line from desktop Excel to Pocket Excel. But let's face it, how many really useful graphs have you ever seen in a spreadsheet anyway? Sure, a graph may seem to be saying something impressive, but don't you often get the impression that people use graphs simply because they can, not because they really mean anything to anyone?

Functioning in a Pocket Excel world

Functions are the meat and potatoes of spreadsheets. *Functions* are the built-in formulas that enable you to perform all sorts of fancy calculations that you wouldn't have a clue how to do on your own.

Pocket Excel has over 100 built-in functions. If you need to calculate "the depreciation of an asset for a specified period using the double-declining balance method," Pocket Excel has a built-in function to do it. Just don't ask me to explain what the double-declining balance method is — I haven't got a clue. But if you need it, it's there waiting for you to dummy up some numbers and act like you really do know what it means. (For more on actually using functions, see "Entering formulas," later in this chapter.)

As bizarre as it may sound, the 100+ built-in functions in Pocket Excel don't come close to the mind-boggling 400+ functions in some desktop spreadsheets. For example, Pocket Excel can't calculate the "cumulative beta probability density function" — whatever that is.

In reality, unless you're really doing strange things with spreadsheets, Pocket Excel will probably have all the functions you'll ever need. If it doesn't, maybe you need to get out into the sunlight a bit more often.

No printing allowed

Pocket Excel is missing one more bit of functionality that you take for granted on your desktop PC. Like all Pocket PC applications, Pocket Excel has no way to print. But like all other Pocket PC applications, there's a simple solution — copy your Pocket Excel spreadsheet to your desktop PC and print it there. Or decide that you really do want a paperless office.

Of course, for every limitation it seems there's someone who just has to find a way around that limitation. If you just can't live without being able to print directly from your Pocket PC, turn to Chapter 3 to see more about how you can print from your Pocket PC using a simple program you can buy.

Creating a Pocket Spreadsheet

Okay, I admit that a bit earlier I said the Pocket PC wasn't the greatest tool for creating a spreadsheet. Your desktop PC's larger screen and more convenient means of input certainly make creating spreadsheets far less of an ordeal than it can be on a Pocket PC. Still, knowing how to create or modify a Pocket Excel spreadsheet on your Pocket PC does provide you with the ability to do so when there's no desktop PC available. Besides, anyone who watches you create a spreadsheet using a stylus is going to know you're not someone to mess with!

So just what does it take to create or modify a spreadsheet on your Pocket PC? Besides a lot of patience, it takes using the tools in Pocket Excel. The following sections show the ones you'll most likely need.

Entering formulas

Pocket Excel uses the same format for formulas that you're familiar with from Excel on your desktop PC. You begin a formula by entering an equal sign (=), and then reference the spreadsheet cells you want to include in the formula. For example, if you want to sum the values from cells A1 through A4, and you want that sum to appear in cell A5, you enter the formula as **=A1+A2+A3+A4** in cell A5. Figure 9-2 shows how this formula appears in the spreadsheet.

Figure 9-2:
When you
enter a
formula in
a Pocket
Excel
spreadsheet,
the value
appears
in the
spreadsheet,
and the
formula
appears just
above the
columns
when the
cell is
selected.

Pocket Excel		8:43	ok
A5		=A1+A2+A3+A4	

	A	B	C
1	123		
2	456		
3	789		
4	67		
5	1435		
6			
7			
8			
9			
10			
11			
12			

Ready Sheet1 ▼ Sum=1435 ▼

New Edit View Format Tools ↑↓

Entering formulas by using arithmetic operators like the plus sign (+) and minus sign (–) is fine for very simple calculations, but to get real power in your formulas, use some of those built-in functions that I mention earlier in "Functioning in a Pocket Excel world." For example, use the SUM function rather than a series of plus signs to sum up a column of 100 different numbers. To insert a function, choose it from the scrolling list of functions and click OK.

Click the 123 button on the onscreen keyboard to make numerical entries somewhat easier by changing to the numeric keypad display.

I don't have the space here to show you how to use Pocket Excel's built-in functions. For that detailed information, refer to a book such as my *Excel 2002 Bible* or one of the other fine Wiley titles that cover Excel in more depth. Even so, I can at least show you how to add those functions to your Pocket Excel spreadsheet. To do so, select Tools⇨Insert Function from the Pocket Excel menu bar, which displays the Insert Function screen shown in Figure 9-3.

If you're not sure which Pocket Excel function you need, use the Category list to cut down the number of functions that are displayed by showing only functions that apply to a specific category. Then, watch the description area below the list of functions. As you highlight a function, the description area provides you with some idea of what the function does.

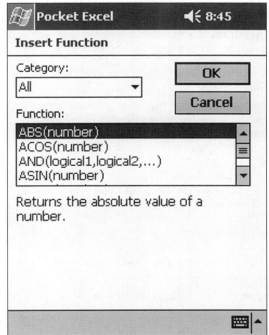

Figure 9-3:
Use this screen to choose from Pocket Excel's built-in functions.

One problem with using functions is that nearly all of them require *arguments* — extra information such as cell references or values you must enter in order to complete the calculation. This doesn't mean that the functions are angry, but you may become frustrated trying to figure out what information is required for each of the arguments — especially when you try to use some of the stranger functions that are available in Pocket Excel. When you select a function to add to your spreadsheet, Pocket Excel includes *placeholders* — names that describe what is needed — for each argument. You have to determine the correct information to replace each of the placeholders. Some of the argument placeholders are easy to understand — such as the year, month, and day values that are required for the DATE function. Other argument placeholders — such as "number" that appears in many functions — are far less clear.

The copy of Excel on your desktop PC includes far more help than simple argument placeholders for entering functions into spreadsheets. I recommend checking the desktop version of Excel if you need more help figuring out what information to enter for each of the arguments in complex functions.

Editing your spreadsheet

We've all heard people blame their mistakes on "computer errors" when in reality computers seldom make errors. Sure, the results may not always be what we expect, but that doesn't mean the computer was wrong. More often the problem is simple human error caused when someone asked the wrong question.

Spreadsheets can easily produce results that aren't what you expect. Until someone invents a computer that does what you mean rather than what you say, this will continue to be a problem. In a Pocket Excel spreadsheet, if you don't get the results you want it's usually because you either entered the wrong information or you have an error in a formula. Either way, you need to edit your spreadsheet to correct the problem.

For some editing chores, you can use the Edit menu commands (see Figure 9-4). For example, if you want to fill a group of cells with a sequence of values, use the Edit⇨Fill command. The other Edit menu commands include:

- **Edit⇨Undo** to return the spreadsheet to where it was before your last entry, and use **Edit⇨Redo** when you realize you wanted that entry after all.

- **Edit⇨Cut** to remove a selection and place it on the Clipboard.

- **Edit⇨Copy** to place a copy of the selection on the Clipboard in addition to leaving it in the spreadsheet.

- **Edit⇨Paste** to add the Clipboard contents to the spreadsheet.

- **Edit⇨Paste Special** to control how the Clipboard contents are pasted — such as just the current values of formulas rather than the formulas themselves.

- **Edit⇨Clear** removes cell contents or formatting.

- **Edit⇨Select All** selects everything in the spreadsheet so that the next command you issue will apply to all of the selection.

- **Edit⇨Find/Replace** to locate all instances of a specific value.

- **Edit⇨Password** sets or changes the password someone will need to open the spreadsheet.

- **Edit⇨Rename/Move** changes the name or storage location for the spreadsheet.

The Edit menu commands aren't very useful when you want to modify a formula. For that you need to attack the problem directly by first selecting the cell you want to modify, and then tapping in the *formula bar* (the area just below the time display in the upper right of the Pocket Excel screen). Figure 9-5 shows how the screen appears when you're editing a formula.

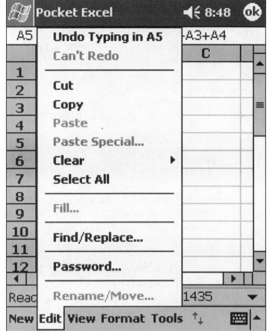

Figure 9-4: Use the Edit menu commands to modify your spreadsheet.

Figure 9-5: Edit formulas directly in the formula bar.

When you're editing (or creating) a formula, you can open the Insert Function screen by tapping on the Insert Function button just to the left of the formula bar. The Insert Function button is the one labeled *fx*. Tap the other two buttons left of the formula bar to enter your changes (the checkmark) or to discard any changes (the X).

If you forget to tap the formula bar before you begin entering something in a cell, you replace the entire contents of the cell rather than editing it. If this happens, immediately select Edit⇨Undo before you do anything else.

Controlling the view

One of the biggest problems with using a Pocket Excel spreadsheet is simply that you can't see very much of the spreadsheet at one time. There's just so much going on to clutter the screen that you don't have a lot of room for useful information.

As Figure 9-6 shows, you can control just how much of that junk appears on the screen by using the View menu options. The five items at the top of this menu are all toggles, so each time you select them they either appear or disappear depending on whether they're currently visible.

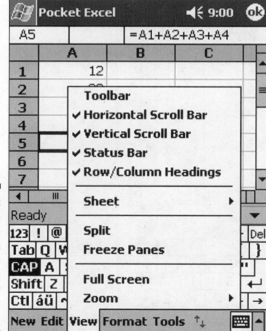

Figure 9-6: Use the View menu commands to regain some valuable screen space.

If possible, place all the cells where you'll need to enter information near the upper-left corner of your Pocket Excel spreadsheet. That way you may be able to hide the scroll bars and still easily input data.

If your spreadsheet has more than one worksheet, use the View⇨Sheet command to select a different worksheet. You can also use the worksheet selector button that appears in the center of the status bar (just above the menu bar) if the status bar is visible.

The View⇨Split and View⇨Freeze Panes commands enable you to see different areas of your spreadsheet at the same time. While you may find View⇨Freeze Panes useful in making certain you're working in the correct row or column, the Pocket PC's screen is really too small for View⇨Split to be of much use.

View⇨Full Screen devotes the maximum possible screen area to displaying your spreadsheet. When you select this command, every Pocket Excel element that can be hidden disappears from view.

Finally, View⇨Zoom lets you zoom in or out on your spreadsheet while leaving all other screen elements normal size. This command is most effective if you combine it with View⇨Full Screen.

Formatting cells

Formatting changes the appearance but not the contents of cells in your spreadsheet. You have an extensive set of formatting options in Pocket Excel. To select the cell-formatting options, first select the cells you want to format. Then choose Format⇨Cells to display the Format Cells screen. This screen has several tabs that you can use to make the following changes:

- ✔ **Size:** Control the row height and column width. Normally, Pocket Excel adjusts these dimensions automatically, but you can change them for more precise control. You can also drag a row or column border to resize them just as you do in Excel on your desktop PC.

- ✔ **Number:** Choose the numeric format used to display numerical values. Choosing the correct numeric format can make the difference between numbers that are impossible to decipher and ones that are instantly recognizable. For example, if a cell is supposed to indicate an important date, 6/26/2000 is probably easier to understand than 36703 (the *date serial number* that corresponds to June 26, 2000 — date serial numbers are simply the number of days since December 31, 1899).

- ✔ **Align:** Control the positioning of text and numbers within cells. By default, numbers line up along the right side of the cell and text lines up to the left. The alignment options even allow you to wrap text to fit within the width of the column.

✔ **Font:** Use a different typeface or other font characteristics such as bold or colored text. You can use any font that is installed on your Pocket PC.

✔ **Borders:** Add lines around cells or a background color. (This tab has nothing to do with a bookstore nor does it have anything to do with going to another country.)

The Format menu has several other commands that you can use to modify your spreadsheet:

✔ Both **Format⇨Row** and **Format⇨Column** enable you to hide or display entire rows or columns and to remove any changes you may have made on the Size tab of the Format Cells screen. Note, though, that removing changes to cell height or row width using the Autofit option only works if you actually have some entries in the same row (or column) when you select the Autofit command.

✔ **Format⇨Modify Sheets** provides you with a tool for adding or deleting worksheets, renaming worksheets, or moving worksheets so they appear in a different order.

✔ **Format⇨Insert Cells** and **Format⇨Delete Cells** are pretty easy to figure out. It's probably no surprise that you use these commands to add or remove cells from your spreadsheet.

Navigating in Pocket Excel

Because so little of a typical Pocket Excel spreadsheet fits on the screen at the same time, you need efficient ways to move around. There are several ways to move to a different location in your spreadsheet:

✔ Use the scroll bars to change the visible area of the spreadsheet. Remember, though, that until you tap a new cell, the cell that was selected remains selected. It doesn't matter that you're viewing a different set of cells — viewing is not the same as selecting!

✔ Use the arrow keys on the onscreen keyboard to move around. Because this method does move the cell selector, it also selects a new cell, and that cell is the one that receives any input when you start typing.

✔ To move a long distance, use the Tools⇨Go To command to display the Go To screen, shown in Figure 9-7. You can enter either a cell address or a name if your spreadsheet has names assigned to cells.

The easiest way to move to a different worksheet is to use the Worksheet Selector button in the status bar.

Figure 9-7:
Use Tools⇨
Go To when
you want
to quickly
jump to a
distant cell.

Exchanging Spreadsheet Data

Pocket Excel uses the same three-ring circus for exchanging data with other computers that you've grown familiar with from other Pocket PC applications. But just in case, your choices are

- **Tools⇨Beam Workbook:** Beams your spreadsheet to another Pocket PC user. Doesn't this almost make you feel like you're back in grade school passing notes?

- **Tools⇨Send via E-mail:** Sends your spreadsheet file as an e-mail attachment. May as well spread the work around, right?

- Finally, if you have ActiveSync set up to synchronize your files, your spreadsheet is copied to your desktop PC when you pop your Pocket PC into the cradle.

Pocket Excel spreadsheets may not be the most exciting way to use your Pocket PC, but they sure can put a lot of power in your pocket. Almost any Excel spreadsheet from your desktop PC will run on your Pocket PC, so maybe one day you can convince your boss that you were late because you had to stop and run some budget numbers on your way to work.

Chapter 10

Managing Your Money

. . . .

. . . .

*P*ocket Money sounds a lot like the change you carry around so you can buy coffee or sodas, doesn't it? "Let's see, I've got two quarters, three dimes, a nickel, and two pennies; I guess it will have to be half a cup of black coffee today. Is the sweetener free?"

Of course, when I talk about Pocket Money here, I'm talking about the little money manager program that's available on your Pocket PC. This handy program helps you keep track of where all your money went and may even help you save enough so you can afford the cappuccino next time.

Some Handy Uses for Pocket Money

Pocket Money is a free download for your Pocket PC so you're probably thinking you should try and get some use out of the program. But maybe you're having a hard time figuring out how you can use it. Well, never fear; I'm going to give you some ideas that will have you reaching for that stylus in no time. Here are just a few of the ways you can use Pocket Money:

✔ If you have an expense account you probably end up paying a lot of business-related expenses like bridge tolls, parking meters, umbrellas, and the like out of your own pocket simply because it's too much trouble to keep track of those miscellaneous expenses. With Pocket Money, you can easily keep track of those items along with a complete record of the date and time of the expense. And after you've entered an expense one time, Pocket Money remembers most of the details so you can enter it far more quickly the next time around. You'll probably end up getting far more than the cost of your Pocket PC back in extra expense money for all those little items that used to be too much trouble to track!

✔ Even if you aren't on an expense account, you can keep better track of your business-related expenses so you don't forget to claim them at tax time. Guess what? Pocket Money is as handy at making sure you get all the business deductions you deserve as it is at making certain that other lucky guy gets his expenses reimbursed.

✔ If you handle petty cash for your organization, you can use Pocket Money to track where all the money goes. There's no sense letting anyone have any questions about whether you're being honest, is there?

✔ If you're the person who's always getting stuck making the lunch run for the office, why not use Pocket Money to keep track of everyone's running bill? That way you're more likely to get paid back on payday — especially if you've got some people with poor memories who always seem to forget at least some of what they owe you.

✔ Pocket Money can also keep track of the stocks in your portfolio. Whenever you go online to check your e-mail, Pocket Money can let you know whether now is the right time to announce your retirement party or to ask for a bit more overtime.

Managing Your Money

If you already use Quicken or Microsoft Money on your desktop PC, you'll find that Pocket Money is quite familiar and easy to use. Pocket Money concentrates on a few basic money management functions rather than trying to cover all the bases. Getting to know Pocket Money takes only a few minutes, and it will be time well spent.

Setting Pocket Money's options

Pocket Money has very few options, but take a quick look at them to help you understand how the program works. To begin, open Pocket Money by clicking the Start button and choosing Programs from the Start menu. Then tap Microsoft Money. When Pocket Money opens, choose Tools➪Options to display the screen shown in Figure 10-1.

You'll probably want to leave all three options selected:

✔ The **AutoComplete+** option makes Pocket Money far easier to use because you don't have to do nearly as much typing. When this option is selected, Pocket Money fills in most entries for you using its best guess based on previous entries. If you eat the same lunch a Joe's Diner a couple times each week, Pocket Money can fill out the whole transaction as soon as it recognizes that you're starting off with "Joe's" as the payee.

↳ The **AutoFill** option also helps you by entering the same amount and category for a payee. You can easily overwrite these entries, but if they are correct you won't have to.

↳ The **Use large font** option simply makes it easier to read the Pocket PC's screen when you're using Pocket Money. There's really no reason not to choose this option.

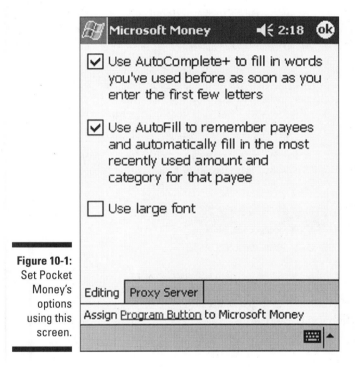

Figure 10-1:
Set Pocket
Money's
options
using this
screen.

Almost no one needs the options on the Proxy Server tab. Those of you who do already know who you are, don't you? *Proxy servers* are special computers that provide access to the Internet while preventing unauthorized traffic. In the case of Pocket Money, the proxy server settings are used only if you set up Pocket Money to track your investments and you need to use a proxy server to access the Internet. Confused yet? Don't worry about it — if none of this sounds familiar, it's a good indicator that it doesn't apply to you.

If you find yourself using Pocket Money a lot, click the Program Button link near the bottom of the page to assign one of the buttons on the front of your Pocket PC to opening Pocket Money. You'll have to decide which of the currently assigned buttons to reassign to Pocket Money. To reassign the front panel buttons on your Pocket PC to any other application, use the Buttons icon on the Personal tab of your Pocket PC's Settings screen.

After you select the three options, tap OK to close the Options screen.

Using a password

For many applications, passwords can be more trouble than they're worth. After all, if someone else uses your Internet account for a few minutes, who cares? (As long as they stay away from your e-mail account, that is.) Most likely your Internet account is set up for unlimited access, so if a friend needs to get on the Internet you're probably quite willing to let him use your Pocket PC and your account.

For Pocket Money, though, a password can be really important because you enter your account numbers and other confidential information you probably don't want to broadcast to the world. And you certainly want to make things a bit harder in case a thief were to steal your Pocket PC.

To add a password that's needed to even open Pocket Money, select Tools⇨Password to display the screen shown in Figure 10-2.

Figure 10-2:
Create a
password
to prevent
unauthorized
access to
your Pocket
Money files.

Enter your password in both boxes and tap OK. You need to enter the same password twice to make certain that you've actually typed in what you thought you did. If the two entries don't match, Pocket Money won't accept them.

Be awfully careful when you're creating a password for Pocket Money. If you forget what you entered, you won't be able to open Pocket Money or access your Pocket Money data. It's a really good idea to close Pocket Money as soon as you've added a password and then re-open the program. That way you can check that your password is correct before you spend a lot of time setting up accounts or entering information. If you can't remember your password, you have to use ActiveSync to remove Pocket Money from your Pocket PC and then re-install it. Any data you've entered in Pocket Money will be lost if you do this.

Setting up a new account

You have to set up an account in Pocket Money before you can use the program. An *account* is simply your checking account, a petty cash account, a credit card, or something similar. You can set up as many different accounts as you need. Each account is separate from all the others, so it's fine to set up special accounts for specific purposes.

To create a new account, click New on the Pocket Money menu bar. This displays the account setup screen, shown in Figure 10-3.

Fill in the blanks on this screen as follows:

✔ In the **Account Name** box, enter a descriptive name for the account. If you're going to be sharing information with Money on your desktop PC, use the same account name as the one on your desktop PC. Enter a name that makes it easy for you to select the correct account so you don't accidentally enter transactions into the wrong account.

✔ Select the type of account from the **Account Type** box. Pocket Money uses the account type to control how it handles transactions, so be sure you choose the correct type. For example, if the account type is a checking account, Pocket Money automatically enters sequential check numbers to record transactions.

✔ Use the **Opening Balance** box to indicate how much money is currently in the account. Here you need to remember that Pocket Money is going to start off with the amount you show, so enter the amount in the account as it exists just before you enter your first transaction. So, for example, if you're going to track your checking account, enter the amount of money shown in your check register just before the first check you're going to record in Pocket Money.

✔ For a credit card or credit line account, use the **Credit Limit** box to indicate your total credit limit for this account.

✔ If the account is an interest-bearing account, enter the appropriate rate in the **Interest Rate** box.

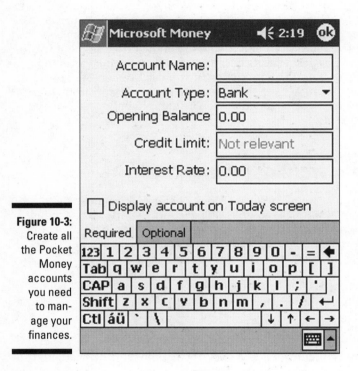

Figure 10-3: Create all the Pocket Money accounts you need to manage your finances.

Next click the Optional tab, shown in Figure 10-4. Here you enter information you may need to access your account.

The information on the Optional tab is optional for a good reason. You don't want to make it easy for someone else to access your accounts without your authorization. If you fill out this tab, make certain you have password protected Pocket Money, as discussed in the preceding section.

Click OK when you have finished setting up the account.

Organizing your money using categories

One of the best ways to keep track of where you've spent your money is to organize things into categories. You can have categories like office expenses, business travel, groceries, entertaining, and that all-important one — chocolate! If you want to use categories in Pocket Money, you have to set them up yourself. To make certain you actually use the categories when you finally do enter transactions, set up at least some basic categories before you start entering transactions.

To create your categories:

1. **Click the View list (the list just below the Start button that indicates what is currently being displayed).**

    If you've just added a new account, the View list is probably showing "Account Manager."

2. **Choose Categories from the View list.**

3. **When the View list indicates Categories, click New to create a new category using the screen shown in Figure 10-5.**

4. **Use the boxes on this screen to enter the information about your categories.**

   Each category must have a unique name — you can't have the same category listed as both an income and an expense category. Slight variations can be used if you can't think of a creative way to name something.

5. **If you want to break down a category further, use the Subcategory of option for the new categories that are a part of the category.**

   For example, you might want subcategories of your Medical category for dental, doctor, and drug-related expenses.

6. **To make a note reminding yourself of something special about a category, enter your note in the Memo text box.**

7. **Click OK when you finish setting up each category.**

Entering your transactions

After you create accounts and set up categories, you can start throwing in some transactions. Now you get to see where the money is really going.

Start by selecting Account Register from the View list. If you've set up more than one account, select the account you want to use from the Account list to the right of the View list. Figure 10-6 shows how your account register appears after you've entered several transactions.

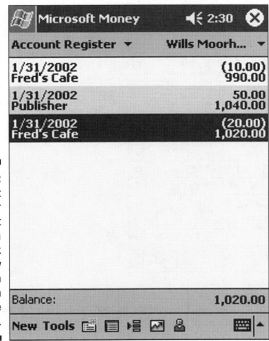

Figure 10-6:
The account register works just like a checkbook to show what's been going on with the account.

To add a new transaction, click New to display the new transaction screen, shown in Figure 10-7. As you begin filling in the Payee box, Pocket Money tries to help out by entering the matching information for the last transaction with this same payee.

After you complete the items on the Required tab, you can use the items on the Optional tab to add more information about the transaction. (The Optional tab is where you select a category to help organize your accounts.)

Use the Void item in the Status box to record checks you wrote but then voided so you don't forget and get in a panic trying to remember what happened to the missing check.

When you're finished entering information, tap OK to complete the transaction.

Figure 10-7:
Use this screen to add new transactions to your accounts.

If you enter a transaction in error, tap-and-hold the transaction, and then tap Delete Transaction. Pocket Money asks to confirm that you really do want to send the transaction to the dump.

You can edit an existing transaction by tapping it to open the transaction screen. Make your changes and then click OK.

The bottom of the transaction screen has a menu item called Split. Use Split to create transactions that are a bit more complicated, such as bank deposits that include funds from more than one payee. When you create a split, you need to allocate the money between different sources. You enter each item in the Split screen, specifying the amount of the item. For example, if you make a bank deposit that includes $500 from your paycheck and $20 you won in the office football pool, you create one item for $500 and one for $20. When you are finished entering the individual items in the split transaction, tap OK to enter the total transaction into the transaction record.

Tracking your investments

Pocket Money can also keep track of your stock market investments. If you have an Internet connection on your Pocket PC, you can even get delayed stock quotes. But your Pocket PC doesn't offer hot stock picks — you still have to rely on your brother-in-law for that type of information.

To add your favorite stocks to the Pocket Money Investments list, select Investments from the View list. Then click the New button and enter the name of the investment and the other details (the stock ticker symbol, the price per share, and the number of shares you own) about the investment. Click OK when you have finished.

Be sure you enter the correct stock market symbol for each of your investments. Pocket Money uses the symbol to locate the current market value.

Figure 10-8 shows how the Investments list looks after I have entered a stock into the list.

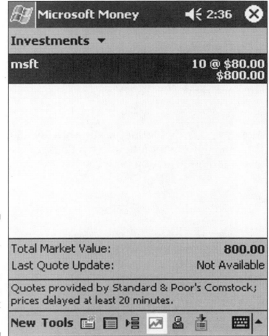

Figure 10-8:
Track your
stock mar-
ket wins
and losses
in Pocket
Money.

After you enter your stocks, select Tools⇨Update Investments command (or click the Update Investments button just to the right of the Tools menu) to get a delayed market price for those stocks. You need an Internet connection through your Pocket PC (see Chapter 12) to get this update.

Sharing the Numbers with Money

If you have Microsoft Money loaded on your desktop PC, you can share the Pocket Money information from your Pocket PC with Money. By sharing this information, you can keep track of expenses on your Pocket PC and then update the files on your desktop PC.

To share information between Microsoft Money and Pocket Money, you must select Money as one of the synchronization options in ActiveSync (see Chapter 7). Unfortunately, if you use a different money management program (such as Quicken) you aren't able to share information between Pocket Money and the other program on an ongoing basis. In fact, you're able to share your Quicken data only if you first load Money on your desktop PC and then import your Quicken data into Money.

If you intend to share information between Pocket Money on your Pocket PC and Money on your desktop PC, make certain you have set up Money on your desktop PC and have established the synchronization before you add information to Pocket Money. Otherwise, you have to remove Pocket Money from your Pocket PC and then reinstall it to add the synchronization option to your Pocket PC.

Data sharing between Money and Pocket Money is strictly a one-to-one relationship. You can't share the same information between a Pocket PC and two desktop PCs, nor can you share information between two Pocket PCs and one desktop PC.

Chapter 11

Calculating the Hard Numbers Easily

*Y*ou've probably got at least one calculator buried somewhere under the papers on your desk. Simple calculators are so common and cheap that people give them away when you renew a magazine or walk into your bank on free calculator day. Why would you possibly need to use your Pocket PC as a calculator?

Actually, having a calculator built into your Pocket PC makes a lot of sense, if for no better reason than your Pocket PC is so useful, you probably have it with you most of the time. As the old saying goes, "A bird in the hand is worth two in the bush."

Calculating the Uses of the Pocket Calculator

You already know a dozen different uses for your desktop calculator, but the calculator in your Pocket PC has some unique uses, too. Here are a few of the ways you can use your Pocket PC calculator:

✔ If you're writing a note on your Pocket PC and need to do some quick calculations to figure out how much more business you'll need to do to increase revenues by 7.8% next year, you can pop open the calculator and get some good numbers. And because you can copy and paste from the calculator, you don't need to retype those numbers.

✔ When you're out for lunch with those stingy people who never seem to remember to add in their part of the tax and tip, you can use the calculator to let them know what their share of the bill really is. Or you can simply choose a better dining companion in the future.

✔ If you're using Pocket Money to manage your finances, you can use the calculator to add up your bank deposits and then copy the results directly into your Pocket Money transaction (see Chapter 10).

✔ Finally, you can gather up all those funky calculators that you got for free and clear a bunch of space on your desk. And because everybody likes to get something for nothing, you could walk around the office giving everyone the gift of a free calculator and make everyone think you're really a nice guy. Just watch out when the office gardener comes by trying to give away zucchini — you'll probably be on the top of his list!

Doing Some Calculations

To open the Pocket PC's calculator, click the Start button and choose Programs from the Start menu. Then tap Calculator in the Programs folder. Figure 11-1 shows the calculator.

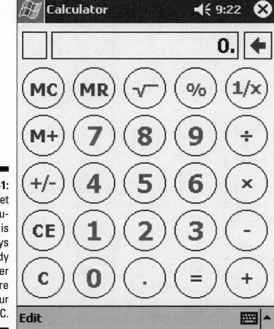

Figure 11-1:
The Pocket PC's calculator is always handy whenever you're using your Pocket PC.

The calculator application on your Pocket PC may look a little different from the one shown in the figures. For example, the calculator on the Audiovox Maestro and on the Toshiba e570 includes a currency conversion feature for those of you who travel in countries where you may need to know how the local prices compare to Euros. Even so, the basics of using the calculator are pretty much the same on all Pocket PCs.

When the calculator is open, tap the keys to enter numbers and perform calculations. As you enter numbers, they appear in the box just above the keys. This box also shows the results of your calculations.

If the onscreen keyboard pops up when you open the calculator, tap the Keyboard icon next to the lower-right side of the menu bar to hide the keyboard. Although you may think the onscreen keyboard could be useful when entering symbols like parentheses in a calculation, the Pocket PC's calculator ignores any such attempts to get fancy. What you see on the face of the calculator really is all you get.

I'm sure you can figure out most of the keys, but there are a few keys that you may not recognize or realize just how powerful they are:

- **M+** adds the current value into memory so you can use it later in a calculation. Because the calculator lacks *nesting* — essentially the ability to perform subcalculations through the use of parentheses — you have to use the calculator's memory if you need to get very fancy.

- **MR** recalls the value that's stored in memory. You can recall the same value as often as necessary, so you can store a value that you want to apply in a series of calculations (such as marking up prices by a set percentage).

- **MC** clears the current value stored in memory. Memory stores a cumulative value, so clear the memory first if you want to replace what is in memory rather than adding to it.

- **+/–** switches the sign of the currently displayed value so that positive numbers become negative, and negative numbers become positive. Use this key if you want to subtract the displayed value from whatever is currently stored in memory.

- **CE** clears the currently displayed value without screwing up your existing calculation. Use this key if you make a mistake entering a value and don't want to go back to the beginning and re-enter all of your numbers.

- **C** clears the entire calculation so you can start fresh.

- **√** gives you the square root of the currently displayed value. Even though most roots are actually a lot closer to round, if you really need a square one for something, this is the place to find it.

✔ **1/x** inverts a number. Essentially, inverting a number means that the calculator divides 1 by the number that is currently displayed. My favorite number to invert is 0.

The rest of the calculator keys are for entering numbers or performing simple calculations.

Even though the Pocket PC's calculator has only a single memory, you can store two values if you're tricky enough. Use the memory keys to store one value and use Edit⇨Copy to store the other. Then use Edit⇨Paste when you want to reinsert the value you stored using Edit⇨Copy.

You can also use Edit⇨Copy and Edit⇨Paste to share values with other Pocket PC applications.

Using OmniSolve When You Need Something More

If you use an HP Jornada series Pocket PC, you've got another far more power-ful calculator you can use. OmniSolve makes your HP Pocket PC function much like a very powerful HP financial calculator. Of course, if another manufacturer made your Pocket PC, you may want to skip the rest of this chapter. Other-wise you may become jealous of all those people using their Jornadas. Or you can go to the LandWare Web site (www.landware.com/catalog/pocketpc/) and buy a copy of OmniSolve for your Pocket PC — in which case you may want to finish reading this chapter after all.

Other calculator programs will run on your Pocket PC if you don't happen to have OmniSolve. You may want to have a look at Chapter 19 to see where you can find one of them to add to your Pocket PC.

To open OmniSolve, click the Start button and choose Programs from the Start menu. Then tap the OmniSolve icon in the Programs folder. And then read the following sections for more information.

Setting OmniSolve's options

OmniSolve is a lot more complex than the Pocket PC calculator, so it has a number of options you can set to control how OmniSolve works. Start by having a look at these options so you know what changes you can make if you want to.

Select Edit⇨Preferences to open the OmniSolve Preferences screen (see Figure 11-2).

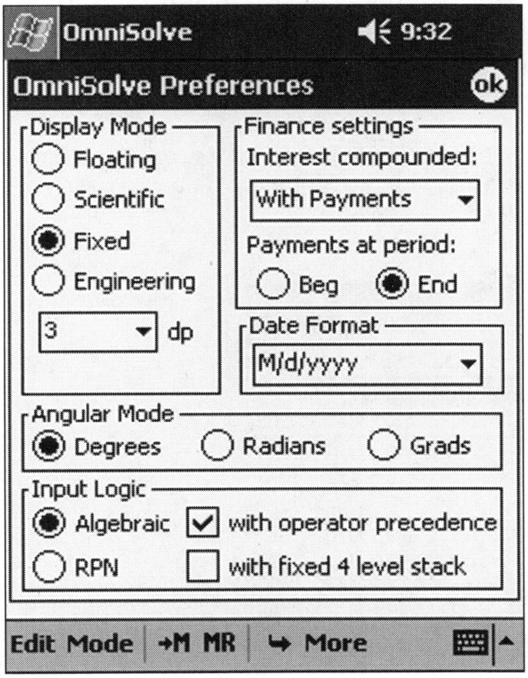

Figure 11-2:
Use the
OmniSolve
options to
turn the
program
into a really
weird
calculator.

Here's a brief, plain-English translation of the groups of settings you can choose:

- ✔ **Display Mode:** Controls how numbers appear in OmniSolve. Each of the options shown suits a certain type of calculation. The dp box selects the number of digits that appear after the decimal point.

- ✔ **Finance settings:** Determines how interest is calculated when you use one of the financial functions. If you're a banker, you probably know what all of the various finance options mean, but for the rest of us, these settings are basically used to squeeze out every last little penny from a borrower.

- ✔ **Date Format:** Selects the way dates are shown. 'Nuff said.

- ✔ **Angular Mode:** Chooses the way angles are expressed. For most people, the default setting of Degrees makes the most sense — Radians and Grads are used mostly by engineers and mathematicians when they want to confuse everyone else.

✔ **Input Logic:** Controls how you enter a calculation and in what order values are processed. If you don't already know what this set of options does, leave them alone or you could end up with a calculator that provides really strange results.

Choosing a calculator mode

As Figure 11-3 shows, OmniSolve offers quite a few different ways to play around with numbers. When you tap Mode on the menu bar, you can choose from many different types of calculations.

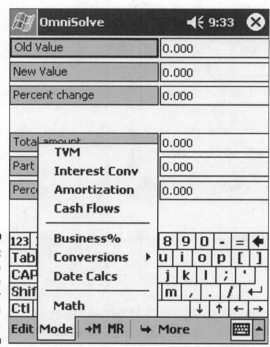

Figure 11-3:
Choose the OmniSolve calculator mode you need.

If you generally use the same OmniSolve calculator mode, use the Edit➪ Startup Application command to make OmniSolve always open in your preferred mode.

The various calculation modes include:

- **TVM** (Time Value of Money): Calculates loan payments, present value, or future value of money.

- **Interest Conv:** Calculates different types of interest rates including nominal, effective, and continuous annual rates as well as the periodic rate.

- **Amortization:** Calculates payment schedules for paying off a loan.

- **Cash Flows:** Returns values such as the *IRR* (Internal Rate of Return) and *NPV* (Net Present Value). You would use these values to determine the value of an investment.

- **Business%:** Calculates items such as profit rates and percentages of totals. Basically, these calculations prove that it's easy to lie using statistics.

- **Conversions:** Performs all sorts of conversions between different forms of measurement — such as between miles and kilometers. There are so many different conversions built into OmniSolve that you'll have to select the type of conversion from a submenu.

- **Date Calcs:** Provides several different ways to calculate the number of days between two dates.

- **Math:** Turns OmniSolve into a good old-fashioned scientific calculator. Although somewhat similar to the standard Pocket PC calculator, the OmniSolve calculator includes many additional functions including the ability to nest calculations using parentheses.

Playing around with fancy calculations

Having a fancy calculator isn't any fun unless you actually play around with it. To see just how useful the various parts of OmniSolve can be when used together, follow along with an example that calculates what 25 miles per gallon translates to in kilometers per liter. Here's how to make this calculation:

1. **Select Mode⇨Math to display the calculator screen.**

2. **Enter** 25 **and tap 1/x to convert the value into gallons per mile.**

3. **Click the →M button and then MS0: to store the value in memory location 0 (see Figure 11-4).**

4. **Select Mode⇨Conversions⇨Volume to display the volume conversions screen.**

5. **Tap the US gallons input box on the left side of the screen and then MR to open the memory list. Tap MR0 to place the stored value in the gallons box.**

6. **Tap the liters box on the left side of the screen to make the conversion into liters.**

7. **Click the →M button and then MS1: to store the value in memory location 1.**

8. **Select Mode⇨Conversions⇨Length to display the length conversions screen.**

9. **Tap the miles input box on the left side of the screen and enter 1 using the onscreen keyboard.**

10. **Tap the kilometers on the left side of the screen to make the conversion into kilometers.**

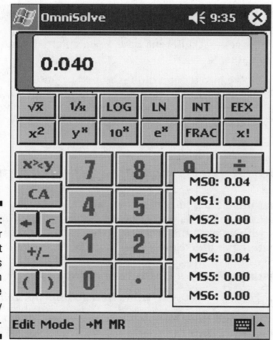

Figure 11-4:
Store your first calculation's results in one of the memory locations.

11. Click the →M button and then MS2: to store the value in memory location 2.

12. Select Mode⇨Math to display the calculator screen.

13. Tap MR to open the memory selector (see Figure 11-5).

14. Select MR2 to recall the value from memory location 2 and place it in the display.

15. Tap the ÷ button to indicate you're going to divide the first number by the second.

16. Tap MR to open the memory recall selector and tap MR1 to recall the value from memory location 1 and place it in the display.

17. Tap the = button to complete the calculation, as shown in Figure 11-6. So now you know: 25 miles per gallon is the equivalent of 10.656 kilometers per liter.

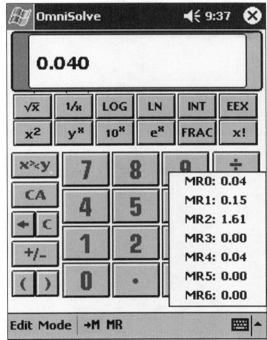

Figure 11-5:
Recall your conversion's results for use in the calculation.

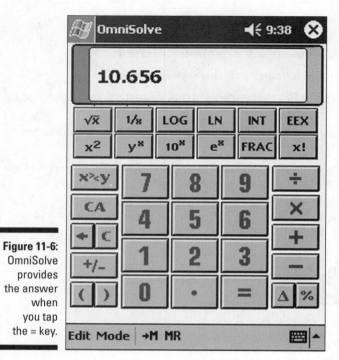

Figure 11-6:
OmniSolve
provides
the answer
when
you tap
the = key.

You probably won't do this type of calculation very often, but it does show how you can combine the different functions of OmniSolve to produce the results you need.

Part IV
The Pocket PC and the Internet

The 5th Wave   By Rich Tennant

"So much for the Graffiti handwriting system."

In this part . . .

You learn how you can use your Pocket PC to access the Internet as well as your local network. Here you'll see just how you can surf the Internet and handle your e-mail virtually anywhere. You'll see how you may be able to make use of both some wireless Internet options as well as the more familiar wired connections.

Chapter 12

Connecting Your Pocket PC

. . . .

. . . .

*I*n the past five or so years, the Internet has gone from being primarily a toy for college students to being one of the most important means of communication throughout the world. The Internet has gotten to the point where even owners of the local used-car lot think they have to have "Internet" in their name. And it's no wonder that this has happened — the Internet really has influenced society in ways no one could've imagined.

At first the Internet was simply a network that allowed certain U.S. government computers and a few university computers to exchange some files. As the Internet grew, more people gained access, and more uses for the network were invented. Today, post offices and long distance phone service providers can tell you that so many people are using the Internet that their business is way down — the Internet is often a much cheaper and faster form of communication.

It's only natural, then, that you probably have thought about how convenient it would be to be able to connect to the Internet through your Pocket PC. In fact, because the Pocket PC is so small and portable, it's now possible to think about something even more radical — using your Pocket PC to connect on the run without even looking for a phone line. In this chapter, I cover the options so you can decide which ones are best for your needs.

But the Internet isn't the only network you may be interested in. You may also want to connect to your company or home network with your Pocket PC. By doing so, you can open up a whole new world of possibilities including much faster synchronization, the ability to remain connected as you roam, and even the option of easily printing documents directly from your Pocket PC.

What You Need to Connect

I'm sorry to be the one to tell you this, but your Pocket PC needs help. That is, your Pocket PC needs some help in order to be able to connect to the Internet. Pocket PCs don't come with the hardware necessary to connect directly to the Internet. For that you're going to have to get some extra pieces, which I go over in the following sections.

Is it real (time) or synchronized?

Sure, you can download Internet content to your desktop PC and share it with your Pocket PC, but that's hardly a real time Internet connection. When you set your ActiveSync options you can choose a couple of Internet-related options:

- ✔ **Favorites:** Downloads a recent copy of Web pages to your Pocket PC whenever you synchronize with your desktop PC. This is not a live version of the page, but rather the latest one that was downloaded from the Internet to your desktop PC. If you were browsing the Internet in the last few minutes, or if you have your desktop PC set up to automatically update your favorite Web sites frequently, the copy that's loaded onto your Pocket PC may be quite recent. But if you try to click one of the links on the page while you're viewing the page on your Pocket PC, nothing happens. With no live connection, there's no way to follow those links.

- ✔ **AvantGo:** Also downloads recent copies of Web pages to your Pocket PC whenever you synchronize with your desktop PC. In fact, the AvantGo item works very much like the Favorites item with one major difference: With AvantGo, you're offered a list of Web sites that are intended to be of interest to Pocket PC users. But here, too, you're dealing with a static view of a Web page rather than one that's truly live.

To see how to set up Web pages for offline browsing on your Pocket PC, see "Offline Pocket Browsing" in Chapter 13.

Just how important is the difference between live (online) and static (offline) viewing? There's an easy answer for that question: It depends.

Obviously, a lot of Web pages don't change very often. You probably don't expect a Web page that contains the text of an old Norwegian folktale to be much different today than it was yesterday. The same story probably remains pretty much the same for quite some time. If you download a copy of the page today, it will still be just the same as the copy you downloaded last month.

On the other hand, a Web site that brings you the latest news changes constantly. The copy you downloaded some time ago may not tell you what you really want to know. For example, if a severe storm is threatening your area, last hour's weather status probably doesn't do you much good. You may not know that a tornado was about to strike if you were depending on the weather report showing that the storm is still 50 miles away.

And, of course, there's e-mail to throw into the picture, too. If you're trying to negotiate a big deal with someone and you're using e-mail messages every few minutes to clinch the deal, it would certainly help to be able to keep things moving while you're commuting. (You don't want your competitor to step in and make a better offer to steal away the business.) But not being connected on the go may prevent you from responding until it's too late.

Understanding the Pocket PC hardware realities

If being able to connect your Pocket PC to the Internet is such a big deal, why don't Pocket PCs simply include the necessary pieces to make the connection? After all, don't the Pocket PC manufacturers realize you want to be able to connect?

Unfortunately, this is one of those problems that is a lot more complex than it seems. When it comes to connecting a Pocket PC to the Internet, a solution that's perfect for me may not work at all for you. Indeed, a solution that works perfectly for you in some cases may be totally useless in others. Here are some reasons why:

- ✔ Different models of Pocket PCs don't always share the same expansion capabilities. Some Pocket PCs have built-in expansion slots while others can be expanded only by using an add-on adapter sleeve.

- ✔ Different types of expansion slots appear on different Pocket PC models (taking into account both built-in and add-on expansion slots). You have to get expansion cards that fit the type of slot that's available on your model. Unfortunately, sometimes even models from the same manufacturer have different types of slots.

- ✔ The most common type of expansion slot on Pocket PCs is the CF — *Compact Flash* — slot. Currently you can get a *wired modem* — a modem that plugs into a standard phone line — or a *digital phone card* that plugs into a digital cell phone, to fit the CF slot.

  CF slots come in two sizes that are called *Type 1* and *Type 2*. The only really important difference between these two is the thickness of the cards that fit into the slot. All Type 1 cards fit into any Type 2 slot, but Type 2 cards are too thick to fit Type 1 slots. Currently the CF slot communication options all are Type 1 size and fit any CF slot. Still, check that you're getting a card that fits your Pocket PC before you plunk down your money.

PC Card slots are much larger than CF slots. Currently the only Pocket PCs that can use a PC Card device are the Compaq iPAQs and the Casio E-200, and then only if you add the PC Card sleeve.

✔ *Wireless modems* are currently available as a PC Card device or as a CF device. Unfortunately, the CF wireless modems still offer a peak data rate of only 19.2Kb.

✔ *Bluetooth* adapters enable your Pocket PC to connect wirelessly to your Bluetooth-enabled cell phone. The rub here is that there are very few Bluetooth-enabled cell phones around, and yours probably isn't one of them.

✔ Digital phone cards are specific to certain brands and models of cell phones. You must get the correct one for your phone.

✔ CF slot devices can be used in PC Card slots using an inexpensive adapter. There's no way to go in the opposite direction, however.

So what's the bottom line? As of right now, you need at least a CF slot (or a serial cable and external modem) to connect your Pocket PC to the Internet. You also need a modem or cell phone adapter, and you need equipment that's compatible with your Pocket PC and with whatever Internet service provider you choose to use.

Okay, so there *is* one more option for connecting your Pocket PC to the Internet. A very few cell phones include a built-in infrared modem that communicates with a Pocket PC via the IR port. This option is available only on some models of *GSM* (Global System for Mobile Telecommunications) cell phones, and it requires careful alignment between the IR ports on your Pocket PC and your GSM phone. Even if you do happen to have the correct type of GSM phone, you probably aren't going to find using the infrared modem option to be a lot of fun (unless you've got at least three arms so you can hold the Pocket PC in one, the phone in another, and the stylus in the third).

Understanding the service availability realities

Before you get your hopes set on one type of Internet connection option for your Pocket PC, you've also got to consider another very important factor. Namely, will you even be able to use the hardware in the area where you are? Here are some very important considerations:

✔ You probably take it for granted that you can plug a regular wired modem into most regular phone jacks and make a connection. While this is mostly true, you do have to be aware that some phone jacks can kill your modem. Digital phone lines — such as the ones in many businesses — produce voltages that will fry your modem. So if you want to use your wired modem, you may not be able to do so from your office or hotel room unless you can plug into an analog phone line. You'll definitely want to check this before plugging in.

✔ Wireless modems typically require *CDPD* (Cellular Digital Packet Data) service. Unfortunately, CDPD coverage is not available in all areas. You'll most likely find good coverage in large metropolitan areas, but it's not widespread enough yet that you can take it for granted.

✔ Digital phone cards require a digital phone and digital service. If your cell phone is analog, you won't be able to use a digital phone card. If your cell phone is digital, but the signal in your area is only analog, you won't be able to connect with a digital phone card.

✔ Wireless connections today are much slower than wired ones. In fact, a typical wireless connection speed is 14.4 Kbps or even slower. Most wired modems are 56K modems.

✔ Wireless modems typically require a separate service contract from your cell phone contract, which can get quite expensive — especially when you consider that a digital phone card generally allows you to connect with little or no extra charge other than your airtime. If you have a cell phone contract that leaves you with a lot of unused airtime each month, the difference could be considerable.

The reality is that you typically get a much faster connection if you go with a wired connection, but you have to find a phone jack to plug into. Wireless service eliminates that problem, but coverage can be spotty even in an area that supposedly is well within the coverage map. You aren't likely to be uploading or downloading huge files with your Pocket PC, so the connection speed may not be as important as your ability to actually connect where it's convenient.

Check with wireless service providers to see what service is offered in your area before you get too hung up on selecting one type of Internet connection for your Pocket PC. There's no sense in wasting time researching options that simply aren't available to you.

Choosing Your Hardware Options

After you've decided on the type of service you want to use to connect your Pocket PC to the Internet, you need to pick out the hardware. By picking the type of service first, you won't waste time buying the wrong equipment.

You may want to consider more than one option. For example, you may want to buy a wired modem so you have the fastest and cheapest service when a telephone line is available, and one of the wireless options for when you're on the go.

CF wired modems

Compact Flash (CF) wired modems may not be the coolest way to connect your Pocket PC to the Internet, but they offer some real advantages over any other option. Not only are CF wired modems inexpensive and fast, but you can connect through your regular Internet account that you use on your desktop PC. But even if you were to set up a separate Internet account just for your Pocket PC, unlimited access is generally quite reasonable — or even free, in some cases.

You can also use CF wired modems in a PC Card slot, such as the one in your laptop PC, using an inexpensive PC Card adapter.

Table 12-1 lists three different CF wired modems you can buy for your Pocket PC.

Table 12-1	CF Wired Modems	
Manufacturer	*Web URL*	*Product Name*
PreTec Electronics Corp.	www.pretec.com/	CompactModem
Socket	www.socketcom.com	Socket 56K Modem CF Card
Pharos	www.pharosgps.com/	CompactFlash 56K Modem Card

You can buy a CF wired modem directly or through one of the many Web sites that specialize in outfitting your Pocket PC. A couple of good sites include Handango (www.handango.com) and Mobile Planet (www.mobileplanet.com).

CF digital phone cards

If you already have a digital cell phone, a CF digital phone card may be available for your phone. These phone cards plug into your Pocket PC and your cell phone and let you connect to the Internet wherever a digital cell phone signal is available.

One excellent place to find digital phone cards is the Socket Digital Phone Card Web site at www.socketcom.com. Be sure to click the link entitled "How to choose the correct Digital Phone Card kit" to make certain you get the right equipment to match your cell phone model. Socket also offers a number of other Pocket PC add-ons you may want to check out while you're visiting the Web site.

Be sure to check the accessories that are available directly from your Pocket PC's manufacturer. Casio, for example, offers digital phone cards for their Pocket PC models at a very attractive price. Of course, if you happen to own an Audiovox Maestro Pocket PC and an Audiovox CDM-9100 cell phone, the necessary connection cable is included right in your Pocket PC's box.

PC Card wireless modems

If your Pocket PC supports it, a PC Card wireless modem is about the coolest way to connect your Pocket PC to the Internet. With a PC Card wireless modem, only a small antenna sticks out from your Pocket PC, and you can concentrate on your browsing rather than worrying about wires.

PC Card wireless modems were actually designed for use with laptop PCs, so if you buy a PC Card wireless modem for your Pocket PC, you'll also be able to use it with your laptop PC.

To use a PC Card wireless modem, you must subscribe to a *wireless IP service plan* from a carrier such as AT&T Wireless, GoAmerica, or Verizon Wireless. These plans can be very expensive, so it pays to shop around for the best deal.

Table 12-2 lists several PC Card wireless modem manufacturers where you can buy a wireless solution for your Pocket PC.

Table 12-2	PC Card Wireless Modems
Manufacturer	*Web URL*
Enfora	www.enfora.com
Novatel Wireless	www.novatelwireless.com/
Sierra Wireless	www.sierrawireless.com/

Before buying a wireless modem, you may want to check with the wireless service provider. Often the service providers offer a package deal that includes a wireless modem as well as the wireless Internet access.

If you want to break away from the low speeds offered by most wireless connections in the past, see whether anyone is offering 1XRTT service in your area. This type of service has the potential to transfer data at up to ten times the speed of the typical CDPD wireless connection.

As this is being written, Audiovox has announced that they will soon be releasing a version of the Maestro Pocket PC with a built-in cell phone and wireless modem. This unit, which will be available from Verizon Wireless and Sprint PCS, will be able to use the high-speed 1XRTT data network. According to the Audiovox executive I spoke with, the primary physical difference between this unit and the standard Audiovox Maestro Pocket PC is that the cell phone and wireless modem circuitry fills up the space normally occupied by the CF slot. This means that you will lose the CF slot (but you will still have the SD Memory slot), but the entire unit will be no larger than a normal Audiovox Maestro.

Connecting through your network

In addition to the options covered so far, you have another way to connect your Pocket PC to the Internet — through your network. See "Networking Your Pocket PC" later in this chapter for more information about this topic.

Setting Up Your Pocket PC Connection

After you've got the hardware and arranged for any service that may be required, you can set up the connection on your Pocket PC so you can actually begin browsing the Internet and sending e-mail.

Setting up the different types of hardware is pretty easy. Each has a few quirks, though, so I've broken the whole mess down into specifics for each one to try to prevent a little confusion. Keep in mind that you can also use the Connection Wizard found in the Start Here section of the Pocket PC Companion CD-ROM to set up a connection instead of setting up the connection yourself. Even so, I think that it's important for you to understand how to set up a connection manually so that you will have a better chance of understanding and correcting any problems that may arise with your connections.

You can have only one active connection at a time. If your Pocket PC is sitting in the synchronization cradle, be sure to remove it from the cradle before you use any other type of connection like a modem.

Be sure your Pocket PC battery is fully charged before you go online. Most Pocket PCs run on battery power when they aren't sitting in the synchronization cradle, and your modem uses power from your Pocket PC's battery, so you'll want a fully charged battery — especially if you plan on being connected for any length of time more than a few minutes. You may also want to consider some of the optional power sources (such as solar cells), which I discuss in Chapter 21.

Setting up a wired modem connection

Setting up your wired modem to work with your Pocket PC will probably seem fairly familiar — especially if you've ever added a modem to your desktop PC. Your Pocket PC automatically recognizes your new modem, so all you have to do is set up the connection.

Be sure you've pushed the modem fully into the expansion slot before you begin.

Here's the step-by-step procedure:

1. **Click the Start button and choose Settings. Then tap the Connections tab (see Figure 12-1).**

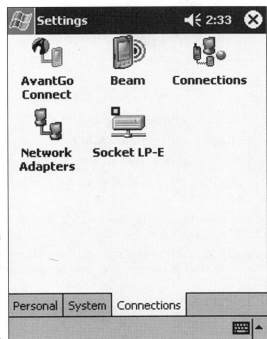

Figure 12-1:
Every new connection begins on the Connections tab.

2. **Tap Connections to open the Connections screen, shown in Figure 12-2.**

   This screen lists the connections you've set up on your Pocket PC.

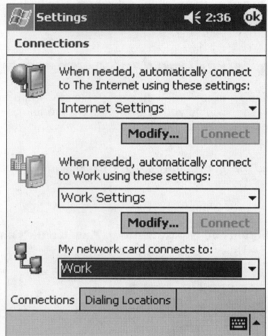

Figure 12-2: Use this screen to select a connection or edit an existing one.

3. **Tap Modify under Internet Settings to begin adding a new connection.**

   You see the Internet Settings screen (see Figure 12-3).

4. **Tap New to begin setting up a new connection.**

   You see the Make New Connection screen (see Figure 12-4).

5. **Enter a descriptive name for this connection in the first box near the top of the screen.**

   Make this name distinctive enough that you can tell your different connections apart when you're ready to connect.

6. **Choose which modem you want to use from the Select a modem list. If you have more than one type of modem, you see several options in this box.**

Figure 12-3:
Choose the connection for accessing the Internet.

Figure 12-4:
You're finally ready to begin configuring your new connection.

7. Select 57600 from the Baud Rate drop-down list.

All wired Pocket PC modems use this setting.

8. Click the Advanced button and then tap the TCP/IP tab, as shown in Figure 12-5.

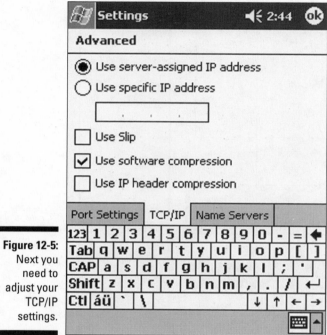

Figure 12-5: Next you need to adjust your TCP/IP settings.

9. Remove the check from the Use IP header compression checkbox.

If this box is checked, you may have a bit more difficulty connecting.

10. If your ISP has specified DNS addresses for you to use, click the Name Servers tab. Select the Use specific server address option button and then enter the addresses in the first two address boxes.

Figure 12-6 shows this tab after the Earthlink DNS addresses have been entered.

11. Click OK and then click Next to continue.

12. Enter the correct dial-up number for your ISP.

If you're setting up a connection to use while you're traveling, be sure to enter the correct area code (and country code if you'll be in another country).

Figure 12-6:
Use these
settings if
your ISP
specifies
specific
DNS
addresses.

13. **Click Next and then click Finish.**

    Your connection setup is nearly complete, but you can't do the final setup until you use the connection the first time.

14. **Tap-and-hold the new connection and select Always Dial from the pop-up menu.**

    You can skip this step if you have only one connection.

15. **Tap OK twice to close the connections settings.**

16. **Tap the Start menu, choose Internet Explorer, and then tap a link to a Web page to open the Network Log On screen.**

17. **Add your user name and password to the top two boxes.**

    You probably don't need to fill in the Domain box unless your ISP has specifically told you to do so.

18. **Decide whether you want to have your Pocket PC save your password so you don't have to enter it each time you want to connect.**

    Leaving the Save password checkbox empty provides a bit more security, but means that you'll always have to enter your password to connect.

19. **Tap the OK button and wait while your Pocket PC attempts to connect to the Internet.**

Your Pocket PC should be able to connect on the first try. If it can't connect, here are some things to check:

✔ Make certain you remembered to connect the phone cord both to your modem and to the phone jack. If you didn't, maybe you'll at least be lucky enough that no one saw you.

✔ You did remember to take your Pocket PC out of the synchronization cradle, didn't you? Your Pocket PC can have only one active connection at a time, and a connection to your desktop PC will prevent your Pocket PC from opening the modem connection.

✔ Check your user name and password. Some ISPs require you to add a prefix before your user name. Earthlink, for example, usually requires you to add ELN/ before your user name.

✔ Verify that you've entered the correct dial-up phone number. It's amazing how easy it can be to enter the ISP's customer service number instead of the dial-up number. By the way, you can ignore the "T" that appears in front of the phone number on the Connect To screen — it simply indicates that the modem will dial the number using tone dialing.

✔ Finally, if all else fails, tap the Dialing Options button and then the Dialing Patterns button. Make certain that the For local calls, dial: box contains at least the letter *g* (and anything else necessary to reach an outside line). If the *g* is missing, your Pocket PC insists that it is dialing, but the modem won't really be sending any tones over the phone line.

Breaking the connection

When you're finished using the connection, disconnect to free up the phone line. (Your Pocket PC eventually disconnects after a period of inactivity, but this can take half an hour or more.)

To break the connection, tap the connection button in the title bar, as Figure 12-7 shows, and then tap End.

Even though modems use very little power when they aren't in use, you can extend your battery life a bit by removing the modem when you aren't using it.

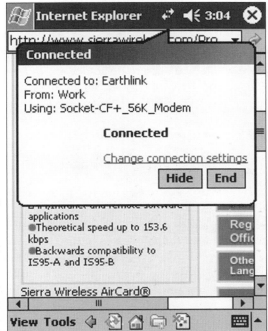

Figure 12-7:
Always
disconnect
when you're
done using
your
Internet
connection.

Setting up a digital phone card connection

Digital phone cards enable your Pocket PC to connect to the Internet through
your digital cell phone without using a modem. This connection works only
when you have a clear digital signal, but because it goes through your cell
phone, there is typically little or no extra charge beyond your cell phone's
airtime to use a digital phone card connection.

In spite of the fact that a digital phone card connection doesn't use a modem,
setting up a digital phone card connection is an awful lot like setting up a
wired modem connection. But there are a few important differences that I'll
point out as you step through the following procedure:

1. **Click the Start button and choose Settings. Then tap the Connections
   tab.**

2. **Tap Connections to open the Connections screen.**

3. **Tap New Connection under Internet setting to begin adding a new
   connection.**

   You see the Make New Connection screen.

4. **Enter a name for this connection.**

5. **Tap the Modem tab.**

6. **Tap New.**

7. **Choose your digital phone card from the Select a modem list.**

   Here's the first place where you need to do something different than if you were setting up a wired modem connection. In this case I'm using a Socket digital phone card, which is listed as Socket-CF+_DPC_Generic_Card_Rev_.

8. **Leave the 19200 selection alone in the Baud Rate list box.**

   Digital phone cards typically connect at 14400, so you don't need to change this setting.

9. **If your ISP has specified DNS addresses for you to use, click the Advanced button and then click the Name Servers tab.**

10. **In the Name Servers screen, select the Use specific server address option button and then enter the addresses in the first two address boxes.**

    You can skip this step if your ISP doesn't require you to use specific DNS addresses or if you're using your cell phone service provider's Internet access service.

11. **Click OK, and then click Next to continue.**

12. **Enter the correct dial-up number.**

    If you're using your cell service provider's Internet service, you may enter something like **#777** — the access number for the Verizon Wireless Internet access service.

13. **Click Next to display the screen shown in Figure 12-8.**

14. **Remove the check from the Wait for dial tone before dialing checkbox.**

    Cell phones don't use a dial tone, so you need to tell your Pocket PC to just go ahead and dial without waiting for the dial tone.

15. **Click Finish to close the connection setup screen.**

16. **Tap OK to return to the Connections screen.**

17. **Make certain your new connection is selected under Internet settings and tap OK.**

18. **Open Internet Explorer and tap a link for a Web page.**

    This will display the Network Log On screen.

19. **Add your user name and password to the top two boxes.**

    If you're using your cell service provider's Internet access, you'll probably use a generic user name and password. For example, Verizon Wireless has all users enter **qnc** for both the user name and the password (make certain you enter this in lowercase).

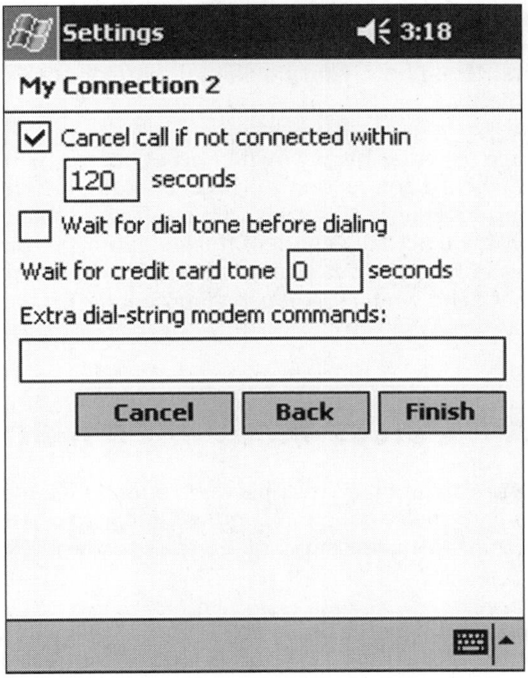

```
┌─────────────────────────────────────┐
│ ▓ Settings              ◀€ 3:18      │
│ ─────────────────────────────────── │
│ My Connection 2                      │
│ ─────────────────────────────────── │
│ ☑ Cancel call if not connected within│
│   ┌──────┐                           │
│   │ 120  │  seconds                  │
│   └──────┘                           │
│ ☐ Wait for dial tone before dialing  │
│                                      │
│ Wait for credit card tone ┌──┐       │
│                           │0 │ seconds│
│                           └──┘       │
│ Extra dial-string modem commands:    │
│ ┌─────────────────────────────────┐  │
│ │                                 │  │
│ └─────────────────────────────────┘  │
│   ┌────────┐ ┌────────┐ ┌────────┐   │
│   │ Cancel │ │  Back  │ │ Finish │   │
│   └────────┘ └────────┘ └────────┘   │
│                                      │
│                                      │
│                                      │
│                                      │
│                            ▓▓▓ │▲    │
└─────────────────────────────────────┘
```

Figure 12-8:
Cell phones
don't
provide a
dial tone.

20. Tap the OK button and wait while your Pocket PC attempts to connect to the Internet.

After you tap the connect button, your Pocket PC should connect in a few seconds. If you have problems, here are some things to check:

✔ Make certain your cell phone has a digital signal. If the D disappears from the display once you try to connect, you may be in a marginal signal area. Sometimes it helps to fully extend the cell phone antenna and to hold the cell phone up in the air. Of course, this *does* make it a bit harder to hold your Pocket PC and use the stylus, but who said things were going to be super easy?

✔ If you're using your cell service provider's Internet service, you may want to verify that they haven't changed the access number or the user name and password.

✔ You may need to move to a different location. Cellular phone service does have a well-deserved reputation for dropouts and other service interruptions. Sometimes you just need to find a site where you have a more consistent digital signal.

When you're finished using your digital phone card connection, remember to disconnect so you don't use up airtime. Also, be sure you unplug the digital phone card connections from both your Pocket PC and your cell phone to save battery life.

Even if your cell service provider has its own Internet access, you may need to set up a digital phone card connection that accesses the Internet through your ISP's dial-up number. Some mail servers are configured to allow only you to use the mail server if you actually connect through your ISP. In some cases this restriction applies only to the outbound mail server, so you may find that you can receive but not send e-mail if you use your cellular provider's Internet access.

Setting up a wireless modem connection

Wireless modems are pretty much a cross between a modem and a cell phone. As such, setting up the connection is quite similar to setting up a wired modem connection with a few small differences thrown in just to keep things interesting.

One of the most important differences to keep in mind with a wireless modem connection is simply that the wireless modem is always set up as a separate account with the CDPD service provider. The wireless modem doesn't use your cell phone's account or airtime.

In most cases the CDPD service provider will program the wireless modem before providing it to you. This is a process that is very similar to setting up a new cell phone. Essentially, the wireless modem must be uniquely identified by its *Equipment ID (EID)* number. If the service provider didn't program the wireless modem for you, it will be necessary to provide this information during the setup process. Your wireless service provider will tell you how to determine the EID.

As far as setting up your Pocket PC is concerned, once the wireless modem is activated by the service provider, you can follow the same sequence of steps shown earlier for setting up a digital phone card connection. If there are any special requirements for using your carrier's service, you can be assured that they will assist you in making sure you have configured everything properly.

Networking Your Pocket PC

In addition to connecting to the Internet, you may also have an interest in connecting to your local network. In fact, you may want to connect your

Pocket PC to your network for many of the same reasons that you may want to network your desktop PCs:

- Sharing information using almost any type of networking is typically far quicker than the USB connection most Pocket PCs use for ActiveSync connections. This is especially true if you want to store a lot of stuff (like several CDs' worth of music) on your Pocket PC's storage card.

- You can easily access shared network folders so that you can copy, delete, or rename files from your Pocket PC. This can be really cool since you don't even need to borrow someone's desktop system to move stuff around on the network.

- Very few printers have infrared ports, so even if you add a third-party printing application to your Pocket PC, printing from your Pocket PC isn't going to be easy. But since printer sharing is pretty common on networks, printing from your networked Pocket PC is simple.

- If your network offers Internet access, there's no reason that you cannot also share that connection with your Pocket PC. This is especially true if your network has a high-speed Internet connection because there are few high-speed Internet connection options available for the Pocket PC.

Understanding your network connection options

In order to do all this neat stuff on your network, your Pocket PC must first be connected to the network. There are a number of different ways to make this connection, so let's take a look at some of the options to see which is the best choice for you.

Getting wired

Let's face it — most network connections use wires. It's just a fact of life that the vast majority of networks have cables running all over the place. I suspect that many of those cables aren't really connected to anything, but with the typical rat's nest of wires, who can tell?

As you might suspect, connecting your Pocket PC to this type of network is pretty easy. All you need is a network adapter that fits your Pocket PC and the right cable. One of the best wired network adapters you can find is the Socket 10/100 Ethernet CF Card (www.socketcom.com). As the name implies, this is a CF card that provides high-speed wired access directly to your network. If you have ever transferred a couple of CDs' worth of music files to your Pocket PC using the USB cradle, you'll really appreciate the difference this card can make. Imagine how nice it would be to cut a ten-minute file download to around ten seconds!

Most networks have a box known as a hub, switch, or router, which handles network traffic. If your network has one of these, you will need a standard Cat-5 network cable to connect the Socket 10/100 Ethernet CF Card to your network.

Suppose, though, that you just have your desktop PC and your Pocket PC. In that case, you can connect your Pocket PC directly to your desktop system without going through another box. But there is a catch — you need a different cable if you want to connect two PCs directly. The cable you need in this case is a *crossover* cable. This isn't something fancy — it's just a network cable with a couple of wires crossed inside.

If you really want to save money on your network cables when connecting your Pocket PC directly to another PC, Socket will give you a free Crossover Connector Kit when you register your Socket 10/100 Ethernet CF Card. This kit even has everything you need to connect a Pocket PC and a laptop with no extra cables.

Crossover cables and regular network cables look exactly the same, but they sure don't work the same. To avoid confusion, always add your own label that says "crossover cable" to any crossover cable you buy. Otherwise you're sure to find yourself trying to use it as a standard cable some day and wondering why things don't work.

Look Ma, no cables!

If you somehow can't quite see yourself putting up with some cable dangling off your Pocket PC every time you want to access your network or the Internet, you'll love the products I'm going to cover now. *Wireless networking* is exactly that — network connections that don't use wires. Rather, wireless networking functions by way of small radios that slip into your Pocket PCs so that you can wander around without dragging some long cable.

There are actually several different wireless networking products on the market, but few of them are actually useful for Pocket PC users. The reason for this is simple — your Pocket PC probably doesn't have the larger PC Card slot needed for many wireless networking products. You need something that is specifically designed for the Pocket PC and its CF expansion slot.

Wireless networking products come in several different flavors. Right now the one flavor that seems to have the broadest support as well as the best compatibility between different brands is the standard known as 802.11b. Regardless of the standard you choose, it's very important that all of the components of your wireless network adhere to the same standard. If you ignore this or think that 802.11a and 802.11b sound pretty close (for example), you'll end up with a bunch of expensive pieces that simply won't talk to each other.

Configuring your wireless connection

Even if you have set up your own wired network in the past, you probably aren't familiar with setting up a wireless network. The whole process is fairly simple and you can be up and running in just a few minutes. Let's take a look at a typical wireless network configuration.

In this case I am using Proxim Harmony 802.11b CF cards in my Pocket PCs, and a Proxim Harmony 802.11b Access Point to allow them to access the network. You can learn more about these items at the Proxim Web site (www.proxim.com).

Here's how to quickly set up your wireless network:

1. **Connect the Access Point to the hub, switch, or router on your network.**

   The Access Point connects with an ordinary Cat-5 cable. You'll want to place the Access Point as high as possible to maximize the range.

2. **Place your Pocket PC in the sync cradle and make certain that ActiveSync connects to your Pocket PC.**

3. **Insert the CD-ROM that came with the wireless network cards and install the drivers.**

   Typically the driver setup will run automatically once the CD-ROM is inserted into the drive. Make certain that the drivers are fully installed on your Pocket PC before continuing.

4. **Remove your Pocket PC from the sync cradle and turn it off.**

5. **Insert the wireless network card into your Pocket PC.**

   Your Pocket PC will automatically turn itself back on once the card is inserted.

6. **Tap the Start menu and choose Settings.**

7. **Tap the Connections tab and then the Network Adapters icon.**

8. **Tap the wireless network card, as shown in Figure 12-9, and then tap Properties.**

9. **Enter the correct settings for your network. Figure 12-10 shows a typical setup for networks that use Internet Connection Sharing.**

In some cases you may be able to use the *Use server-assigned IP address* option, but you will probably find that setting the network card to specific IP addresses works better on small networks like you might have at home or in a small business.

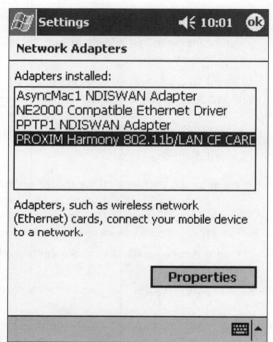

Figure 12-9: Choose your wireless network card.

10. **Tap the Name Servers tab and set the name server addresses, as shown in Figure 12-11.**

    If your ISP has specified specific addresses for the DNS and alternate DNS settings, enter those addresses — otherwise leave these two fields blank. If you know the IP address for the PC on your network that has your ActiveSync connection, enter that address in the WINS field as shown in the figure. This will enable your Pocket PC to connect to that PC a little more quickly.

11. **Tap OK as many times as necessary to close all of the screens. Then press the Reset button to restart your Pocket PC and apply the changes.**

12. **Tap the Start button and choose Settings.**

13. **Tap the System tab and then tap the Wireless LAN Setting icon.**

    If you use a different brand of wireless network card, you may find that this icon has a different name and some different options. If so, you'll need to follow the directions that came with the wireless network card.

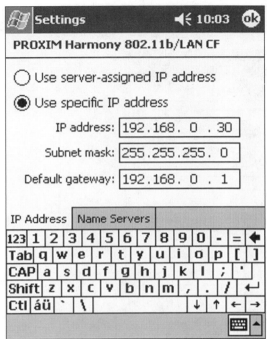

Figure 12-10:
Select the
correct IP
addresses.

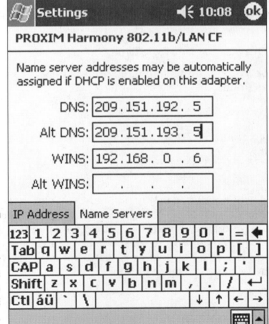

Figure 12-11:
Set the
name server
addresses
according to
your ISP's
directions.

14. **Tap the Configure tab, as shown in Figure 12-12.**

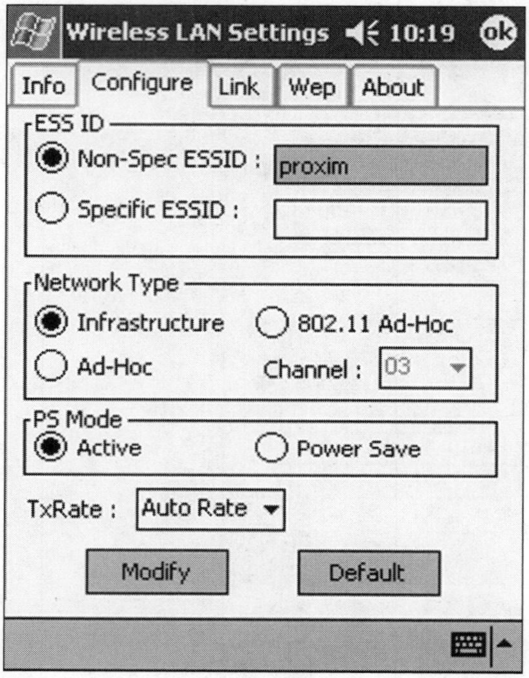

Figure 12-12:
You need to specify the type of network.

15. **Select Infrastructure as the Network Type.**

   The other Network Type options apply to wireless networks that do not include an Access Point.

16. **Tap OK.**

Your wireless network should now be functional. Next we'll look at how you can use the connection.

Using your wireless connection

Now that your wireless connection is set up, I'm sure you can't wait to try it out. The first thing you will want to do is make an ActiveSync connection between your Pocket PC and your desktop PC. To do so, open the Start menu and choose ActiveSync (you may have to open the Programs folder and open ActiveSync from there if it doesn't appear on the Start menu). Tap Sync to make the connection, as shown in Figure 12-13.

If you cannot connect to your desktop through your wireless connection, open the Connections icon on the Connections tab (tap Start and then Settings first). Make certain that you have set the network card setting to connect to your network. In Figure 12-14, I have specified that I will use the Work setting.

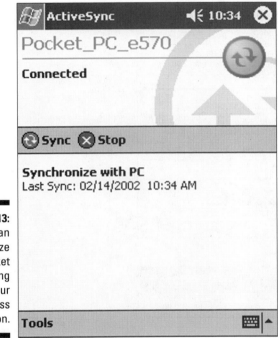

Figure 12-13: You can synchronize your Pocket PC using your wireless connection.

If you find that your Pocket PC can connect to your network but cannot use the wireless connection to access the Internet, make certain that Internet Connection Sharing is enabled on your network. Also, if you are using a Proxim Harmony 802.11b Access Point, don't select the This network uses a proxy server to connect to the Internet option on the Proxy Servers tab of the Modify Settings screen for the connection.

If you want to access files on your network using your wireless network connection, you can do so using File Explorer on your Pocket PC. To do so, open File Explorer and then tap the Open Path icon on the menu bar (this is the icon at the right end of the File Explorer icons) to display the Open dialog box, shown in Figure 12-15.

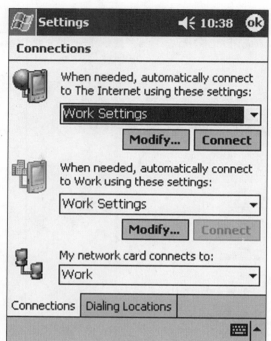

Figure 12-14:
Use the
Connections
settings to
choose your
connection
options.

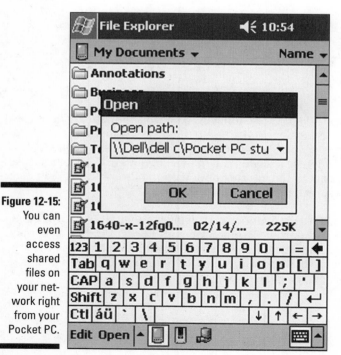

Figure 12-15:
You can
even
access
shared
files on
your net-
work right
from your
Pocket PC.

In order to access network files from your Pocket PC, you will need to make certain that several conditions are satisfied:

✔ There must be some shared folders on the network.

✔ You'll need to know the correct network address for the folder. I usually find that it is easiest to look at the address bar on my desktop system to determine the proper address. The address starts out with two back slashes, then the computer name, then the share name, and then the path. Like I said, it's easier to look at the address bar on your desktop to see a proper example.

✔ You may need to enter a user name and password, but this depends on the way your network is configured.

Another cool way to use your wireless network connection is for printing on shared network printers.

Using Bluetooth cards

Even though Bluetooth sounds like what you get from eating blueberry pie, Bluetooth is actually another method of creating a wireless connection. Bluetooth connections can be used for many of the same tasks as the 802.11b options mentioned earlier, but the two have a number of important differences:

✔ Bluetooth and 802.11b networks are incompatible. You cannot interchange components between these two.

✔ Bluetooth connections have a much shorter range — typically about 10 meters compared to about 400 meters for 802.11b.

✔ Bluetooth cards typically use far less power than 802.11b cards. This can prolong the battery life of your Pocket PC (assuming the shorter range is acceptable for your needs).

✔ Some cell phone models — notably from Ericsson and Nokia — have Bluetooth capabilities built in, making it possible for your Pocket PC to access the Internet through your cell phone wirelessly.

Unfortunately, I was unable to obtain either a Bluetooth-equipped cell phone or a Bluetooth Access Point for testing during the writing of this edition. I did try our Bluetooth cards from Socket (www.socketcom.com) and TDK (www.tdksys.com). These allowed me to connect my Pocket PC and my laptop PC via a Bluetooth connection. And my teeth are still white!

Working remotely

If you have a Pocket PC and a wireless connection, you have options that can get you out of the office. That in itself might be worth the cost of a Pocket PC!

No one would claim that a Pocket PC can do everything that a desktop PC can do. But with the options I'll show you next, your Pocket PC can do virtually anything that your desktop PC can do.

Controlling your desktop with NetOP Remote Control

Figure 12-16 shows something that probably looks a little familiar, yet not something you're used to seeing on your Pocket PC — an ordinary Windows desktop. In this case I'm looking at the icons on the desktop of one of the PCs on my network using NetOP Remote Control (www.netop.com).

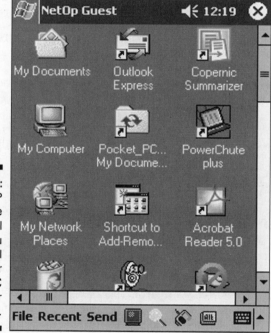

Figure 12-16:
NetOP
Remote
Control
enables you
to control
your
desktop PC
from your
Pocket PC.

NetOP Remote Control can do far more than simply show your desktop's screen on your Pocket PC. Indeed, when NetOP Remote Control is running you can use anything on your desktop system using your Pocket PC. You can run the programs on your desktop, change settings, and even perform file-management functions.

It helps to use your imagination a bit when you use a program like NetOP Remote Control. Sure, there are the obvious business applications for this type of program, but there are a lot of ways to have some fun, too. For example, you can use your 802.11b wireless network connection to access your desktop system while you're sitting out in your backyard with your Pocket PC. Then you can play music through your home stereo system connected to the line out from your desktop system's audio card. Your Pocket PC can control Windows Media Player and even adjust the volume.

If you use NetOP Remote Control (or any other remote control software) to allow remote access to your desktop PC, make certain that you activate the security features included in the program. Otherwise someone else might be able to gain control of your desktop system and do all sorts of mischief.

Using VPN with your Pocket PC

If you open up your network so that it is easy to access, it's convenient for you and the other people who need access to get in and work on the network. Unfortunately, it's just as easy for the people you don't want to gain network access to get in and play around.

Network security is a serious issue (and one that is far too large to discuss effectively here). But ease of use is also a big issue. If accessing your network requires you to stand on your head while reciting the fifth paragraph of *War and Peace* backwards, you probably are going to find all sorts of reasons why you don't bother to use the network.

How can you balance the need for effective security with the desire for easy remote network access? One very effective method is to use something called *Virtual Private Networking* (VPN). This is a method of using a public network (such as the Internet) as a means of connecting to your network without the security problems. Essentially, VPN handles all of the security issues so that only those people you authorize can access your network. In effect, VPN makes your network totally private while at the same time it allows controlled access through public networks.

To learn more about VPN products you can use on your Pocket PC, I suggest you visit the Columbitech Web site (www.columbitech.com). This is also a good source for more information about general wireless security issues.

Chapter 13

Surfing with Pocket Internet Explorer

*I*f you see a dog that's singing a Mozart opera, you're probably amazed enough that the dog can sing that you don't notice if he's a little off-key. In some ways, the singing dog is a lot like Internet browsing on a Pocket PC. It's so amazing that you actually can surf the Web on a Pocket PC that you're willing to put up with a few "off-key" compromises.

Even though surfing the Web on your Pocket PC will never be quite the same as browsing with a huge desktop monitor, there's a lot to be said for both the convenience and sheer coolness of being able to whip out your Pocket PC and find something on the Web. While everyone else has to wait until they can fire up their desktop PC, you're able to go online whenever you want. That alone is worth the price of admission, isn't it?

Introducing Pocket Internet Explorer

Pocket Internet Explorer is a Web browser designed for the small screen of the Pocket PC. A *Web browser* is just a program that displays Web pages more or less about the way the Web page designer intended. On your desktop PC you probably use Internet Explorer, Netscape Communicator, or Opera as your Web browser, but none of those is able to run on a Pocket PC. Pocket Internet Explorer, of course, is similar to Internet Explorer, but there are a lot of differences.

Understanding the Pocket Internet Explorer screen

Figure 13-1 shows the Pocket Internet Explorer screen similar to the one that you'll probably see the first time you open Pocket Internet Explorer (your Pocket PC will have a link to its manufacturer's Web site as the second item on the list). You don't need to be connected to the Internet to see this screen because it's stored right on your Pocket PC. In fact, you don't need to connect until you actually want to visit a Web site.

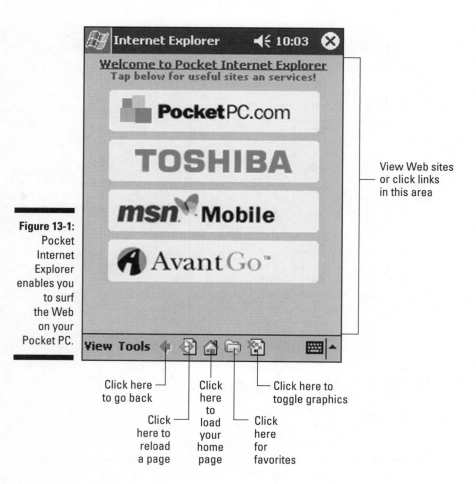

Figure 13-1:
Pocket
Internet
Explorer
enables you
to surf
the Web
on your
Pocket PC.

View Web sites
or click links
in this area

Click here
to go back

Click
here to
reload
a page

Click
here
to
load
your
home
page

Click
here
for
favorites

Click here to
toggle graphics

Right off the bat you'll probably notice that the Pocket Internet Explorer screen looks quite a bit different from any other Web browser you've used in the past. For one thing, there are far fewer buttons and toolbars cluttering up the screen. Since Pocket Internet Explorer has far less room to waste, Web pages tend to have a more compact appearance with far less empty space between the various bits and pieces. (Later in this chapter, in the section "Making the Best Use of Your Screen Real Estate," I show you how to maximize your viewing area.) Even with a more compact view of Web pages, you still need to be able to move around. Fortunately you don't need to learn anything new to navigate Web pages using Pocket Internet Explorer. You can still click a link to load a different Web page ("click" by tapping the link with your stylus). You can still use the address bar to enter a URL (although you have to use View➪Address Bar to display the address bar first because it's normally hidden to give you more browsing room). And you can still scroll to other areas on a Web page using the scroll bars that appear when the Web page is too large for a single screen.

Setting your general options

Pocket Internet Explorer has a number of options that you can set to control how the program works. You may want to have a quick look at these options before you actually begin browsing with Pocket Internet Explorer to be sure that you understand exactly what will work the best for you.

To begin setting the Pocket Internet Explorer options, select Tools➪Options on the Pocket Internet Explorer menu bar to display the General tab (see Figure 13-2).

Here's a brief explanation of the options on the General tab:

 ✔ The **Home page** buttons enable you to choose a specific Web page to view whenever you open Pocket Internet Explorer. Choose Use Current if you're viewing a Web page that you want as your home page. Choose Use Default to return to the Web page shown in Figure 13-1.

 Choosing a Web page that's always available is a good idea. Because your Pocket PC isn't likely to be connected to the Internet all the time, this means choosing a Web page that's stored on your Pocket PC. Because the default Web page is stored on your Pocket PC, you don't need to connect in order to view the page. If you choose an online Web page, Pocket Internet Explorer won't be able to load the page unless your Pocket PC is connected.

 ✔ The **History** options enable you to control how long Pocket Internet Explorer maintains a record of your browsing. The longer links remain in the History list, the more likely you'll be able to find the link when you want to return to that neat page you remember visiting but can't quite remember the URL. Of course, as with most everything else on your Pocket PC, use some moderation in choosing how long to keep things in the history because everything you store does eat up some memory. (For more on the History list, see the section "Browsing your History list" later in this chapter.)

✔ In the **Temporary Internet Files** section, use the Delete Files button to remove any Web pages and their associated files from temporary storage. These files are stored so that you can more quickly reload a Web page that you've visited recently.

✔ If you're really running low on memory, click the **Clear History** button and the **Delete Files** button. You typically won't free up very much room this way, but it may be enough to temporarily solve the problem.

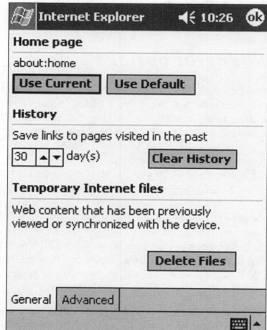

Figure 13-2: This page shows a few of the Pocket Internet Explorer options you can control.

Playing with the advanced options

Next click the Advanced tab, shown in Figure 13-3. Here you find some very useful options.

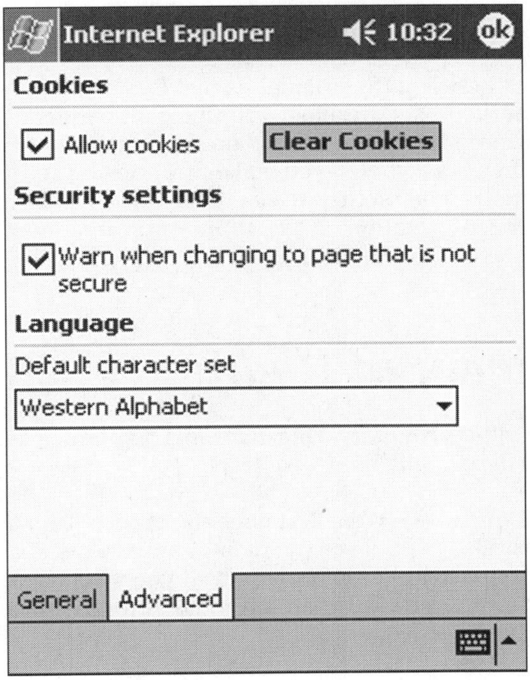

Figure 13-3:
Use the
advanced
options to
control
some very
important
settings.

Here's a quick look at the advanced settings:

✔ The **Cookies** settings let you control those files that Web sites can place onto your Pocket PC when you visit a site. Some people hate the idea that Web sites can use cookies to track some of your Web browsing activity, while others like the convenience that cookies provide — such as the ability to shop online. Choose the cookie settings that make you feel comfortable, and don't forget the milk.

✔ In the **Security settings** section, the Warn when changing to a page that is not secure option is very important on a Pocket PC. On your desktop PC, your browser provides visible feedback to tell you whether the Web page you're visiting is secure. This makes it far safer for you to enter sensitive information because you can easily tell if someone is asking you to enter your credit card number on a page that is not encrypted. But on a Pocket PC it's a lot harder to tell whether the page you're visiting is secure — especially if you've hidden the address bar to get more browsing area. That's why it's a good idea to receive a warning when you go from a secure page to one that isn't secure.

✔ The **Language** selection can be important if you visit a lot of foreign language Web pages. You may need to play around with this setting to see which selection does the best job of displaying the Web pages you visit.

Choosing your connection options

One of the big changes between the original Pocket PCs and the Pocket PC 2002 systems is the method used to select your Internet connection options. On the Pocket PC 2002 systems this option is no longer a part of Pocket Internet Explorer. Rather, it's a choice you make by choosing settings after you open the Connections icon on the Connections tab of the Settings screen. See Chapter 12 for more information on this topic if you somehow skipped that chapter in your haste to get surfing.

Surfing the Connected Web

Okay, let's stop this fooling around and start surfing! It's time to see what Web browsing on a Pocket PC is really like.

To begin having some fun on the Web, first click the Start button and choose Internet Explorer. Most likely you'll see the default home page shown back in Figure 13-1, but you may also see a different page if you've chosen a new home page. Figure 13-4 shows how Pocket Internet Explorer appears after an online Web page has been loaded.

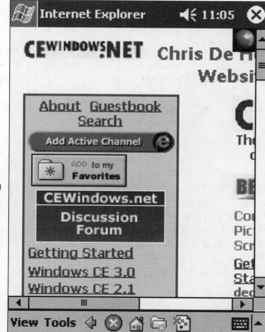

Figure 13-4:
The CEWindows .net Web site is a good source of online Pocket PC information.

Entering URLs

A unique address, called a URL, identifies all Web sites. If you want to view the Dummies Books Web site, for example, you can enter the address www.dummies.com and your Web browser finds and loads the page you've asked for.

Like all Web browsers, Pocket Internet Explorer has an address bar that you use to enter URLs. But unlike most other browsers, Pocket Internet Explorer usually has the address bar hidden so you have a bit more space for viewing Web page content. When you want to enter an address, you first have to display the address bar so you have a place for the address.

To display the Pocket Internet Explorer address bar, select View➪Address Bar from the menu bar. This option is a toggle, so you use the same command a second time to make the address bar go away again. Figure 13-5 shows Pocket Internet Explorer after I've displayed the address bar, entered a URL, and clicked the Go button to load a new page.

Figure 13-5:
Use the address bar to enter Web page URLs.

The down arrow at the right side of the address bar displays a list of URLs you've visited. To return to one of those Web sites, click the down arrow, tap the URL of the site you want to visit, and click Go.

Following links

Almost all Web pages include links that you can follow to visit other Web pages. It is, in fact, those links that inspired the name "Web" in the first place. The Web really is an endless web of links that lead here and there. Links are also one of the most fun things about the Web. You never know where you'll eventually end up if you start following interesting-looking links.

Links can have several different appearances. Figure 13-6 shows a Web page with a couple of different types of links.

In Figure 13-6, you can tell which words are links because they are underlined and appear in a different color from regular text. The underlined text clearly leads you to the Web page for Developer One Agenda Today for the Pocket PC. Tapping on the underlined text moves you to the new page.

Figure 13-6:
Tap links to journey to additional Web pages.

If you accidentally tap a link and find yourself on the wrong page, click the Back button (the left-pointing arrow on the menu bar) to return to the previous page.

Going home

After you've followed a bunch of interesting-looking links, you may find yourself yearning to return to the sanity of home — your home page, that is. When you get this urge, just click the little house symbol on the Pocket Internet Explorer menu bar. Pocket Internet Explorer reloads your home page. Too bad it can't also bring you your slippers at the same time.

Reloading pages

Although no one knows for certain, there's a rumor that a certain Mr. Murphy watches when you download Web pages and that he knows the absolute worst time to interrupt the proceedings. Why else would Web pages refuse to load?

Fortunately, Web browsers have a tool designed to fight Mr. Murphy's plan — the Reload button. Any time you need to reload a Web page, click the Reload button (the button with the two curved arrows in the middle of the Pocket Internet Explorer menu bar), and Pocket Internet Explorer sends a new request for the page to the Web server.

The Reload button helps in several different instances:

- If you haven't turned off loading of pictures (see "Getting rid of graphics" later in the chapter) but all you see are placeholders where images belong on a Web page, hit Reload to ask for the page and images to be sent again.

- If you're viewing a Web page with frequently updated contents — such as news headlines or stock prices — tap Reload to see an updated view.

- If you're trying to access a Web site that won't respond because too many people are trying to view it at the same time, clicking the Reload button may be all it takes to hit that small window of opportunity when the server will actually respond and send you the page.

Viewing the page properties

Unless you're really nosey, there's probably not a lot of reason to view the properties of the Web pages you're visiting. Still, you can find out a few useful pieces of information by clicking View⇨Properties. For example, you can see the address (or URL) of the page you're viewing and see whether it is secure. Secure Web pages have a URL that begins with https:// while non-secure pages begin with http://. You can verify which you are viewing by noting what the Security line just above the URL says.

Make certain you're on a secure Web page before you enter confidential information like credit card numbers.

Sending a link

As you surf the Web, you're bound to come across Web pages that you'd like to share with someone else. Pocket Internet Explorer provides a very easy way to do this by allowing you to send the URL in an e-mail message. The recipient can then click the link and view the page.

To send a Web page link to someone, first make certain that you're viewing the page you want to send. Then select Tools⇨Send Link via E-mail. Address your message and include an explanation so the recipient knows why you're sending the link. Chapter 14 covers e-mail on your Pocket PC in more detail.

Pocket Internet Explorer doesn't include an option for sending a complete Web page to someone — you can send only the link to that page. And because you can send only a link, the page may have changed or even disappeared before your e-mail message recipient tries to view the page. If it's important that he sees the same information you're seeing, you may want to open Internet Explorer on your desktop PC and send the page — not just the link — from there. Or you may want to copy the information as discussed in the next section.

Copying information you want to keep

One thing that's certain about the Web is that you can't trust it to remain the same. Pages are updated or can disappear with no warning, and this can mean that important information may not be there when you return. If you want to preserve what you've seen on a Web page, the most reliable way to do so is to save the page on your own computer.

Pocket Internet Explorer doesn't offer you a way to save a Web page on your Pocket PC, so if you want to save the information from a site, you need to use a slightly different approach. What you have to do is to copy the information you want and then paste it into your own document.

To copy information from a Web page in Pocket Internet Explorer, follow these steps:

1. **Open the Web page that contains the information you want to borrow.**

2. **Drag your stylus across the information you want so that you select the information. Alternatively, use Tools⇨Select All Text to select all the text on the page.**

    Unfortunately, while you can save the text from a Web page, you cannot save any images from the page.

3. **Select Tools⇨Copy to copy the selected data to the Clipboard.**

4. **Open the document where you want to add the information and select the Paste command.**

    You find the Paste command on an Edit menu, a Tools menu, or on some other menu depending on the application you're using.

You'll probably find that you need to do a bunch of cleanup to remove the junk that got pasted into your document along with the stuff you wanted.

Browsing your History list

Pocket Internet Explorer keeps a record of the URLs of the Web pages you visit so that it's easier for you to return to those same pages. Consider how often you've probably thought that you'd like to return to a site you visited earlier, but you couldn't quite remember the correct URL. Maybe you visited the page a few days ago and just now realize that it contained some information you really need.

To use the History list, select View⇨History. As Figure 13-7 shows, this displays a list you can scroll through. You return to a page by tapping the correct link.

You can view the URLs by tapping the down arrow to the right of Page Title and selecting Address, which may be helpful if you want to return to the main page on a Web site rather than to a page you've already visited. This may also help you locate the information you need if the page you visited earlier has disappeared.

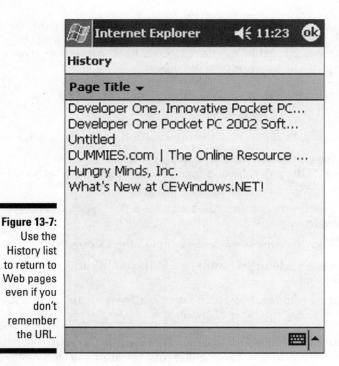

Figure 13-7:
Use the
History list
to return to
Web pages
even if you
don't
remember
the URL.

Playing favorites

Even though you can browse through your History list to find links to Web
pages you've visited, the History list is not the most ideal way to store links
to Web pages you'll want to visit in the future. Not only do links disappear
from the History list after a certain period of time, but all the History list links
can be instantly cleared away with a tap of your stylus.

Pocket Internet Explorer provides a better way to store the Web page links
you really don't want to lose. You save them as *favorites* and they'll remain
available until you decide to get rid of them.

Viewing your favorite Web sites

To return to your favorite Web sites, you use the Favorites list instead of the
History list. To display this list, tap the Favorites button — the button that
looks like a folder with an asterisk — at the right side of the Pocket Internet
Explorer menu bar.

You can also use the Favorites list for offline viewing of Web pages. See
"Getting favorites from your desktop PC" later in this chapter for more
information.

Saving favorite Web sites

So how do your favorite Web sites magically get onto your Favorites list? Simple: You put them there using the Add/Delete tab of Favorites (see Figure 13-8).

Figure 13-8: Add your own favorite Web sites to the list.

You've probably noticed that this screen asks which items you want to delete. To add a Web site to the list, you've got to do just a bit more:

1. **Open the Web page you want to add to your list of favorites.**

2. **Tap the Favorites button.**

3. **Tap the Add/Delete tab.**

4. **Click the Add button.**

5. **If you want, modify the page name to something more descriptive.**

6. **Click Add.**

If you're having a hard time figuring out which Web sites to add to your list of Favorites, here are some ideas:

✔ Include the login page for your online stockbroker. That way you're able to quickly access your account and make those trades as soon as you hear some interesting news.

✔ If you travel a lot, add the online ticket reservation sites for your favorite airlines. If you have a wireless connection, you're able to quickly book a flight if you find you need to change your schedule at the last minute.

✔ Add a weather forecasting site and you're able to see whether it's a better idea to fly off to the mountains for skiing or to the coast for some sunshine.

✔ Of course, you want to include www.dummies.com so you can find out when your favorite author comes out with a new title. You wouldn't want your collection to be incomplete, would you?

Offline Pocket Browsing

Connecting to the Internet may not always be practical, but that shouldn't keep you from viewing Web pages that contain interesting or useful information. You may, for example, want to catch up on the weather forecast or some local news stories while you're riding to work in your car pool even though everyone else just wants to listen to a talk show or the sports. You could, of course, use a wireless Internet connection if you have one available, but there's no reason why you can't do a little browsing even when you can't connect.

The key to offline browsing on your Pocket PC is ActiveSync. Using this tool, you can set up your desktop PC to automatically download certain Web pages to your Pocket PC so that you can view them when it's convenient for you. That way, your Pocket PC will have your weather, news, or whatever you want all ready when you grab it on your way out the door in the morning. And you won't have to listen to some fat turkey spouting his latest conspiracy theory about a government cover-up of UFOs and how they're causing all the chickens to produce green eggs.

Using AvantGo

AvantGo is a free service that provides *channels* — essentially Web pages with specialized content — designed specifically for the Pocket PC. These channels provide information intended for offline viewing. For example, you can view an AvantGo channel that provides a local weather forecast based on a ZIP code you enter.

To use AvantGo, you click Options in the ActiveSync window on your desktop PC. Then make certain that you select AvantGo as one of the synchronization options. Your desktop PC then connects to the Internet and downloads the latest AvantGo channel information.

After you've set up AvantGo in ActiveSync, tap the AvantGo link in Pocket Internet Explorer on your Pocket PC. You have the opportunity to select the types of information you'd like to view offline on your Pocket PC. In some cases you need to specify information like your ZIP code before you're able to view that information.

After you've configured your AvantGo selections, ActiveSync automatically updates the channels whenever you synchronize your Pocket PC with your desktop PC. Because this synchronization is automatic, you don't have to actively download Web pages to update your Pocket PC. You can just grab your Pocket PC from its synchronization cradle and go.

Getting favorites from your desktop PC

Even though AvantGo has hundreds of channels, that's a tiny fraction of the Web sites on the Internet. You probably have quite a few Web sites that you like to keep track of, and most of them aren't AvantGo channels.

You can still have your favorite Web sites available for offline viewing on your Pocket PC even if they aren't AvantGo channels. You just have to go through a few simple steps to set up the synchronization, but when you're done, you have those Web pages available when you're on the go and not connected. Here's how to set up your desktop PC and your Pocket PC to make this happen:

1. **Open ActiveSync on your desktop PC (if it isn't already open) and then click the Options button.**

2. **Make certain that the Favorites option is selected, and click OK.**

3. **Open Internet Explorer on your desktop PC and go to a Web page you want to make available for later offline viewing on your Pocket PC.**

4. **Select Favorites⇨Add to Favorites from the Internet Explorer menu to display the Add Favorite dialog box.**

   You can also use the Tools⇨Create Mobile Favorite command as an alternate way to save a Web page for offline browsing on your Pocket PC. If you select this alternate method, though, you won't be able to select certain options such as whether to include any linked pages.

5. **Select the Make available offline checkbox.**

   Selecting this checkbox causes Internet Explorer to save the contents of the Web page rather than simply a link to the Web page. This step is necessary to have something to see on your Pocket PC.

6. **Click the Create in button to drop down the lower part of the dialog box so you can view the list of locations where you can save the Web page.**

7. **Click the Mobile Favorites folder as the place to save the Web site.**

8. **Click the Customize button and then Next (if the Offline Favorite Wizard introduction screen appears).**

9. **Choose whether you want to include any linked pages. Click Next to continue.**

   Rather than downloading linked pages, you may want to select specific pages that are linked to the current page and set up separate Mobile Favorites links to those specific pages. That way, you can download just the pages that are important to you and minimize the storage space requirements.

10. **Choose the I would like to create a new schedule option.**

    Selecting the new schedule option is very important because otherwise you'll have to manually choose to update the page rather than have it updated automatically.

11. **Click Next.**

12. **Select the update schedule that works best for you.**

    No matter when you are setting up the schedule, make certain that you specify a time that updates the page *before* you take your Pocket PC out of the synchronization cradle — otherwise you'll be viewing content that could be nearly a day old.

13. **If you want your desktop PC to automatically connect at the scheduled synchronization time, select the If my computer is not connected when this scheduled synchronization begins, automatically connect for me option.**

    Be aware, though, that choosing this option can cause your desktop PC to connect and remain connected even after the page has been updated. Still, if you don't select this option, the page may not always be updated when you expect. Click Next after you've decided which setting works best for you.

14. **If you need to enter a user name and password to access the site — perhaps to get a stock portfolio update from your online broker — make the appropriate entries on the final Offline Favorite Wizard screen.**

15. **Click Finish to conclude the process.**

After you've added your favorite Web sites to the Mobile Favorites folder, set up a synchronization schedule, and set up ActiveSync to synchronize those pages with your Pocket PC, you'll be able to view your favorite Web pages at your convenience.

 Not all Web pages require periodic updating to be useful on your Pocket PC. You can also add Web pages to your Mobile Favorites folder even though those pages remain relatively unchanged over a long period of time. Just make certain you click the Make available offline checkbox so that the content and not just the link is stored.

Making the Best Use of Your Screen Real Estate

I doubt whether anyone complains that the screen on the Pocket PC is too large. When you're viewing Web pages in Pocket Internet Explorer, it's pretty clear that Web site designers probably aren't giving too much thought to how their pages look on the Pocket PC's screen. You've got to make the most of a small area, and fortunately Pocket Internet Explorer has a few tricks up its sleeve to help you out.

Getting rid of graphics

One thing you can do to fit more text onto your Pocket PC's screen is to choose to not display the graphics that appear on most Web pages. After all, do you *really* want to view all those banner ads? You can turn off the graphics by tapping the Show Pictures icon on the Pocket Internet Explorer menu bar. Another plus: Your Web pages load faster because you aren't downloading any images. You can tap the button again to once again display the graphics.

Expanding the usable screen area

Even if you want to see the images on Web pages, you can still make better use of the little bit of screen that you've got. Tap the View menu and then use the following options:

   ✓ Choose **Fit to Screen** to make Pocket Internet Explorer scrunch things together by reducing wasted space. When you select this option, you won't need to scroll nearly so much because Pocket Internet Explorer uses as little space as possible to display the Web page contents.

✔ Choose **Address Bar** only when you need to enter a URL, and then deselect this option once you've loaded the Web page. The address bar is necessary only while you're entering an address, and hiding the address bar gives you a touch more room for viewing Web pages.

✔ Tap **Text Size** and choose the size of the characters used to display Web pages. Selecting a smaller size fits more onto the screen at one time, but if you go too small, you may need to get stronger reading glasses. Of course, you can choose a larger text size if you have trouble reading the text, too.

Browsing the Web on your Pocket PC can be a lot of fun — whether it's online or offline browsing. Your Pocket PC certainly makes it possible to surf the Web at times and places where doing so would otherwise simply be impossible.

Chapter 14

Keeping Track of Your E-Mail

● ●

In This Chapter

▶ Setting up your e-mail account

▶ Creating and sending messages

▶ Synchronizing messages with your desktop PC

● ●

*T*here's certainly no denying that e-mail has become an important part of life for most PC users. Far more messages are sent via e-mail on a daily basis than anyone could have imagined just a few years ago. You probably use e-mail a lot, and being able to use your Pocket PC for e-mail would most likely come in handy for you.

Your Pocket PC is especially well-suited to helping you manage your e-mail. Its pocket size is small enough to take with you so you can deal with e-mail messages when you would otherwise be wasting time waiting for something else to happen. It's also convenient because you can whip out a message when a thought hits rather than waiting until you're back at your desk. And because your Pocket PC can share e-mail messages with your desktop PC, you don't have to stay late at the office to handle a rush of messages that arrived just before quitting time.

Connecting to Your Mail Server

E-mail messages move over the Internet much like letters travel through the postal system. E-mail moves a lot faster than ordinary mail, of course, but there are certain similarities. First, all e-mail messages need to be sent to a specific, unique address. In addition, e-mail messages travel through *mail servers* — the electronic equivalent of post offices. Just as it's necessary for the post office to know that you've built a house and are now living at a particular street address, it's also necessary for you to establish your e-mail address with a mail server.

Sending and receiving e-mail messages with your Pocket PC requires that you first set up your Pocket PC with the proper mail server and address information. So let's start by setting up and configuring your Pocket PC to use e-mail.

Setting up your e-mail account

You'll probably want to set up your Pocket PC to use the same e-mail account as your desktop PC so you can more easily share e-mail between the two.

You can use two basic types of e-mail with your Pocket PC: online and offline. *Online* (Web-based) e-mail services typically require that you read, compose, and send messages while you're online using a Web browser. Your Internet service provider (ISP) probably also provides you with a more traditional e-mail account that enables you to handle your e-mail offline. *Offline* e-mail servers are also known as IMAP4 or POP3 mail servers, depending on the particular mail protocol they use. You have to select the correct mail server type when you're setting up e-mail on your Pocket PC, but it should be quite easy to get the server type from your ISP.

The Pocket PC Inbox is primarily designed to work with the more traditional type of e-mail account rather than with Web-based e-mail. If you want to use Hotmail — an online e-mail service — you can use the MSN Mobile link in the Mobility section of the Pocket PC Companion CD-ROM to sign up for MSN Mobile and a Hotmail account. You will then be able to use your Hotmail account just like the more traditional e-mail services.

To set up your e-mail account on your Pocket PC, follow these steps:

1. **Click the Start button and choose Inbox.**

2. **Tap Services⇨New Service on the Inbox menu bar to display the E-mail address screen.**

3. **Enter your e-mail address in the text box.**

4. **Tap Next to display the Auto Configuration screen, shown in Figure 14-1.**

   At this point your Pocket PC will attempt to connect and configure itself correctly.

5. **Click Next to continue and to display the User Information screen, shown in Figure 14-2.**

6. **Enter your user name and your password if you want your Pocket PC to be able to send and receive e-mail automatically.**

   If you either skip the password or don't check the Save password option, you have to enter the information manually each time you want to access the mail server.

7. **Click Next to display the Account Information screen.**

8. **In the Service type box, select the type of mail server your ISP provides.**

   In most cases the default POP3 is the correct choice.

Figure 14-1:
Wait until
the Status
box says
Completed
before
continuing.

Figure 14-2:
Use this
screen to
enter your
user name
and
password.

9. **Enter a name for this mail service in the Name box.**

10. **Tap Next to display the Server Information screen.**

11. **If the server names are not filled in, enter the correct names that were supplied by your ISP.**

    In most cases you won't enter anything into the Domain box. The domain setting primarily applies if you send and receive e-mail through a Windows NT network mail server.

12. **To adjust the settings for this mail server, tap Options to display the Options screen, shown in Figure 14-3.**

Figure 14-3:
Choose your
e-mail
options.

13. **Select the mail service settings that work best for you.**

14. **Click Next to display the next screen.**

15. **Choose the options to control how much of each message you want to download.**

    If you're using your Pocket PC as a companion to a desktop PC, you'll probably want to accept the default settings. That way you're able to identify and respond to urgent messages from your Pocket PC, while your desktop PC downloads all messages completely — including any attachments.

16. **Tap Next to display the final screen.**

17. **Tap Finish to complete the setup.**

Choosing your message options

Before you begin using a new mail service, at least review the message options that are selected for the mail service so you can be sure Pocket Inbox is handling mail the way you prefer.

To check the message options, select Tools⇨Options from the Pocket Inbox menu bar. Then click the Message tab (see Figure 14-4).

Figure 14-4:
Set the message options the way you want them.

Here's a brief description of these options:

> ✓ Use **When replying, include body** to include the original message when you send a reply to someone. If you don't select this option, people have a very hard time remembering which message you're replying to.

When you include the original message in your reply, cut down the clutter by deleting those parts of the original that aren't needed to convey the message.

- ✔ If you include the body text in replies, make certain that both the **Indent** and **Add leading character** boxes are selected. Using these options makes it easier for the recipient to recognize the text you're replying to. Don't try to get fancy with the leading character, either. Everyone recognizes the greater than (>) symbol as signifying a reply. If you decide to use a different character, you'll only confuse people.

- ✔ Use **Keep copy of sent mail in Sent folder** to keep a record of messages you send. It's tempting to try to save storage space by not selecting this option, but then you won't have any way to determine whether you've actually sent a message or simply thought you should and then forgot.

- ✔ Select an option for **After deleting a message** to determine how you want Pocket Inbox to respond when you are finished with a message. You may need to experiment with the three possibilities to see which fits your way of working.

- ✔ Finally, use the **Empty deleted items** selections to tell Pocket Inbox what to do with messages you delete.

Getting e-mail addresses

Way back in Chapter 4, you play around with the Pocket PC address book to add contact information for the people you deal with. Now that you're about to use e-mail on your Pocket PC, you begin to reap the benefits from those efforts.

Pocket Inbox can use the e-mail addresses contained in your Contacts list. It can also use online address books to verify e-mail addresses. To control how these options work, select Tools➪Options from the Pocket Inbox menu bar and click the Address tab, as shown in Figure 14-5.

Use the drop-down list to determine which fields in the Contacts list to use for e-mail addresses when you enter a name rather than an e-mail address. In most cases this won't matter because you'll probably use a single e-mail address for the majority of your message recipients. Where this can make a difference is if you regularly send e-mail to a group of people and have separate home and work e-mail addresses for each of them. In that case, you can use one e-mail address field for their home address and a different one for each person's work address.

If you only use your Pocket PC to read and compose e-mail messages, and then use ActiveSync to transfer those messages to Outlook on your desktop PC for sending, make certain you don't select a mail server for verifying e-mail addresses on your Pocket PC. If you do select this option, your Pocket PC may lock up when it searches for the mail server and can't find it. For a refresher on using ActiveSync, you may want to refer to Chapter 7.

Figure 14-5:
Select the
e-mail
address
sources you
want to use.

Setting your message storage location

If you have a memory storage card for your Pocket PC, you can use the storage card to store any messages and any attachments. To select this option, select Tools⇨Options from the Pocket Inbox menu bar and click the Storage tab.

Although it seems like a memory storage card should be the perfect place to store your e-mail messages and any attachments, there's a fundamental problem with this idea. If you connect directly to the Internet from your Pocket PC in order to send and receive e-mail, you'll probably need to use your Pocket PC's CF expansion slot for your modem or your digital phone card. As a result, the CF expansion slot isn't likely to be available for your memory storage card while you're using your Internet connection. Of course, if you have a memory storage card that fits into a different expansion slot, then a memory storage card may be a good idea.

Sending and Receiving E-Mail

E-mail was really one of the great inventions of the computing age. E-mail made it possible to send a quick message at any time and have that message delivered almost instantly. But unlike other forms of communication, e-mail is also cheap and has the ability to bridge time differences between people any-where in the world. You can send a message to your friend half way around the world when it's convenient for you, and you don't have to worry about waking them with an expensive phone call. They, of course, can respond when they're available — whether that's right now or hours from now.

Your Pocket PC has the ability to make e-mail even more convenient. Now you can use e-mail almost anywhere and at any time.

Creating a message

Creating an e-mail message is a very simple process. It's almost the same as writing out a quick note except that you need to add the recipient's address and a subject line to an e-mail message.

To create an e-mail message, tap New on the Pocket Inbox menu bar. This opens a message form like the one I'm using in Figure 14-6. Then, follow these steps:

Figure 14-6:
Enter your e-mail message using the message form shown here.

1. **Tap the down arrows to the right of the subject line to display the Cc, Bcc, and Service fields in addition to the To and Subj fields.**

2. **Enter the name of the recipient or his e-mail address in the To field.**

   You can click on To if you want to select the message recipients from your address list. If you click To, you see only those people in your address list who have e-mail addresses.

3. **Use the Subj line to briefly describe your message.**

   Coming up with a good subject line can be a real art because you want to distill your meaning down into just a few words. The message recipient needs to be able to grasp how important the message is from seeing the first few words of the subject line — long subject lines probably won't display completely in his or her Inbox.

   The Bcc (blind carbon copy) field is a really handy tool. People you list only in the Bcc field get the message, but their name and e-mail address don't appear on their copy of the message, nor on anyone else's copy. You can use this to great advantage if you need to send the same message separately to a whole bunch of people, because no one knows who else was listed in the Bcc field of the message, and therefore won't know who else got the message. The Bcc field offers two other advantages, too. If you print an e-mail message, the message header normally prints at the top of the message, and the header contains a list of the recipients. By using the Bcc field for most recipients, you reduce the amount of paper needed to print the message. Also, by using the Bcc field, you eliminate the problem of someone responding by clicking the Reply All button because if no recipients are shown, you're the only person who gets the reply.

4. **After you've finished composing your message, click the Send button to place the message into your Outbox folder.**

   Items in the Outbox folder go out the next time the mail server is contacted.

Sending and receiving messages

If you configured Pocket Inbox to automatically send and receive e-mail, you don't have to do anything special to send the messages from your Outbox. Those messages go out and any new messages are received as soon as your Pocket PC connects to the mail server.

You can, however, tell your Pocket PC to send and receive messages immediately by clicking the Send/Receive button (the button with two envelopes at the right side of the Inbox menu bar). Depending on your settings, you may need to connect to the Internet manually, and you may need to enter your mail server's user name and password.

Organizing messages in folders

By default, Pocket Inbox creates several folders for organizing your e-mail messages. Figure 14-7 shows the typical array of folders you see if you click the View list just below the title bar.

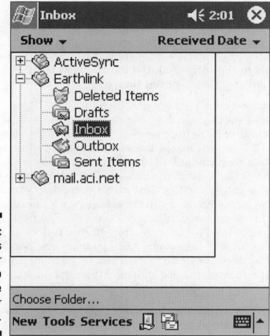

It's easy to see the purpose of each of the default folders. But you may want to be a bit more organized by creating new folders to hold specific messages. For example, you may want one folder to hold all incoming messages relating to one of your projects. You can add new folders by selecting Tools⇨Manage Folders from the Pocket Inbox menu bar and then tapping New.

Don't try to change the meaning of the default folders. Not only will Pocket Inbox ignore you, but it will continue to handle messages according to the folder they're located in. That is, any messages that are in the Outbox folder will be sent to the mail server the next time you connect — no matter if you'd rather do something else with them. Some things just can't be changed!

Getting the entire story

If you want to get a quick overview of the status of your messages, simply tap Tools⇨Status.

Don't depend on the Message Status screen to tell you if you have any incoming messages waiting to be retrieved. Pocket Inbox has no way to determine whether you have any incoming messages until you actually connect to the mail server.

Exchanging Messages with Outlook

Just as you can use your Pocket PC for offline browsing without having an Internet connection on your Pocket PC, you can use your Pocket PC for offline e-mail. In both cases the key component is ActiveSync, because ActiveSync allows your Pocket PC and your desktop PC to share important information in a controlled manner.

Because you need to use Outlook on your desktop PC to share e-mail with your Pocket PC, the Pocket PC Companion CD-ROM includes a full version of Outlook 2002. If you have not already installed Outlook 2002, you will need to get out your Pocket PC Companion CD-ROM and do so before you can continue. (Although you can continue to use Outlook 2000 if you have that installed.)

After you install Outlook 2002 on your desktop PC, you can share e-mail messages between your Pocket PC and your desktop PC by selecting the Inbox option in ActiveSync. To do so, open ActiveSync and click the Options button. Then make certain that Inbox is selected. If you like, you can click the Settings button for more precise control over the way e-mail is shared.

You can share e-mail only between your Pocket PC and one desktop PC. If you use two different desktop PCs, carefully choose one for sharing e-mail messages because you'll use just that one desktop PC.

Part V
Multimedia Time

The 5th Wave — By Rich Tennant

"Well, here's what happened—I forgot to put it on my 'To Do' List."

In this part . . .

Now it's time to have some fun with your Pocket PC. In this part you'll see how you can read all sorts of new electronic books on your Pocket PC, why a Pocket PC can be a great musical companion, how to make your Pocket PC into the perfect partner for your digital camera, and why your Pocket PC is the ultimate handheld game machine. You will also see how to do some things you never dreamed of doing with your Pocket PC, such as watch TV shows.

Chapter 15

Reading eBooks

*I*t's pretty clear to anyone who uses a Pocket PC that having a computer that fits easily into your shirt pocket opens a whole new range of possibilities. The *eBook* represents a great example of just how much these new ideas can change the way we do ordinary things. In this case, that ordinary thing is something you're doing right now in the old traditional way — reading a book. If this were an eBook, you wouldn't be looking at ink printed on paper, but rather words on your Pocket PC screen.

Understanding eBooks

People have been reading text on computer screens for as long as there have been computer screens. It's reasonable to ask, therefore, just how eBooks are different from the plain old text you've been seeing since you started using computers. Actually, there are several differences:

✔ Because your Pocket PC is about the size of a paperback book, it's easy to hold your Pocket PC in your hand while you read an eBook. This makes reading eBooks far more like reading a "real" book than like reading text on a computer screen.

✔ The Microsoft Reader program you use to read eBooks allows you to search, bookmark, and annotate eBooks. You can even ask for the definition of unfamiliar words as you're reading.

✔ Many popular books — including current best-sellers — are available as eBooks but not as plain text files because the eBook format allows publishers to control the distribution of titles so both the authors and publishers can earn the money they deserve from their efforts.

✔ With your backlit Pocket PC screen, you can read an eBook in the dark without trying to find a flashlight that doesn't have dead batteries.

eBooks are stored in a highly compressed format that greatly reduces the amount of storage space that's needed. This format also allows publishers to control who can read an eBook. Because of the special format, you need a special program to read eBooks. On your Pocket PC, that program is Microsoft Reader.

eBook Connections maintains a Web site, www.ebookconnections.com/ ReadersPrimer, that contains an excellent introduction to the world of eBooks. At this site you find up-to-date information on just about anything you may want to know about eBooks.

If you are a budding author who wants to let other people read your work without all of the hassles involved in traditional publishing, the main eBook Connections Web site (www.ebookconnections.com) has links to several eBook publishers. You may find that one of these eBook publishers will provide you with the opportunity to publish your work (and make a little pocket change at the same time).

Downloading eBooks

In order to read an eBook on your Pocket PC, you've got to first get those eBooks into your Pocket PC. The process is similar to copying other files to your Pocket PC, but there are a few differences.

Copying eBooks to your Pocket PC

The first eBooks you're likely to try out are the free samples included on the Pocket PC Companion CD-ROM. You may as well see whether you like reading eBooks on your Pocket PC before you spend time and money on other eBooks, right?

Files you copy directly from a CD-ROM always have their *read-only* file attribute set. This doesn't present any problems when you want to read eBooks on your Pocket PC, but it does produce a cryptic error message when you later decide to free up some storage space on your Pocket PC. To prevent this problem, first copy the eBook files from the CD-ROM to your desktop PC hard drive. Then right-click the copied files and choose Properties. Remove the check from the Read-only checkbox and click OK. Now you can copy the files from your hard drive to your Pocket PC and you won't have any problems when you later want to delete an eBook.

Table 15-1 lists the titles that are included on the Pocket PC Companion CD-ROM.

Table 15-1	eBooks on the Pocket PC Companion CD-ROM	
Author	*Title*	*File*
Louisa May Alcott	*Little Women*	lwmen10.lit
J. M. Barrie	*Peter Pan*	peterpan.lit
Ernest Bramah	*Kai Lung's Golden Hours*	kailung.lit
Emily Bronte	*Wuthering Heights*	heights.lit
Francis Hodgson Burnett	*Secret Garden*	sgarden.lit
Edgar Rice Burroughs	*Tarzan of the Apes*	tarzan.lit
G. K. Chesterton	*Innocence of Father Brown*	gkctiofb.lit
Frederick Douglass	*My Bondage and My Freedom*	douglass.lit
Arthur Conan Doyle	*Study in Scarlet*	asis.lit
Zane Grey	*Riders of the Purple Sage*	riders.lit
Washington Irving	*Legend of Sleepy Hollow*	losh.lit
Jerome K. Jerome	*Three Men in a Boat*	jerome.lit
Jack London	*Call of the Wild*	cotw.lit
Machiavelli	*Prince*	mprince.lit
Raphael Sabatini	*Captain Blood*	blood.lit
H. H. Munro	*Unbearable Bassington*	sakibass.lit
Robert Louis Stevenson	*Treasure Island*	treas10.lit
Bram Stoker	*Dracula*	dracu10.lit
Mark Twain	*Tom Sawyer*	sawyr10.lit
Jules Verne	*Around the World in 80 Days*	80days.lit
H. G. Wells	*Time Machine*	timemach.lit
Oscar Wilde	*Importance of Being Earnest*	ernest.lit

To copy any of the eBooks to your Pocket PC, follow these steps:

1. **Be sure your Pocket PC is connected to your desktop PC and open ActiveSync if it isn't already open.**

2. **Click the Explore button in ActiveSync.**

3. **Open Windows Explorer on your desktop PC and navigate to the folder where the eBook files are located.**

   On the Pocket PC Companion CD-ROM this is the \MS\APPS\MSReader\ \EBOOKS folder, but if you followed the earlier tip about removing the read-only file attribute you may have copied the files to a folder on your hard drive.

4. **Select the files you want to copy in Windows Explorer, and then drag-and-drop them into the My Documents folder, which is open in the ActiveSync Explore window.**

Be selective about which eBook files you copy to your Pocket PC. Unless you have added a memory storage card and are copying the files to the storage card, the 7.24MB of eBook files on the ActiveSync CD-ROM may not all fit in your available storage memory at the same time.

Building your eBook library

You aren't limited to the selection of eBooks from the Pocket PC Companion CD-ROM, of course. You can also download eBooks from a number of different Web sites. One such site, the eBook Directory, is found at www. ebookdirectory.com.

You find links to many more eBook vendors at the eBook Connections Web site, www.ebookconnections.com/. Some sites offer a selection of free eBooks in addition to titles you can purchase.

Unfortunately, many things fit loosely into the definition of eBooks. A lot of what are called eBooks aren't designed to be read on your Pocket PC. When you download eBooks, make certain you are downloading files that are specified as being Microsoft Reader–compatible files. Otherwise you'll be wasting your time (and maybe money) downloading files you can't use on your Pocket PC.

Understanding digital rights management

When you buy a printed book, the mere fact that it is printed on paper and bound together means that it is really only convenient for one person to read that copy at a time. If you think the printed book is really good, you may tell a friend about it so he can buy his own copy. Or you may loan him your copy when you're finished reading the book. But it's unlikely that you will both share one copy at the same time — that would be pretty inconvenient, wouldn't it?

But as you have seen earlier in this chapter, eBooks are a slightly different type of product than printed books. The eBooks you found on the Pocket PC

Companion CD-ROM were just as easy for you to copy as any other file. Unfortunately, this ease of copying means that some people feel that it is okay to give other people free copies of any eBooks they may buy. Needless to say, there isn't a lot of incentive to write and publish a book if people are giving away hundreds of copies for each copy that is sold!

In the past, the ease with which eBooks could be copied and shared has made it difficult to find a lot of really good books in the eBook format. You may have noticed that the eBooks on the Pocket PC Companion CD-ROM are all old books written long ago. There aren't any of today's best-sellers sitting there just waiting for you to download for free.

In an attempt at making publishing books in eBook format more popular, Microsoft has made the Microsoft Reader Activation Pack available (on the Pocket PC Companion CD-ROM). This software adds something known as *digital rights management* (DRM) to your Pocket PC's Microsoft Reader program. Why should you care about this? It's simple, really. Once you have run the Microsoft Reader Activation Pack (by clicking the Download link, shown in Figure 15-1), your copy of the Microsoft Reader can then use eBooks that are copy protected. That is, you will be able to buy premium-quality books to read on your Pocket PC because those books cannot be copied and shared with other people. In effect, this makes the premium eBooks that you buy act more like printed books. And this gives publishers and authors an incentive to publish more premium eBook titles, so everyone wins.

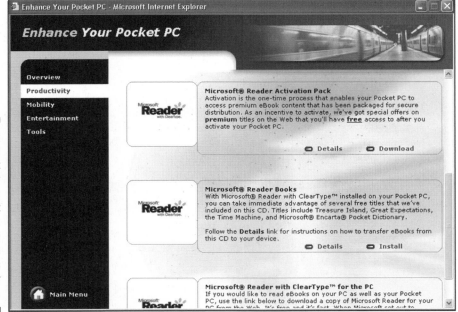

Figure 15-1: Run the Microsoft Reader Activation Pack so that you can read the premium eBook titles on your Pocket PC.

Managing your eBook library

Managing your eBook collection is easy. The main things are to control where your eBooks reside on your Pocket PC and to delete eBooks you no longer need to free up space for other uses. Here are some points to consider:

✔ A memory storage card is an excellent place to store your eBooks. You don't need any other accessories like modems to read eBooks, so you could keep your entire eBook collection on a memory storage card that you pop in whenever you want to view your library. Remember to place the eBook files in the My Documents folder on the memory storage card.

✔ You may encounter a cryptic error message if you try to delete an eBook by using tap-and-hold and selecting Delete from within Reader. If you do, this probably means that the file is set to read-only mode and you can't delete it from within Reader. If this happens, you'll need to use this next method to delete the file.

✔ You can use the File Explorer on your Pocket PC to delete or move files. Even so, you may find that it's easier to click the Explore button in ActiveSync on your desktop PC and then manage those files from your desktop PC.

✔ Backing up your eBooks on your desktop PC (as you saw in Chapter 7) is an excellent idea — especially if you have purchased some premium titles. That way, you will be protected in case anything happens to the file on your Pocket PC.

Reading an eBook

Some people build up big collections of fancy-looking books but never read a single one of them. You'll probably be far more practical about your eBook collection — especially because eBooks just don't have the same panache as a library full of leather-bound law books.

To open an eBook, follow these steps:

1. **Click the Start button and choose Programs.**

2. **Tap Microsoft Reader to open the library (see Figure 15-2).**

3. **Tap a book title to open that book.**

   Figure 15-3 shows that I've opened *Around the World in 80 Days*.

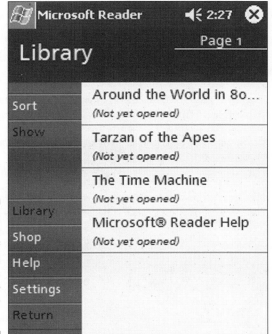

Figure 15-2:
The library
shows all of
the eBooks
that are
currently
on your
Pocket PC.

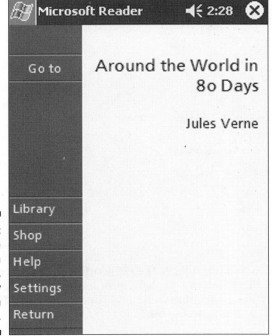

Figure 15-3:
After you've
opened an
eBook,
you're ready
to begin
reading.

Navigating an eBook

Reading an eBook is most definitely different from reading a bound paper book or even from reading a text document on your desktop PC. For one thing, how do you flip the pages?

As Figure 15-3 shows, the title page of each eBook contains several options you can tap to navigate your way through the book. To begin at the beginning, tap Go to and then tap Begin reading on the menu that pops up. The Microsoft Reader program also keeps track of how far you've read and the last page you were viewing — so there's no need to try to dog-ear any of the pages!

When you begin reading, the Microsoft Reader program shows several things on each page (see Figure 15-4), and you can use these to navigate your way through the book:

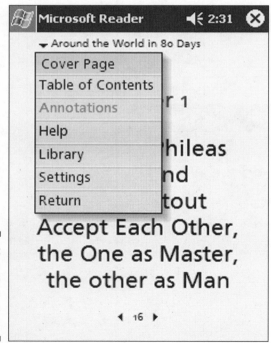

Figure 15-4:
You can navigate using the arrows on the page.

> ✔ The down arrow just to the right of the book title pops up a menu (shown in Figure 15-4) that you can use to return to the beginning, open your list of annotations, view the guidebook, open the library, change the view settings, or return to the last page you were viewing.

- ✔ The left arrow (by the page number) returns you to the next lower-numbered page. This may not be the last page you were reading if you jumped to a page from an annotation or from the index.

- ✔ The right arrow displays the next higher-numbered page. The current page number appears between the two page navigation arrows.

Tapping the right or left arrow to move through the pages soon gets tedious. That's why all Pocket PCs offer alternative methods for navigating the pages of an eBook. Here's what you'll find on your Pocket PC:

- ✔ On some Pocket PCs, you can use the rocker switch on the left side of the Pocket PC to page through the book. Each time you flick the switch up or down you move one page backwards or forwards through the book.

- ✔ On all Pocket PCs, use the Navigator button on the front of the Pocket PC to move through the book. Pressing on the right side or the lower side of the button moves you forward, while pressing on the left side or the top side of the button moves you back.

- ✔ If your Pocket PC has both the rocker switch on the left side of the Pocket PC and the Navigator button on the front of the Pocket PC, you can even switch off between the two if your finger gets tired of paging through the book.

One thing that is very different about reading eBooks on your Pocket PC compared to reading a text document on your desktop PC is that eBooks always jump an entire page at a time. You won't see the line-by-line scrolling that's common when you're viewing text documents.

Adding notes and such

Have you ever found yourself writing notes on one of those sticky notepads and then placing the note into a book you were reading? Eventually it becomes almost impossible to read the book without knocking the notes out of place. And even if they stay where they belong, it can be really hard to remember where you made a note about this and where you made one about that.

When you're reading an eBook it's really easy to add your own notes to the text and to later go back and refer to those notes. To do so, tap the word or phrase you wish to annotate and then select Add Text Note from the pop-up menu that appears, as shown in Figure 15-5.

Type in your note as shown in Figure 15-6, and then tap outside the notepad area to complete your note.

Figure 15-5:
Use this
menu to add
bookmarks
and notes
to your
eBooks.

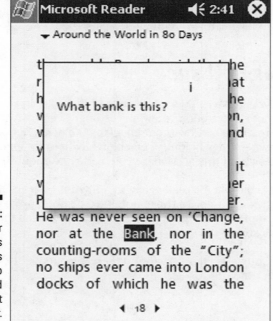

Figure 15-6:
Add your
own notes
to eBooks
to help
you find
important
points later.

After you've added notes to the text you can review your notes using the annotation index. When you open the index, tap the note you'd like to see, and the Reader opens the note as well as the page where you've added the note. You will also see a small Note icon next to any line that contains a note.

Tap the Keyboard icon to hide the onscreen keyboard when you're viewing existing notes, enabling you to view the eBook page in addition to simply seeing the note itself. You can also tap the *i* in the upper part of the notepad to see the note in context.

You can also add highlighting, a bookmark, or a drawing to the text by selecting the proper choice from the pop-up menu that appears when you select text. If you want to quote the text exactly, you can copy the selected text.

Listening to Audio Books

There are times when it simply isn't convenient to try to read, but when you'd still enjoy listening to something more intelligent than your average, overweight, self-absorbed talk radio host. After all, "ditto" is simply not the stuff of interesting conversation, is it?

Your Pocket PC can come to the rescue by enabling you to listen to *audio books*. These recorded books and other types of content (like in-depth news reports) can be played back on your Pocket PC.

Using the Audible Player

One way to listen to audio books is to install the Audible Player on your Pocket PC. To use the Audible Player, you must first load it onto both your desktop PC and your Pocket PC. Some Pocket PCs include a version of the Audible Player, but you can easily download the most recent version by visiting the Audible Web site at www.audible.com/. When you install the Audible Player, it integrates with Microsoft Reader on your Pocket PC, and any audio book content you download appears in the Reader's library.

The download from Audible also includes the Audible Manager software for your desktop PC. This software makes it easy to download and manage content from the Audible Web site. Both the Audible Player and Audible Manager are free downloads. The Audible Web site includes some free content and a lot of items that you must pay for.

After you install the Audible Player and download some audio books to your Pocket PC, you may find that listening to an audio book is even easier than reading an eBook. You simply open Microsoft Reader and then select the audio book from your library. Tap the Play button (it is the single right arrow in the toolbar), and the audio book begins playing. If you pause or stop the playback, the Player remembers where you left off and resumes at the same point when you restart the playback later.

Using Windows Media Player

Your Pocket PC can also play Windows Media Player–compatible content. This type of material is not played using the Microsoft Reader, but rather with the Windows Media Player that is built into your Pocket PC. You can find a huge variety of Windows Media Player content on the Web at sites such as Audiohighway (www.Audiohighway.com).

The headphones that came with your Pocket PC make audio books easier to understand and help you to avoid disturbing other people who don't want to listen to your audio book.

Reading Laridian PocketBible

The Bible is probably the most popular book of all time, so it's only natural that it would also be a popular thing to read on your Pocket PC. Laridian (www.laridian.com) makes it easy for you to read and study the Bible through their PocketBible for the Pocket PC (see Figure 15-7).

You may well wonder what advantages there might be to reading the Bible on your Pocket PC as opposed to simply picking up a printed version. Actually several come to mind:

✔ You can read and study from multiple translations of the Bible on your Pocket PC. This makes it easy to compare the different versions so you can more easily understand passages that may seem a little confusing.

✔ You can find what you want using the find features in PocketBible. This makes it much easier to find references to specific topics.

✔ You can add your own notes, with hyperlinks to Bible verses so that it is easy to keep track of your references.

✔ Additional reference books (such as dictionaries) are available from Laridian. This is especially useful if you want to study the text or prepare talks on biblical topics.

Your Pocket PC is also a lot smaller and easier to carry around than a printed Bible — especially when you consider all of the extra books (such as different translations) you can get from Laridian. Your Pocket PC won't get any heavier when you add those extra books, either!

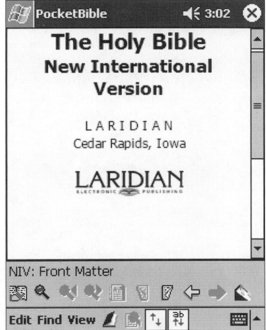

Figure 15-7:
You can
even read
the Bible
on your
Pocket PC.

Chapter 16

Using Your Pocket PC for Music

*A*s if you really need it, this chapter provides you with yet another great way to use your Pocket PC and to eliminate the need for another piece of equipment. Your Pocket PC is a great replacement for those little carry-about music players — especially because your Pocket PC works even better than any of those devices and can be easily expanded to play far more music, too.

Using Windows Media Player

Your Pocket PC uses a special version of Windows Media Player to play music and other multimedia files. You can also use Windows Media Player on your desktop PC to create copies of music files for use on your Pocket PC.

Copying music illegally can get you into a lot of trouble. Recording companies and artists quite rightly wish to protect their property by enforcing their rights under copyright laws. These laws generally prohibit you from making copies of music and then selling, trading, or giving away those copies. Making a copy of music you have purchased — such as an audio CD — for your own private use on a device such as your Pocket PC is generally considered acceptable. Unfortunately, no one really knows what the courts may decide tomorrow, so be very careful when it comes to copying any music, no matter what the source.

Transferring music to your Pocket PC

Audio CDs are a great medium for distributing music. They're relatively small, fairly immune to casual damage, and they produce very high-quality sound. But unless you've got awfully big pockets, audio CDs aren't all that great as a portable music source. Not only are they too big, but they're also prone to skipping even when played in really good portable CD players.

Audio CDs hold uncompressed sound recordings, which means that a complete recording can use up to 650MB of space on an audio disc. Your Pocket PC, of course, probably has nowhere near that much storage room. Windows Media Player can compress audio tracks to a fraction of their original size. Some sound quality is lost when compressing an audio track, but you don't notice the difference when listening to music on your Pocket PC, anyway. But even with compression, you likely won't be able to copy an entire audio CD to your Pocket PC unless you add a memory storage card. See "Expanding Your Pocket PC's Musical Capabilities" later in this chapter for more information.

Windows Media Player 7 (or later) has everything you need for copying music to your Pocket PC. If you're still using an earlier version of Windows Media Player on your desktop PC, you can get a free upgrade to the latest version. To do so, click Help⇨Check for Upgrade in your current version of Windows Media Player.

To copy music from an audio CD to your Pocket PC, follow these steps:

1. **Open Windows Media Player on your desktop PC.**

2. **Insert the audio CD into your CD drive.**

3. **Click the Copy from CD button to display the tracks on the audio CD.**

   If you have an Internet connection, Windows Media Player attempts to obtain the track information from a music database located on the Internet.

4. **Make sure the tracks you want are checked. Then, click the Copy Music button to first copy them to your desktop's hard drive**.

   Figure 16-1 shows how the Windows Media Player appears while copying the tracks.

5. **Next click the Copy to CD or Device button.**

   Windows Media Player examines your Pocket PC to see how much space is available and then displays the music files in the currently open media library as well as those on your Pocket PC.

6. **Select the tracks you want to copy to your Pocket PC and then click the Copy Music button. Figure 16-2 shows how this process appears as files are being copied.**

Figure 16-1:
Copy the
music
tracks to
your
desktop
PC's hard
drive first.

Figure 16-2:
When the
music is on
your hard
drive, you
can copy it
to your
Pocket PC.

Creating a play list

After you have the music files on your Pocket PC, you can create a play list
by selecting the music you want to hear. If you have enough storage to store
several different complete audio CDs on your Pocket PC, you may even want
to create several different play lists.

To set up a play list, follow these steps:

1. **Click the Start button on your Pocket PC and choose Windows Media from the Start menu.**

2. **Tap Select on the menu bar, and then tap the plus sign (+) at the far lower-left side of the toolbar.**

3. **Select the songs you want to include (see Figure 16-3), and then click OK.**

   In this case, I want to include several of the songs.

4. **Tap OK.**

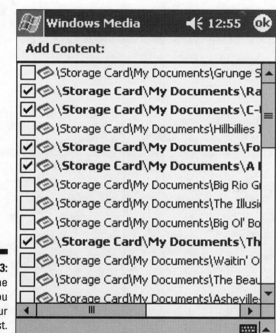

Figure 16-3: Choose the songs you want in your play list.

Playing your music

After you set up your play list you can listen to the music. Figure 16-4 shows the Windows Media Player ready to begin playing.

To hear the recording in stereo, use the headphones that came with your Pocket PC. You can also play back the music through a set of small battery-powered amplified speakers like the ones often used with desktop PCs.

Figure 16-4:
It's time to enjoy the music you've stored on your Pocket PC.

Music playback can be a major drain on your Pocket PC's battery. Be sure that you're starting out with a fully charged battery and that you've turned off the backlight on your Pocket PC.

If you're using the headphones that came with your Pocket PC, look for a small *R* on one earpiece and a small *L* on the other. That way you'll be certain that the right and left channels are playing in the correct ear.

Setting the Windows Media Player options

You can make your Pocket PC a little more convenient as a music player by customizing the buttons on the front of your Pocket PC so that they have special functions when you are playing music. You don't have to worry about screwing up the normal operation of your Pocket PC — the buttons assume their special functions only when Windows Media Player is open.

To set up these special functions, tap Tools➪Settings➪Buttons on the Windows Media Player menu bar, which displays the Options screen.

To assign a function to one of the buttons, first choose the function from the drop-down list. Then press the button you want to use for the function. You can remove an assigned function from a button by selecting <None> from the list and then pressing the button. Tap OK when you're finished.

Expanding Your Pocket PC's Musical Capabilities

The Pocket PC is easily expanded to provide even more music playback capabilities. Let's take a quick look at a couple of options you may find quite interesting.

Adding storage space

You may have noticed (in Figure 16-2) that my Pocket PC had a lot of room for storing music. One of the problems with using a Pocket PC as a portable music player is that there isn't a lot of room for music files in the standard storage space that comes built into a Pocket PC. Fortunately, it's easy to expand your Pocket PC's capacity using a memory storage card. In my case, I added a 128MB SD memory card from Kingston to allow my Pocket PC to store several hours of music.

Table 16-1 lists several manufacturers of memory cards that you can get for your Pocket PC.

Table 16-1	Memory Cards to Expand Your Pocket PC's Music Storage
Manufacturer	*Web site*
Delkin Devices	www.delkin.com/
Kingston Technology Company, Inc.	www.kingston.com/
Lexar Media	www.lexarmedia.com/
PreTec Electronics Corp.	www.pretec.com/
SanDisk	www.sandisk.com/

Different Pocket PCs have different types of expansion slots. Make certain you know the exact type of slot in your Pocket PC before you buy an expansion card. For example, the HP Jornada Pocket PCs use a CF Type 1 card, but can't use a CF Type 2 card nor SD memory cards without an expansion sleeve. The Audiovox Maestro, the Casio E-200, and the Toshiba e570 all use CF Type 1 and Type 2 cards as well as SD memory cards. The Compaq iPAQ uses an adapter sleeve that you buy according to the type of expansion card you want to use.

Playing music through your car radio

If you have tried listening to the music you play on your Pocket PC using earphones, you already know that the tiny speaker in your Pocket PC really doesn't do much justice to the music. Actually, it would probably be fair to say that as far as music is concerned, the Pocket PC's speaker stinks!

On the other hand, in most areas it is illegal to wear earphones while you are driving (it's also dangerous, of course). But there you are with several hours of your favorite music in your Pocket PC, and there's nothing good on the radio. What can you do (other than put up with the lousy Pocket PC speaker, that is)? How about playing the music through your car radio?

The SoundFeeder from Arkon Resources (www.arkon.com) sends a stereo signal from your Pocket PC right to an FM radio. In most cases this is probably going to be your car radio, but any FM radio will do.

Since the SoundFeeder works with any FM radio, you can even bring along the music for a party right there on your Pocket PC. Any home stereo or even a boombox will do.

Finding Music Online

In addition to copying music from an audio CD, you can also find a lot of music online that you can play on your Pocket PC. In some cases you can download free music tracks, but you also find artists who sell their own music at a reasonable price online.

Recent legal battles have made finding online music download Web sites more of a challenge than it used to be. You can usually find files by searching for MP3 or WMA downloads using your favorite online search engine. If you're really dedicated to finding music files, you may want to download the Copernic 2001 search tool from www.copernic.com. The Copernic 2001 Pro version that I use has a specific MP3 search category to make finding online music much easier.

Here are a few other sites where you can find music to download:

- ✔ www.mp3charts.com
- ✔ www.mp3board.com
- ✔ www.playdude.com
- ✔ www.mp3netseek.com
- ✔ www.soundhub.com

Chapter 17

More Pocket PC Multimedia

*I*f you've got a digital camera in addition to your Pocket PC, you've probably given some thought to using the two devices as partners. After all, your Pocket PC is a computer, and digital images are in their natural element on a computer. Why not use your Pocket PC to put those finishing touches on your digital images? On the other hand, you have probably never given any thought to watching your favorite TV shows on your Pocket PC, and you may not have thought that your Pocket PC would be any good for giving a PowerPoint presentation, either. By the end of this chapter you'll see that these are some of the more unusual and fun ways to use your Pocket PC — as well as an excuse to get some more fun toys to play with.

Sharing Photos with Your Digital Camera

In order to work with digital images on your Pocket PC, you first have to move those images from your digital camera to your Pocket PC. This can be very simple in some cases and very difficult in others — depending on a number of hardware and software factors I show you in the following sections. For example, in some cases you may be able to simply share a memory storage card, while in others you may even need to bring your desktop PC into the act between your Pocket PC and your digital camera.

Most digital cameras store images in JPEG, BMP, or TIFF file format. Of these, JPEG is often better to work with on a Pocket PC than the other two if for no better reason than the fact that JPEG images are generally *compressed* so they take less storage space.

Sharing digital images on memory cards

The most straightforward method of sharing digital images between your digital camera and your Pocket PC is to use a memory storage card that is compatible with both units. If this is an option, you can typically just pop the memory card out of the camera, plug it into your Pocket PC, and you're ready to go — almost.

Your Pocket PC generally needs a bit of help finding files that are stored on a memory card if those files aren't stored in a folder called My Documents. Digital cameras, of course, typically have no need for folders, so they often store image files on the memory card without using any directory structure. Therefore, you may need to explicitly tell whatever software you're using on your Pocket PC to look on the storage card for image files because they won't be stored in the Pocket PC's preferred location.

Of course, life is often more complicated than we may like. Not all digital cameras use the same types of memory cards as the ones that may be compatible with your Pocket PC. And even digital cameras that do use the same type of memory card as your Pocket PC may not be able to handle a memory card with as much capacity as the ones you can use in your Pocket PC.

If you want to share memory cards between a digital camera and a Pocket PC, you may want to spend some time researching memory card compatibility *before* you buy a digital camera. Then get a camera that uses the same memory cards as your Pocket PC. Of course, if you've already got that digital camera, you may just get lucky and find out that it can use the same memory cards as your Pocket PC.

Connecting to your digital camera

As an alternative to sharing a memory card between your digital camera and your Pocket PC, you may want to transfer images another way — by connecting your Pocket PC and your digital camera. This, however, may be even trickier to arrange than sharing a memory card.

Here are some possible ways you may be able to transfer images by connecting your Pocket PC and your digital camera:

✔ Some digital cameras support sending images via infrared. This may or may not work with your combination of digital camera and Pocket PC, but it's more likely that the two will be compatible if they're both from the same manufacturer.

✔ The one foolproof method of transferring image files from your digital camera to your Pocket PC is to first transfer them from your digital camera to your desktop PC. You can use the software that came with your digital camera to do this. Then use ActiveSync to send those files to your Pocket PC. Of course, this sort of defeats the whole idea of using your Pocket PC as your digital camera's companion, but it is a sure-fire approach.

Editing Photos on Your Pocket PC

Digital imaging is one place where the various Pocket PC manufacturers pretty much leave you on your own. You aren't going to find highly sophisticated photo-editing software bundled with your Pocket PC. Fortunately, though, you can easily correct this problem by adding an inexpensive piece of software to your Pocket PC.

Downloading and installing new software on your Pocket PC is really pretty simple, but it's a subject that I don't really cover in detail until Chapter 19. If you want to try out the software shown in this chapter, you may want to hold off until you've had a chance to read Chapter 19 (or you can skip ahead, of course).

Realize that no matter how good the software is, your Pocket PC is far more suited to fairly simple image-editing tasks than it is to professional-level photo manipulation. There's a reason most graphic artists use desktop PCs with large monitors. Editing photos is just a lot easier when you can see more detail, and the Pocket PC's screen is simply too small to show a lot of detail.

Of course, digital photo editing is a subject that can easily take up several complete books. Rather than try to cover the topic badly in a few pages, I'm simply going to show you one of the tools that is available for the Pocket PC so you can get an idea of the possibilities.

The tool I've selected is Pocket Artist from Conduits Technologies. You can download a trial version from `www.conduits.com/`. Figure 17-1 shows an example of the items that are available on the Pocket Artist Menu⇨Tools menu.

When you take photos with your digital camera, you often find that some adjustment of the brightness, contrast, or colors can really improve the images. As Figure 17-1 shows, Pocket Artist gives you easy access to these adjustments.

If you want to go beyond basic adjustments and get creative, Pocket Artist provides tools to help there, too. For example, Figure 17-2 shows the list of tools that appear when you tap the Paintbrush icon on the toolbar.

No matter where you manipulate images — on your Pocket PC or on your desktop PC — working with a copy of important files rather than with the original is always a good idea. You can easily go too far and then want to go back several steps. Making a copy is the safest way to ensure you can always go back to the original.

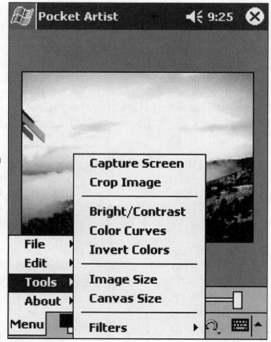

Figure 17-1: Pocket Artist gives you all the basic image-editing tools you need to fix up your digital photos.

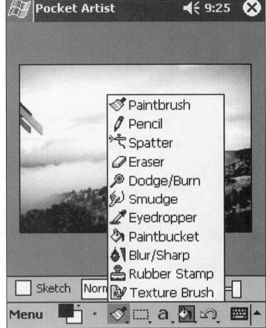

Figure 17-2:
Pocket
Artist also
goes well
beyond the
basics with
tools for
artistic
manipu-
lation.

Displaying Your Photos

If you've ever tried to show people the digital photos you've taken, and tried to use the display screen on your digital camera to do so, you know how difficult and frustrating that can be. Not only is the screen too small for good viewing, but cycling through the images usually requires pressing the right buttons.

One alternative is to use your Pocket PC and create a slide show of your images. ACDSee Mobile (www.acdsystems.com) can easily do this, and, as Figure 17-3 shows, it can also display thumbnail views of the images on your Pocket PC.

ACDSee Mobile is one of the few Pocket PC applications that can display TIFF images.

Watching TV on Your Pocket PC

When you think of watching TV, your Pocket PC probably isn't the first thing that pops into your head. Sure, your Pocket PC is a great little tool and it can be a lot of fun, but using it to watch TV? Isn't that a bit off-the-wall?

Well, maybe it is and maybe it isn't. I can actually think of several reasons why you might want to watch TV on your Pocket PC:

✔ A long cross-country flight would be a whole lot more interesting if you brought along a great movie you could watch. With a set of stereo earphones you could even ignore that boring person sitting next to you who wants to keep yapping the whole way, too.

✔ If you are studying a course that is available on video, imagine how handy it could be to be able to watch the course on your Pocket PC? You could spend the time while you're riding to work on the train or in your carpool learning something useful.

✔ If you want to give a presentation that includes a short video segment, imagine how handy it would be to be able to bring along the presentation on your Pocket PC. And as you'll see later in this chapter, it's even possible to show that video on a large-screen TV, on a desktop PC monitor, or even using a digital projector.

✔ Finally, if you get stuck at a party talking to one of those people who just *has* to show you a whole stack of photos of their *really* ugly grandkids, imagine how cool it would be to whip out your Pocket PC and make them watch a video of your dog singing along to an opera recording!

To watch TV shows on your Pocket PC, you need a means of recording, compressing, and transferring those shows to your Pocket PC. The system that I've found that handles this whole process is SnapStream PVS (`www.snapstream.com`). SnapStream PVS uses a TV tuner card installed in your desktop PC to record TV shows from any available source so that you can watch the shows when it's convenient. This program also has a number of other really cool features such as the capability of supplying streaming video to any PC on your network.

Once you have recorded the show using SnapStream PVS, you can then compress that recording and transfer it to your Pocket PC using PocketPVS. Finally, you can view the show on your Pocket PC, as shown in Figure 17-4.

Figure 17-4:
You can view TV shows on your Pocket PC.

PocketPVS uses Windows Media Player on your Pocket PC to display the video.

To hide the Windows Media Player and display the video as large as possible, select Tools➪Settings➪Audio & Video from the Windows Media Player menu. Then select All from the drop-down Full screen list box and tap OK. This also converts the video playback mode to landscape.

At the default settings, you'll need about 1MB of storage space for every minute of video you store on your Pocket PC. This means that you can probably just fit a typical full-length movie onto a 128MB storage card. If you compare the postage stamp size of a 128MB SD memory card with the size of a standard VHS video tape, this has to be one of the more amazing feats of miniaturization around.

If you don't have a TV tuner card in your desktop PC, SnapStream offers some very good ones at quite reasonable prices on their Web site.

Displaying PowerPoint Shows on Your Pocket PC

Okay, I'll be the first to admit that the screen on your Pocket PC is simply too small to be very effective if you want to give a PowerPoint presentation to a crowd. Even if everyone were really friendly, that tiny screen just wouldn't do the job. If you want to make a good impression, your Pocket PC is going to need a little help. Fortunately, that help is finally here.

I've found a couple of very handy adapter cards that can enable your Pocket PC to display an image using a large-screen monitor, a digital projector, or possibly even a large TV set. With these cards, your Pocket PC can show the world (or at least a large group of people) your PowerPoint presentation or pretty much anything else that appears on your Pocket PC's screen.

Your Pocket PC's screen has a resolution of 240 x 320 pixels — far lower than the typical computer monitor or even a TV set. Fortunately, both of the video adapter cards I discuss have the capability to display a much higher resolution when connected to a large display. In fact, in some cases they are able to display up to 1024 x 768 pixels.

The two Pocket PC video display cards I tested are:

- ✔ Margi Presenter-to-Go (www.margi.com)
- ✔ Colorgraphic Voyager VGA CF (www.colorgraphic.net)

Both of the video adapter cards fit into a CF expansion slot, but the two units do have some differences. Here is a list of the most important differences I found:

✔ The Margi Presenter-to-Go requires a Type 2 CF slot, so you will not be able to use this unit with an HP Jornada Pocket PC.

✔ The Margi Presenter-to-Go includes a remote that works through your Pocket PC's infrared port. This makes it possible to control a PowerPoint presentation from some distance away.

✔ The Colorgraphic Voyager VGA CF has the capability to display your show on a TV set that has a standard composite video input (an RCA jack). This means that you can give a presentation even if a large-screen monitor or a digital projector isn't available.

✔ The Margi Presenter-to-Go includes a basic application for displaying PowerPoint slides. The Colorgraphic Voyager VGA CF includes a shareware version of Conduits Pocket Slides for this purpose.

✔ As this is being written, the Colorgraphic Voyager VGA CF has a slightly lower list price than the Margi Presenter-to-Go. You'll want to check for the latest deals to find out the current price before ordering either one, of course.

Figure 17-5 shows an example of how a PowerPoint slide looks on the Margi Presenter-to-Go. The slides I'm using are from a presentation entitled *Nevada Westerns,* produced by the Nevada Film Office (www.nevadafilm.com) and used by permission of the Deputy Director Robin Holabird.

Figure 17-5:
You can display PowerPoint slide shows using a video adapter card.

The basic presentation software that comes with the Margi Presenter-to-Go displays your slides without any animations or transition effects. If you want to spice up your shows (and maybe keep that guy in the fourth row from falling asleep and snoring in the middle of your presentation), you may want to have a look at a couple of more capable pieces of software:

- ✔ Conduits Pocket Slides (`www.conduits.com`)
- ✔ CNetX Pocket Slide Show (`www.cnetx.com`)

Both of these offer the capability to set up transitions between slides. Conduits Pocket Slides offers a few additional features that enable you to modify the presentation, which you can then save and transfer back to PowerPoint on your desktop PC. Figure 17-6 shows how you can use the stylus during a Conduits Pocket Slides presentation to add onscreen annotations.

Figure 17-6: You can even draw on the screen as you give your presentation.

Regardless of the video adapter card and presentation software you choose, using your Pocket PC for presentations will certainly make it a lot easier for you to bring your show along in your pocket.

Chapter 18

Playing Around with Your Pocket PC

You probably didn't buy a Pocket PC just so you could play games. You may even be one of those people who claim you never waste time playing games. Even if this is true, don't you want to have a little bit of fun? Aren't you at least curious to see just how good a Pocket PC game can be?

Everyone needs a little bit of fun in their life. Even if you're an extremely busy person, it's important to relax sometimes. Taking a few minutes to play a game can be just the ticket to helping you calm down, and surprisingly, may be just what you need to help you solve a problem that's been troubling you. By getting your mind off the problems, you may just find the answers to those problems. So go ahead, take a few minutes to have some fun — it's good for you!

 Even if you skipped over my warning about the necessity of using screen protectors to prevent scratching of your Pocket PC's screen in Chapter 2, it is absolutely vital that you take heed of that warning now — before you begin playing games. I can give you a 100 percent guarantee that you will damage your Pocket PC's screen if you start playing games on it without first adding a screen protector. You've been warned, so any damage you do if you aren't using a screen protector should come as no surprise!

Playing Games

When you really need to play a game, you need it right now. After all, who can predict just when they'll need to spend a few minutes kicking back and taking it easy? That's why your Pocket PC comes with a couple of games — so that you can just get to it and have some fun.

One of the problems with writing about the Pocket PC is that after you get beyond the basics, different brands and even different models of Pocket PCs have differences between them. One area where differences may certainly occur is in the games that come bundled with your Pocket PC. If your Pocket PC doesn't happen to include the games shown in the following sections, you may need to download copies from the Web. I know this is a bummer, but that's just one of the hazards of having choices.

Playing Solitaire

Solitaire is probably the all-time favorite computer game. Sure, there are a lot of fun games that have all sorts of fans, but Solitaire has probably burned up more computer time than virtually any other computer game. One reason for this may simply be that versions of Solitaire are available on almost any type of computer. Solitaire is also the only game that is installed on every Pocket PC right out of the box, so it's a game that I know you can play if you want to do so.

Figure 18-1 shows the Pocket PC version of Solitaire. To play Solitaire, click the Start button and choose Programs from the Start menu. Tap the Games folder and choose Solitaire.

In Figure 18-1, I'm playing the Vegas scoring version of the game. To choose your game options, tap Tools⇨Options on the menu bar to display the Options screen.

If you go really deeply into the hole, you can use Tools⇨Options and select a different scoring method to reset your score.

Hunting mines

The Pocket PC Companion CD-ROM offers three games as a free download through a link in the Entertainment section. These three are Hearts, Reversi, and Minesweeper. Although none of these three is installed by default, you can download and install any of them in a few minutes. Figure 18-2 shows what happens when you tap on one of the squares containing a mine in the Minesweeper game.

If you decide to play Hearts or Reversi, you have the option of playing against another Pocket PC user via the infrared link. Figure 18-3 shows the Play options screen that appears when you start Reversi. If you want to play against a human opponent, you choose one of the options in the lower section of the screen.

Figure 18-1:
If only I could figure out how to get my Pocket PC to pay my Solitaire winnings, I'd be happy.

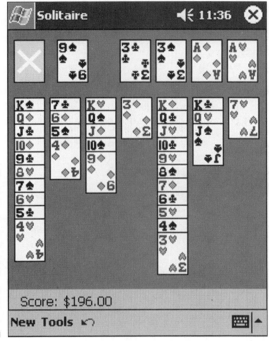

Some Pocket PC manufacturers go a bit beyond the basics when it comes to providing entertainment options. For example, both Casio and HP include some trial versions of some interesting games you might find amusing. But even if your Pocket PC doesn't include these particular games, you can always go to the game manufacturer's Web site and download a trial version of your own.

Golfing in your pocket

Think you've got what it takes to be the next Tiger Woods? If so, check out ZIOGolf 2 on your Pocket PC. Just remember that no matter how much you may want to, bending your stylus around a tree in frustration isn't going to help.

To play ZIOGolf 2, click the Start button and choose Programs from the Start menu. Tap the Games folder and choose ZIOGolf 2.

When you're playing ZIOGolf 2, you control the power of the swing using the "C"-shaped area to the right of the golfer. You can also choose the club, the wind conditions, and the direction of your stroke. What you can't do is to keep your own scorecard. Considering my best two-hole score of 42 strokes, I'm not going to try to tell you anything more about how to play the game — you'll probably do better without my help!

If your Pocket PC doesn't include the demo version, you can download a copy or buy the full 18-hole version on the Web at www.ziosoft.com. You'll also find additional courses you can add to keep the game challenging.

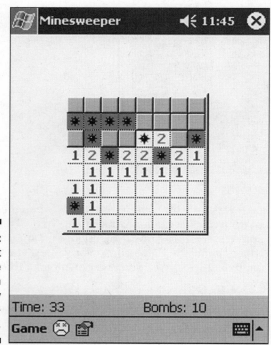

Figure 18-2:
Watch out for the mines when you play Mine-sweeper.

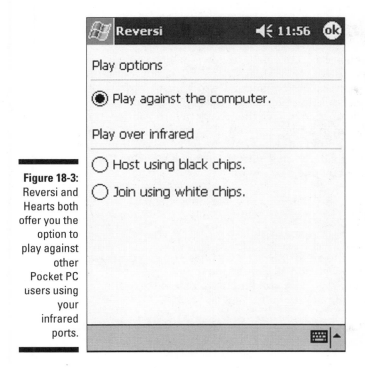

Figure 18-3:
Reversi and
Hearts both
offer you the
option to
play against
other
Pocket PC
users using
your
infrared
ports.

Finding More Games to Challenge You

As you may have guessed, the fertile minds of game developers have created more for the Pocket PC than just the few I've shown you so far. There are dozens of games that have been developed for the Pocket PC.

Pocket PC games come in three or four flavors. Some run on any Pocket PC, so you don't have to worry too much about which version you get. But some games are specifically designed for one processor family and you need to download the correct version for your Pocket PC. When games (or other Pocket PC applications) are designed to run on one processor family, they are usually listed as being for SH3, ARM, or MIPS processors. They may also be listed as intended for a specific brand and model of Pocket PC. All of the Pocket PC 2002 systems use ARM processors — which is the same processor used in the original Compaq iPAQ Pocket PC. If a game says that it is intended for either the Pocket PC 2002 or for the Compaq iPAQ, you will be able to play it on your Pocket PC 2002 unit.

Downloading Pocket PC games

Most Pocket PC games are quite small, so downloading them from the Web is one of the best ways to get them. Many Pocket PC games are free, but you'll also find shareware games and commercial products at various sites. *Shareware* programs come in several varieties, but all share one common thread — you get the chance to give them a try before you buy them. If you like the game, you send in a small amount of money to register your copy. Registration may add extra features, allow the game to continue to be used after it has expired, or simply ease your conscience knowing that you aren't stealing the fruits of someone else's work.

Some Web sites list several varieties of games in a single listing. If you see notations like PPC and HPC (or something similar), the programs you want are those listed as PPC.

One of the first places to go for Pocket PC games you can download is the Pocket PC Downloads Web site at `www.microsoft.com/mobile/pocketpc/downloads/default.asp`. Here you find up-to-date links to the Pocket PC download areas of a number of interesting places.

For freeware and shareware Pocket PC games you can download, one of the best places is the Tucows Web site at `pda.tucows.com/wince/`.

Looking at some other Pocket PC games

The games you can play on your Pocket PC run the gamut from deceptively simple to extremely complex. Some of the best of them are the ones that seem very simple but end up requiring a lot of strategy if you're going to do well.

Next we'll look at some really great games that will really get you itching to play.

Trying out Hexacto Full Hand Casino

If you love to play casino games but you can't always do so — either because a casino isn't next door or because it costs too much, you'll love Hexacto Full Hand Casino. As Figure 18-4 shows, this program includes four different casino games: Blackjack, Roulette, Slot Machine, and Video Poker.

Just how good are the games in Full Hand Casino? Well, I'm not going to tell you how many hours I've spent playing them, but Figure 18-5 shows a sample of the Slot Machine game so you can see for yourself.

Trying out Hexacto Tennis Addict

Hexacto realizes that not everyone is a casino game fan. That's why they have released several other games for the Pocket PC including the Tennis Addict game, shown in Figure 18-6. As this figure shows, Tennis Addict changes your Pocket PC's screen into landscape mode for a more enjoyable playing experience.

Figure 18-6:
Tennis Addict gives you a chance to play a rousing game of tennis without ever breaking a sweat.

You'll find a whole bunch of really fun games at the Hexacto Web site (www.hexacto.com). Just don't blame me if you end up spending all of your time playing.

Part VI
Working with Pocket PC Add-ons

The 5th Wave   By Rich Tennant

"I think my body's energy centers ARE well balanced. I keep my pager on my belt, my cell phone in my right pocket, and my Pocket PC in my inside left breast pocket."

In this part . . .

You'll see where to find Pocket PC programs, how to install them, and how to make the ones you want fit into the available space. You'll learn what you need to make traveling with your Pocket PC a truly enjoyable experience by adding the right pieces to make your Pocket PC into a great traveling companion.

Chapter 19

Finding Pocket PC Applications

. . . .

. . . .

*O*ne of the greatest features of the Pocket PC is that it's a real PC. That is, your Pocket PC isn't limited to performing just one or two dedicated functions. By adding new programs, you can use your Pocket PC for virtually unlimited purposes. In fact, almost anything that can be done with a desktop PC can also be done with a Pocket PC.

Getting the right programs for your Pocket PC can be a little confusing. In this chapter, I help clear up some of that confusion so that you're able to get what you want from your Pocket PC.

Understanding What Will Run on the Pocket PC

Your Pocket PC uses an operating system called Windows CE 3.0. From this name you may get the impression that any of your Windows programs from your desktop PC can run on your Pocket PC, but this simply isn't so. Windows CE 3.0 may be related to the version of Windows that runs on your desktop PC, but the relationship isn't quite close enough to allow you to share most of your programs.

Here are some important things you need to know about what will run on your Pocket PC:

> ✔ If a program is specified as being specifically for the Pocket PC, it will almost certainly run on your Pocket PC — unless the specifications also indicate that the program is for a specific processor.

- All of the Pocket PC 2002 models use the ARM processor, which was introduced originally in the Compaq iPAQ. Therefore, virtually any program that is intended for the iPAQ Pocket PCs will run on every Pocket PC 2002 system.

- If a program is designed for SH3-based Pocket PCs, that generally means it will run on HP Jornada 540 series Pocket PCs. This type of program will not run on the Pocket PC 2002 models.

- If a program is designed for MIPS-based Pocket PCs, that generally means it will run on Casio E-125 Pocket PCs. Once again, these programs will not run on Pocket PC 2002 units.

- Many programs designed for Windows CE 2.0 will also run on the Pocket PC, but it's best to try before you buy. Windows CE 2.0 programs swap the positions of the Pocket PC's Start button and the program's menu or toolbar, but this change is temporary. After you exit the Windows CE 2.0 program, your Pocket PC returns to normal.

- Some programs are listed as being for "palm-sized" PCs. This term could mean many things. For example, it may mean that the program is really for the Palm PC OS (operating system) and is totally incompatible with your Pocket PC. Don't buy one of these programs unless you get some assurance you can get your money back if it doesn't work on your Pocket PC.

- If a program says that it's for Windows CE HPC or HPC/Pro devices, it probably won't work on your Pocket PC unless it specifically says that it also runs on PPC devices. You may even see other variations on this jargon jungle, so always watch for the PPC or Pocket PC designation.

One of the most important things to ask when buying Pocket PC software is whether you can try the program to make sure it works before you plunk down your money. Many Pocket PC programs have demo or trial versions you can check out before buying. If you can't get a trial first, make certain you can get a refund if the program won't work on your Pocket PC.

Finding Pocket PC Software on the Web

Most Pocket PC software is distributed by way of downloads from the Internet. One of the big reasons for this is simply that Pocket PC software tends to be very compact compared to desktop PC software. An awful lot of function can be packed into a very small package when it's a package intended for the Pocket PC.

The Web sites that distribute Pocket PC software tend to fall into two major categories: Web sites that belong to software developers and Web sites that offer software from many different manufacturers. Each has advantages and disadvantages:

✔ A software developer's Web site generally offers only those products produced by that one company, which limits your choices somewhat compared to the more general sites.

✔ A Web site that offers software from a variety of manufacturers gives you more choices and often uses a rating system to help you decide which products best suit your needs.

✔ The software developer's Web site may have the most recent updates sooner than the general sites. You may also find *beta* versions that enable you to test features that will appear in upcoming release versions (beta software is software that isn't quite ready for prime time — it's a test version that may contain a number of bugs and other gremlins to make life interesting for the testers).

Figure 19-1 shows the Web site of Developer One, a Pocket PC software developer. You can find this site at `www.developerone.com/`.

Figure 19-2 shows a more general Web site — that of Handango — where you'll find Pocket PC software from a number of different manufacturers. You can find the Handango Pocket PC software Web site at `mobile.handango.com/`.

Figure 19-1:
Developer
One sells
their own
software for
the Pocket
PC on their
Web site.

Figure 19-2:
The Hand-
ango Web
site offers
Pocket PC
software
from many
manu-
facturers.

Some other good Pocket PC software download sites include:

- ✔ www.microsoft.com/mobile/pocketpc/downloads/default.asp
- ✔ pda.tucows.com/
- ✔ www.pocketgear.com/

Getting down to business

Chapter 18 introduces many different types of games for your Pocket PC.
Games may be a lot of fun, but playing games doesn't get your work done. If
you want to get down to business with your Pocket PC, plenty of programs
are available to help you do so.

Here is just a sample of some of the types of business-related programs you
find for the Pocket PC:

✔ Several developers have filled an important gap in the suite of built-in Pocket PC applications by creating database programs. These types of programs can be extremely useful for anyone who needs to keep track of lots of information, such as an inventory listing or the status of rooms in a large convention hotel.

If you want to use a large database on your Pocket PC, the built-in storage memory will likely need to be expanded using a memory card.

✔ A number of developers have created Pocket PC programs that are loaded with tons of different unit conversions, which can be quite useful for anyone working on a large international project or for someone ordering supplies for a building project.

✔ Closely related to the conversion programs are the applications that turn your Pocket PC into a super-sophisticated calculator. Anyone involved in science or in financial calculations will certainly find these programs quite useful.

✔ Finally, there are even programs that enable you to send a fax from your Pocket PC. Even though e-mail capability is built into the Pocket PC, remember that some people don't have an e-mail address, so being able to send them a fax may be the only way to quickly get written information into their hands.

Chapter 22 shows some specific examples of some very useful business-related Pocket PC programs. Figure 19-3 shows one Pocket PC business program, Pocket Database from Surerange. One difference you'll notice between programs for your Pocket PC and those for your desktop PC is that Pocket PC programs tend to be far less expensive, making it a lot easier to justify adding that handy units conversion program or that database program you could really use.

Adding some utilities

Utility programs are the Rodney Dangerfield class of Pocket PC applications — they don't get the kind of respect they deserve. But that's to be expected because most people don't want to put a lot of thought into the inner workings of their Pocket PC. Still, the utility programs do have a lot to offer:

✔ Closing down programs on a Pocket PC isn't always easy because your Pocket PC is supposed to close unneeded programs when something else needs the memory. Still, it's really nice to have a utility program that allows you to easily switch between open programs and to decide for yourself which ones to shut down.

✔ Because memory space is so important on a Pocket PC, several utilities were designed to help you manage memory. Some seek out useless files that can be deleted, while others make it possible to cram more into memory by compressing data into less space.

✔ Since many important documents are only available in PDF format, you may want to be able to read those types of documents on your Pocket PC.

✔ If you often use your Pocket PC to perform complicated tasks that require a whole series of precise steps, you'll certainly find a scripting utility quite useful. A scripting utility enables you to create a script that goes through the whole process for you so you don't have to keep on repeating it yourself.

These are just a few examples of the broad range of useful utility programs you'll find for your Pocket PC. Figure 19-4 shows one of these utilities, Adobe Acrobat Reader.

Many utility programs are ones you use only occasionally. Rather than using up memory on your Pocket PC by keeping them loaded all the time, you may want to load them when you need them and then remove them after you're done using them. You can always use ActiveSync to reload these programs from your desktop PC as necessary.

Abbreviation	Meaning
Adm	admiral
adv	adverb
AEC	Atomic Energy
aet	aetatis or aged
AH	anno Hegirae or
AI	artificial
AIDS	acquired immune
AL	American
Ald	alderman
AM	ante meridiem or
AM	amplitude
AM	Artium Magister or
AMDG	ad majorem dei
anon	anonymous
ANZAC	Australian and
AOH	Ancient Order of
AP	Associated Press
APO	Army Post Office

🗔 Database   ◀€ 12:12   ⊗

File Edit View Record Search

Figure 19-3: A database program is a very handy addition to your Pocket PC.

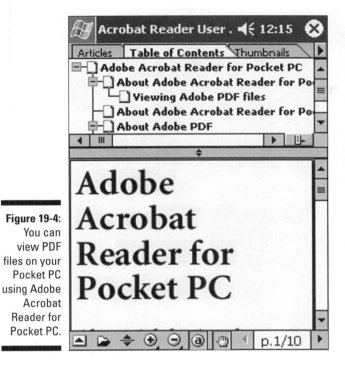

Figure 19-4:
You can view PDF files on your Pocket PC using Adobe Acrobat Reader for Pocket PC.

Loading Programs You've Downloaded

When it comes to installing new programs on your Pocket PC, your Pocket PC and your desktop PC really are companions — you generally need your desktop PC to help install programs on your Pocket PC. There are a few rare exceptions, but most programs must first be loaded onto your desktop PC and then added to your Pocket PC.

Here I step through a typical Pocket PC program installation so you know what to expect when you want to add new programs to your Pocket PC:

1. **Open Windows Explorer and locate the installation program.**

   Make note of the location that the program is saved to when you download the program. If you obtained the Pocket PC program on CD-ROM or diskette, obviously you'll find the installation program there.

2. **Open the installation program.**

   This screen serves one very important purpose — it tells you which program you're trying to install.

3. Click Next to continue.

You now probably have several steps that may include accepting a license agreement, choosing where to store the files on your desktop PC, and choosing where you want the program to appear on your desktop PC's Start menu. Continue through these steps until you see a message similar to the one shown in Figure 19-5.

Figure 19-5:
This message indicates you've completed the desktop PC setup and are ready to begin the Pocket PC setup.

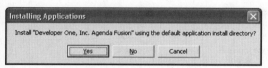

4. In most cases you want to click Yes to begin installing the program onto your Pocket PC.

The one exception is if you want to install the program onto a memory storage card. If so, you would click No and then step through designating the directory where you do want to install the program on your Pocket PC.

5. When you see the message shown in Figure 19-6, you've finished with your desktop PC and need to look at your Pocket PC's screen to see whether you need to do anything there.

Typically there's nothing required on your Pocket PC, but a few programs make you disconnect your Pocket PC and press the reset button.

6. Tap OK to finish.

Be sure to read the user's manual, installation notes, or any other documentation that comes with your Pocket PC programs. Often you find some excellent tips that help you make the most of the program you just installed.

Figure 19-6:
Be sure to
look at your
Pocket PC's
screen to
see whether
you still
need to do
anything
to com-
plete the
installation.

Freeing Up Memory

There's an old saying that basically says you can't be too thin or too rich. When it comes to Pocket PCs, you can say that you can't have too much memory. Your Pocket PC differs in one very fundamental way from your desktop PC — your Pocket PC must store all programs and data in memory at all times. Your desktop PC, on the other hand, can put unused stuff out on a disk somewhere until it's needed.

This difference between your Pocket PC and your desktop PC is an important one. The difference means that you can't simply add new programs whenever you want without making certain there's enough room for them. On a desktop PC with gigabytes of disk space, you'll probably outgrow your desktop PC long before you need to worry about it. On a Pocket PC, available space can be an issue almost as soon as you start adding new programs.

Unloading programs you don't need

One of the great things about having your desktop PC and your Pocket PC as partners in installing Pocket PC software is that you can typically remove programs from your Pocket PC and yet still have them available if you later decide to reinstall them. And because you may have to unload some programs when you want to try out some new Pocket PC software, this can be a real lifesaver!

There are two primary ways to unload programs from your Pocket PC. You can either remove them using just your Pocket PC, or you can use ActiveSync on your desktop PC to remove them. Both methods work, so it's really up to you to figure out which you prefer.

Unloading programs using ActiveSync

If you want to remove programs from your Pocket PC by working through ActiveSync on your desktop PC, here's what you need to do:

1. **Place your Pocket PC in the synchronization cradle and open ActiveSync if it isn't already open.**

   Of course, if you are using a wireless network connection for your Pocket PC, you can skip the part about placing it in the synchronization cradle since your network connection is likely much faster than the USB connection — meaning that the wireless connection is a better option for installing and removing most programs.

2. **Select Tools⇨Add/Remove Programs from the ActiveSync menu.**

   ActiveSync examines your Pocket PC to see which programs are currently installed and then displays the Add/Remove Programs dialog box (see Figure 19-7).

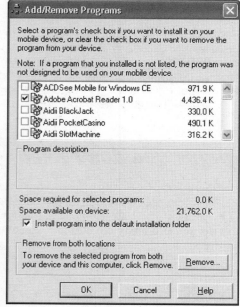

Figure 19-7:
You can add or remove programs from your Pocket PC using ActiveSync on your desktop PC.

3. **Remove the check from any programs you want to uninstall from your Pocket PC.**

    You can also add a check to any of the listed programs you do want to install.

    Don't click the Remove button — doing so removes the program from both your Pocket PC and your desktop PC.

4. **Click OK to make the changes.**

    Be sure to look at your Pocket PC's screen to see whether you need to do anything else like reset your Pocket PC.

Using ActiveSync on your desktop PC to remove programs from your Pocket PC has another advantage you may not have considered. By using ActiveSync, you can be sure that you still have the option to reinstall the program if necessary. If you uninstall a program directly on your Pocket PC as shown in the next section, it's possible to remove programs and not be able to reinstall them without first downloading the installation program from the Web.

Unloading programs directly on your Pocket PC

If you'd rather work directly on your Pocket PC, you can uninstall programs without using your desktop PC, which may be your only choice if you're away from your desk but need to download a large file directly into your Pocket PC using your Internet connection.

Here's how to unload programs directly from your Pocket PC:

1. **Tap the Start button on your Pocket PC and select Settings.**

2. **Click the System tab and then tap the Memory icon.**

3. **In the Memory Settings screen, tap Remove Programs to display the list of programs that are currently installed in your Pocket PC's storage memory (see Figure 19-8).**

4. **Select any of the programs you want to uninstall and then click the Remove button.**

5. **Tap OK when you have removed everything you want and are finished.**

You've probably noticed that neither using ActiveSync on your desktop PC nor using Remove Programs directly on your Pocket PC offers you the option of removing all the programs on your Pocket PC. That's because the basic applications on your Pocket PC — things like Pocket Word and Pocket Excel — are loaded permanently into your Pocket PC's *ROM* (Read-Only

Memory). Even though these items are loaded into permanent memory, it is possible to update them using special software that can modify *Flash ROM* — a special type of ROM included in all Pocket PC 2002 systems specifically so that updates can be made if necessary.

Deleting unneeded files

Of course, programs aren't the only files that can eat up memory space on your Pocket PC. It's a sure bet that there are a lot of other files you don't need anymore that are simply wasting space.

You have several ways to remove unneeded files from your Pocket PC. For example, if you've loaded a bunch of eBooks into the Microsoft Reader library, you can delete those books when you're done with them using the tap-and-hold method. You then select Delete from the pop-up menu, and you've sent them off into digital nothingness.

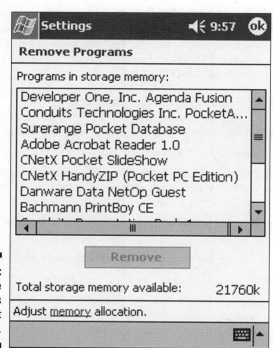

Figure 19-8:
Choose the programs you want to remove.

You may think that the Find link on the Memory settings screen offers a good way to find and delete unneeded files. If so, you'd be half right. Sure, you *can* use the find tool to locate files, but you can't delete them once you've found them.

A better way to find and delete files is to use the File Explorer, shown in Figure 19-9. Here you can not only locate but also delete files.

To open File Explorer, click the Start button and choose Programs. Then tap the File Explorer icon.

To view your files sorted by size (or some other sort order), tap the sort list just below the time display and choose the sort order you prefer.

Using a memory card to hold extras

No matter how hard you try, sometimes it's just not possible to squeeze everything you need into your Pocket PC's built-in memory. That's when you need to look for an alternative.

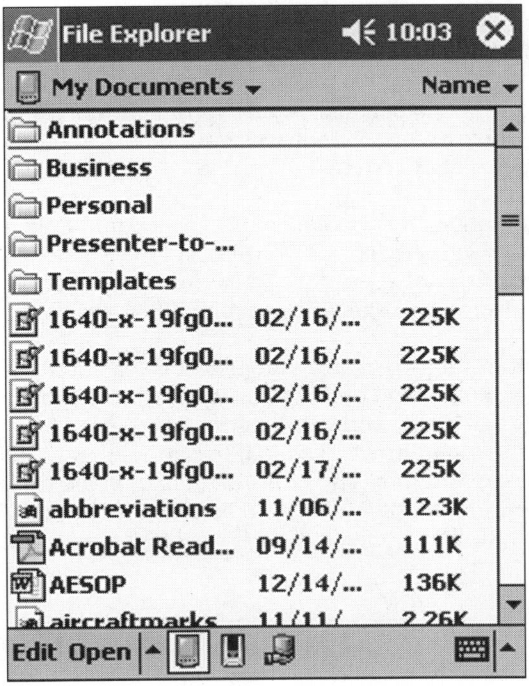

Figure 19-9:
Use File Explorer to manage the files on your Pocket PC.

File Explorer	◀€ 10:03 ✕
My Documents ▾	Name ▾

📁 Annotations		
📁 Business		
📁 Personal		
📁 Presenter-to-...		
📁 Templates		
📄 1640-x-19fg0...	02/16/...	225K
📄 1640-x-19fg0...	02/16/...	225K
📄 1640-x-19fg0...	02/16/...	225K
📄 1640-x-19fg0...	02/16/...	225K
📄 1640-x-19fg0...	02/17/...	225K
📄 abbreviations	11/06/...	12.3K
📄 Acrobat Read...	09/14/...	111K
📄 AESOP	12/14/...	136K
📄 aircraftmarks	11/11/	2.26K

Edit Open

All Pocket PCs are expandable, but it can be tricky getting the right pieces to fit your particular Pocket PC. You need to be sure that any memory card you buy will actually fit your unit.

- ✔ The most common type of memory expansion on the Pocket PC is the CF (or Compact Flash) memory card.
- ✔ Most Pocket PC 2002 systems have a second expansion slot specifically designed for SD (Secure Digital) memory cards.
- ✔ Compaq Pocket PCs present a special challenge when you want to expand your memory; you need to buy an expansion sleeve that pops onto the back of the Pocket PC.

If you really want to expand the storage capabilities of your Pocket PC, you may want to consider the IBM Microdrive. The 1GB Microdrive is the better choice of the Microdrive models for Pocket PC use because it actually uses less power than the smaller capacity units. Note, however, that the IBM Microdrives are not compatible with the HP Jornada Pocket PCs.

Using HandyZIP

Almost anyone who uses a PC has encountered *zipped* — compressed — files at some point. By using one of the popular ZIP utilities such as WinZIP (www.winzip.com) you can compress files so that they take less room and so that they are faster to send via e-mail. Because of the far more limited storage space on a Pocket PC, being able to compress your files is even more important than it is on your desktop system.

Unfortunately, the ZIP utility that you use on your desktop PC won't work on your Pocket PC. To work with ZIP files on your Pocket PC, you'll need a ZIP utility such as HandyZIP (www.cnetx.com) designed specifically for use on your Pocket PC. Figure 19-10 shows an example of HandyZIP at work with a ZIP file.

Outlook 2002 has built-in security features that block certain types of file attachments. If you send an e-mail message containing an attachment that Outlook 2002 considers to be potentially dangerous, the recipient will not be able to open or save the attachment — even if the attachment really is safe. One of the best ways to avoid this type of problem is to place the attachment into a ZIP file and then send the ZIP file as the message attachment. Outlook 2002 doesn't block ZIP file attachments, so the recipient will be able to open and save your attachment.

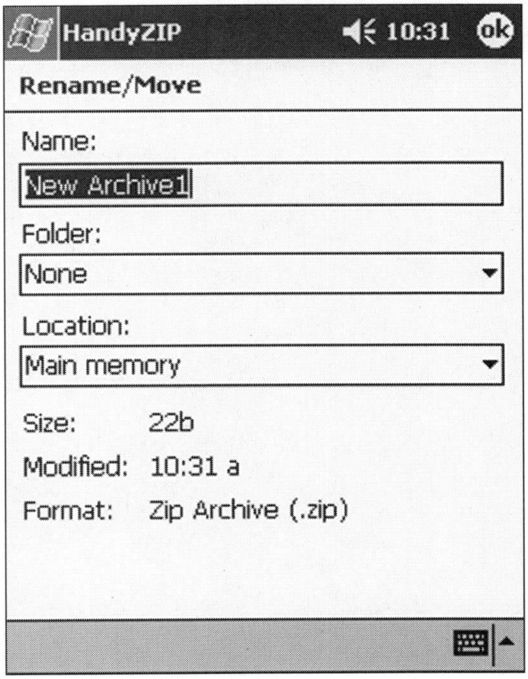

HandyZIP ◀€ 10:31 **ok**

Rename/Move

Name:
New Archive1

Folder:
None ▼

Location:
Main memory ▼

Size: 22b

Modified: 10:31 a

Format: Zip Archive (.zip)

Figure 19-10:
Use Handy-
ZIP to work
with ZIP
files on your
Pocket PC.

Chapter 20

Traveling with Your Pocket PC

. . . .

. . . .

*Y*ou probably wouldn't think of taking your desktop PC along on a trip, and even a laptop PC isn't all that convenient as a traveling companion. Your Pocket PC, though, is just the right size to bring along almost anywhere you're going. What's more, your Pocket PC can really make traveling a whole lot more enjoyable.

Your Pocket PC as a Traveling Companion

Traveling can be a lot of fun. Traveling can also be stressful — especially if you don't know where you're going or you can't speak the local language. Your Pocket PC is a really great tool for helping you cope with the problems that can make travel less enjoyable than it should be.

Using your Pocket PC while traveling

Normal life doesn't stop simply because you've hopped onto a plane for some far-off vacation spot. Sometimes it even seems as though more stuff happens when you try to get away for a few days. If you've ever returned from a trip and found that you have 362 e-mail messages waiting for you, you know exactly what I mean.

Your Pocket PC can help you keep things under control even when you're off on a trip. Here are some things your Pocket PC can do for you while you're traveling:

✔ Your Pocket PC can help tame the e-mail monster by letting you send and receive e-mail on the go. You can quickly delete the 50 percent of messages that are simply junk mail, and you can handle the small percentage of messages that really can't wait for you to get back. The rest can simply wait until you get home, but at least you won't have nearly so many to deal with when you do get back.

✔ You can use your Pocket PC to check local weather forecasts so you know what to plan. After all, there's no sense trying to plan a day at the beach if a sudden cold snap is coming in tomorrow. Maybe that wax museum won't be quite as lame as you thought.

✔ If you suddenly get the urge for a great ethnic meal, you can use your Pocket PC to find restaurant ratings on the Internet for the area in which you're traveling. Not all of your vacation meals have to come out of a fast food bag, do they?

✔ If the place you're visiting turns out to be really boring, you can log on to your favorite cheap tickets Web site and find out what other destinations are available at the last minute and at bargain prices. Who knows, maybe you'll find round-trip tickets to Aruba for $100 if you're willing to take off in two hours.

✔ Finally, if you get a hot tip, you can whip out your Pocket PC and access your online stockbroker. You may even pay for the whole trip with a single trade!

Pocket PC travel considerations

Traveling with your Pocket PC should be as simple and carefree as possible. If your Pocket PC is going to make travel easier and more fun, dealing with problems along the way is about the last thing you want to do. Here are some things to remember to make your Pocket PC a better traveling companion:

✔ Pocket PCs can run only as long as they have power. Because virtually all Pocket PCs use built-in batteries, you can't just pop into the local drugstore and get new batteries for your Pocket PC. Make certain you bring your AC adapter along so you can recharge your Pocket PC's batteries when necessary.

If you're going to be traveling in a foreign country, you probably need an adapter to plug in the Pocket PC's AC adapter. These adapters for foreign outlets can be hard to find on the road, so I suggest visiting the iGo Web site (www.igo.com) to buy the right adapters before you leave.

✔ You may want to consider one of the solar panel options I mention in Chapter 21. That way you can avoid the whole funny electrical outlet mess while you show everyone just how green you really are.

✔ Connecting to the Internet while you're on a trip can be a real experience. Research the local access numbers before you go so you know how to access your ISP. You also need to know what toll-free numbers are available because local access numbers have a tendency to change frequently.

✔ If you're using a digital phone card to access the Internet through your cell phone, make sure you know the access number for your cell phone service provider's Internet service, which may save you from paying expensive long distance charges.

✔ If you're going to be traveling in a foreign country, check out your Internet access options before you go. Some countries require special types of modems, and you may well find that your cell phone can't connect. Even if you're able to connect easily, make certain you aren't paying expensive international long distance rates to access the Internet.

✔ It's even possible that some countries may consider your Pocket PC or some of its accessories — especially things like GPS receivers — to be spying equipment. You can lose your Pocket PC or even be thrown in jail if the local authorities are feeling especially hostile towards foreigners. If you're in doubt about countries you'll be traveling through, check with your travel professional before bringing along your Pocket PC.

✔ Finally, a Pocket PC can look pretty attractive to a thief. Be sure to set a system password before you go (see Chapter 2), and don't put your Pocket PC down anywhere where it becomes an easy target.

Finding Your Way — Without Asking for Directions

No one really likes to stop and ask for directions. Sure, there are some people (men and women) who make a joke about how members of the opposite sex (again, men *and* women) will drive on into oblivion because they refuse to ask for directions, but the ones making that joke probably couldn't tell whether a map were upside-down or backwards, anyway.

One of the problems with asking for directions is simple — the directions most people give are usually so poor that no one could follow them even if they wanted to. When people give directions they tend to forget to include a lot of important details. I don't want to know that I'm supposed to turn by Mrs. Jones' apple tree; I want to know that I need to follow Highway 101 for 2.3 miles and then turn right onto Crosspointe Boulevard.

Reading maps on your Pocket PC

Road maps are the standard tool for finding your way around in unfamiliar territory. Of course, finding the right maps and keeping track of them while you're traveling just adds additional complication to what should be an enjoyable trip. To cut down the clutter and make things a bit easier, you can download maps onto your Pocket PC.

Your Pocket PC comes with a program called Pocket Streets that you can use to display maps on your screen. You can use maps from Microsoft Streets & Trips, Microsoft MapPoint, or Microsoft AutoRoute Express Great Britain with Pocket Streets. Pocket Streets doesn't include any maps of its own. You must either download maps from your desktop PC or from the Web (www.microsoft.com/pocketstreets).

If Pocket Streets isn't already installed on your Pocket PC, you'll find a link on the Pocket PC Companion CD-ROM in the Mobility section. Depending on the mapping program you have installed on your desktop PC, you may have been given the option to install Pocket Streets when you installed the mapping program.

Figure 20-1 shows how Pocket Streets shows a map (which happens to be the map to my favorite campground on the Oregon coast). You use the arrows in the lower right of the map display to pan the map, and you use the plus and minus symbols to zoom. If you want to mark a location, you use the pushpin in the toolbar at the bottom of the screen.

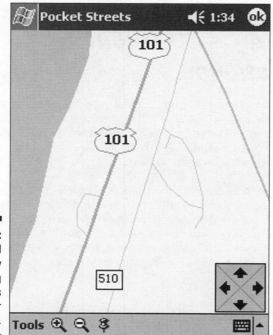

Figure 20-1:
You can find your way by taking along some maps on your Pocket PC.

Connecting a GPS to your Pocket PC

If you've ever been lost, you're going to love adding a *GPS* (Global Positioning Satellite) receiver to your Pocket PC. This innovation has made it possible to always have an accurate fix on your precise position to within 100 feet of your exact location. If you have a GPS and still get lost, you've got to be really trying to get lost!

GPS receivers work by comparing radio signals from a series of satellites that are circling the earth. In order to actually receive these very weak signals, your GPS receiver must be in a position where it can actually "see" the sky directly overhead, which means that a GPS receiver generally won't work inside your house, while you're driving through a tunnel, or even in a forest if the canopy of trees overhead is too dense. It also means that when you first try out your GPS unit, you're likely to find the whole experience a little frustrating if you're attempting to get familiar with it in the comfort of your office. Go outside, and your GPS receiver will begin to work as soon as it can see the satellites.

Getting the right GPS receiver

Several different GPS receiver manufacturers exist, so you have a number of choices in buying a GPS receiver to team up with your Pocket PC. First you need to decide which type of hardware you want. GPS receivers designed for use with the Pocket PC come in two general flavors:

- ✔ Some GPS receivers — such as the Pharos iGPS-180 — connect to your Pocket PC using the serial connector at the bottom of your Pocket PC. That means that the connection is made through the same connector you use to connect your Pocket PC to your desktop PC (your Pocket PC uses the same connector for both serial and USB connections). This type of GPS receiver requires a special cable that is designed for your Pocket PC model. These types of GPS receivers also include an adapter that plugs into the 12-volt power outlet on your car's dash to power both the GPS receiver and your Pocket PC.

- ✔ A number of CF-slot GPS receivers are also available from companies such as Teletype, Pretec, and Pharos. These GPS receivers plug into the CF slot on the top of your Pocket PC so that you can use your Pocket PC and the GPS receiver as a single, compact unit. These units are especially handy for use when you are hiking since they don't depend on being powered by your car.

The CF GPS receivers all have a small jack on the side where you can attach an external antenna. This extra-cost option is intended for situations where the GPS receiver cannot receive a strong enough signal — such as inside a vehicle. My experience has been that the GPS receivers typically do not need the external antenna, so I recommend that you try using the GPS to see whether the external antenna is needed in your situation before spending extra on the antenna.

In addition to choosing between the two types of GPS receivers, you will need to decide on the mapping software that you will use. All of the GPS receivers can be used with Pocket Streets (but you will need to make certain that you have Pocket Streets 2002 SR-1 or later to use a GPS with Pocket Streets). Even though Pocket Streets will work with a GPS receiver, you'll probably find that the software that comes with your GPS receiver offers some advantages. For example:

- ✔ All of the GPS manufacturers provide routing options so that your Pocket PC can give you turn-by-turn directions as you drive. Since the route is drawn on your Pocket PC's screen in a contrasting color, you can easily tell when you're coming up to a turn.

- ✔ Some of the navigation software includes voice prompts so that your Pocket PC will tell you to "turn right" when necessary. The voice prompts are also nice enough to let you know when you are off course — without adding any comments about your map-reading abilities.

- ✔ Another useful option you'll find in some of the programs is a travel guide, which can direct you to points of interest such as notable local restaurants. You won't have to put up with a greasy burger from some roadside fast food place unless that's what you really want.

It can be difficult to decide which features are most important. You may want to visit the GPS manufacturers' Web sites for a rundown of the features included in the current software versions before you make your choice.

Although the GPS manufacturers don't really want you to know this, I have found that any of the navigation software can be used with any of the Pocket PC–compatible GPS receivers. This does not mean, however, that all of the GPS receivers are identical. It simply means that they all adhere to the *NEMA* standard — which is simply the means by which GPS receivers transmit data to computers.

Table 20-1 lists three sources for Pocket PC–compatible GPS receivers. I have tested units from each of these manufacturers, and they all work well with Pocket PCs.

Table 20-1	Pocket PC–Compatible GPS Receivers
Manufacturer	*Web Site*
Pharos Science & Applications	www.pharosgps.com
Pretec	www.pretec.com
Teletype	www.teletype.com

Storing your GPS maps

One of the biggest problems with using a GPS receiver with any type of hand-held device is simply that detailed maps can take a lot of space. And because you probably want the best, most detailed map possible when you're traveling, you'll almost certainly find that storage space on your Pocket PC is suddenly a big issue. Here are some possible solutions:

✔ Try downloading a map that covers a smaller area or one that has less detail.

✔ You can uninstall pretty much everything else from your Pocket PC's built-in storage memory. Of course, this greatly reduces the value of your Pocket PC as a traveling companion, and it still may not even give you enough room for some maps.

✔ You can add a memory storage card to your Pocket PC and store your maps there. This is by far the best solution, and the only one I can recommend (unless, of course, your GPS receiver is already using the expansion slot). This is an especially good solution with those Pocket PC 2002 systems that have two independent expansion slots.

The software user's manual for your GPS receiver has information on the specific procedures necessary to download maps from your desktop PC to your Pocket PC.

Using your GPS receiver

You have two ways to use a GPS receiver along with your Pocket PC: navigating by latitude and longitude and navigating using maps. If you need to navigate to a specific location using latitude and longitude, the GPS receiver can show you this in very fine detail (see Figure 20-2).

Using the software that comes with a GPS receiver, you select View⇨GPS Info (or something very similar) to view the information shown in Figure 20-2.

Use the GPS Info display to identify a precise location even when a map is unavailable for an area. For example, you can use this display to return to the exact spot on a large lake where you caught all those fish on your last fishing trip, and you won't have to worry about leaving any markers that may tip off some other anglers to your favorite hot spot.

Your GPS receiver must be able to locate at least three Global Positioning satellites in order to determine your location. To see how many satellites are currently in view, select View⇨Sat. Info (or something similar). Figure 20-3 shows that eight satellites are currently in view, and four have a strong enough signal to be useful (the bars near the bottom of the display show the signal strength).

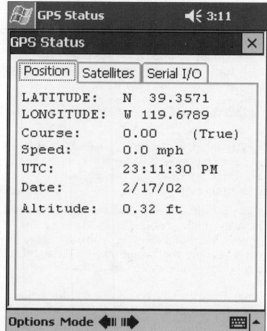

Figure 20-2:
With a GPS receiver attached, your Pocket PC can show your exact location.

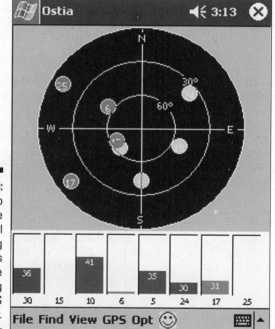

Figure 20-3:
You can also see where the Global Positioning satellites are in the sky using your GPS receiver.

Most of the time you'll want to have your Pocket PC and GPS receiver show your location on a map, which is especially useful if you're trying to find an address. The GPS software can plot a course using the roads on the map and then all you have to do is follow that course. As you move along, the display constantly updates so you can see your current location, making it very easy to see when you need to turn. You can even get voice prompts so you don't have to watch the display.

Trying to navigate with your Pocket PC and a GPS receiver while you are driving can be very dangerous. If possible, have someone else watch the display or make certain that you have a good idea of your route before you begin driving. If your navigation software offers voice prompts, this can also increase the safety factor considerably.

Using your Pocket PC as a pilot's companion

If you happen to be a pilot, you certainly can appreciate the small size of a Pocket PC. Nothing else is quite as cramped as the cockpit of a typical private aircraft. So when it comes to choosing tools to help you plan a trip and find your way, you want something that will do a lot for you and not take up too much room — and if this doesn't describe a Pocket PC, I don't know what does!

I've discovered two very useful programs aimed at Pocket PC owners who happen to also be pilots. While I don't have a lot of room to devote to these two, I would like to give you a quick look at them and then suggest that you visit the manufacturers' Web sites for more information.

The first of these programs is Hahn's FlightPlanner (www.hahnsllc.com), shown in Figure 20-4. This program offers complete flight-planning functions and will even assist you in filing a flight plan.

The next program you should check out is Control Vision's MovingMap (www.controlvision.com), shown in Figure 20-5. This software works with your GPS receiver to provide you in-flight information about your current position as well as real-time weather so you can avoid problems that might disrupt your flight.

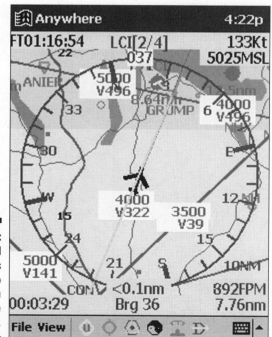

STATION	WEIGHT	MOMENT	
Empty W...	1600	60.7	
Fuel	0	0.0	
Pilot & Co...	0	0.0	
Rear passa...	0	0.0	
Baggage ...	0	0.0	
Baggage ...	0	0.0	
Runup allo...	0	0.0	
=======	====...	====...	
TOTAL:	1600.0	60.7	
STATUS	In Ran...	In Range	
VALID			
MOMENT	MIN	56.0	
RANGE	MAX	75.5	

Weight & Balance - Fligt 8:50

Flight View

Figure 20-4:
Hahn's Flight-Planner will help you handle all of the details necessary in preparing your flight plans.

Anywhere 4:22p

FT01:16:54   LCI[2/4]   133Kt
037   5025MSL

File View

Figure 20-5:
Control Vision's MovingMap keeps you on course in the air.

Speaking the Language

One of the most difficult things about visiting foreign countries is that they speak all those foreign languages.

Aside from learning the languages that are spoken in the areas where you want to travel, getting a language translator that runs on your Pocket PC may be one of the best ways to deal with understanding what's going on when you're traveling. Getting a quick translation may also be the key to keeping yourself out of trouble, as Figure 20-6 illustrates.

One product I've found for translating between languages on the Pocket PC is the Ectaco Language Teacher (shown in Figure 20-6). This software is available in versions for many different languages.

Ectaco offers demo versions that you can download for free. As always, try out the demo to be sure it works properly on your Pocket PC before you buy the full version.

Figure 20-6: Being able to translate foreign language into something you can understand can come in handy.

In addition to helping when you're traveling, Ectaco Language Teacher can also be handy in helping you in other interesting ways:

✔ You can impress your dinner companions by translating menu items in an ethnic restaurant. Of course, you do run the risk of spoiling their appetite when you tell them what's really in that dish they just ordered.

✔ If you're looking for obscure information on the Web, you may be able to find what you need only on some of the foreign language sites. You can try translating a few key words into other languages and then doing your online search. You still have the problem of translating your results, but you may find information that simply isn't available any other way.

✔ If you need to insult someone but don't want him to know what you said, you can translate your insult into a language he doesn't understand. (Just don't tell him where to find the translator.)

Part VII
The Part of Tens

The 5th Wave By Rich Tennant

MUST HAVE LEFT IT IN MY POCKET WHEN I DID THE LAUNDRY. NOT GOOOD ON A SALES CALL.

In this part . . .

You see the best Pocket PC accessories, see the best Pocket PC business programs, and have some fun discovering the best Pocket PC games.

Chapter 21

Ten Great Pocket PC Accessories

· ·

In This Chapter

▶ Finding out what works with your Pocket PC

▶ Adding storage to your Pocket PC

▶ Finding the best ways to communicate with your Pocket PC

▶ Using your Pocket PC to navigate

▶ Adding a keyboard

▶ Keeping your Pocket PC powered

▶ Protecting your Pocket PC

▶ Mounting your Pocket PC in your car

▶ Connecting your Pocket PC to a big-screen display

▶ Getting the most from your Pocket PC

· ·

*P*ocket PCs are a lot of fun all by themselves, but you can make your Pocket PC even more useful and fun by adding the right accessories. In writing this book, I've had the chance to try out a lot of neat Pocket PC stuff, and now it's time to let you into my playground to see which toys I like the best.

What Will and Won't Work with Your Pocket PC

Before you go out and spend your money on Pocket PC accessories, knowing what will and what won't work with your Pocket PC is pretty important. There's nothing worse than getting all excited about some great gadget, buying it, and then finding out it doesn't work. Here are some guidelines to help you avoid this disappointment:

✔ Make certain you know the type and size of your Pocket PC's expansion slot. The most common one is the CF slot, but SD expansion slots and PC Card expansion slots are also available.

✔ If you're thinking about a CF slot device, remember that some Pocket PC CF slots are Type 1 slots. Some CF devices require the thicker Type 2 slot and won't fit Pocket PCs with Type 1 slots.

✔ Type 1 CF devices can be used in Type 2 CF slots, but not the other way around.

✔ CF devices can be used in PC Card slots using an inexpensive adapter, but PC Card devices can't be made to fit a CF slot.

✔ Pocket PCs generally have a serial connection, but you may need to buy a special cable from your Pocket PC's manufacturer to connect to standard serial devices (like external modems).

✔ Even if you have the correct cable, some serial devices won't work with a Pocket PC. Anything that needs special driver software works only if it includes a driver specifically designed for the Pocket PC. Drivers intended for the version of Windows on your desktop PC won't work on your Pocket PC.

✔ Some devices are designed to work with specific Pocket PCs. If the package lists specific models but not the particular Pocket PC you own, ask before you buy (and get an assurance that you can return the item if it doesn't work for you).

One sure way to find Pocket PC accessories that work with your Pocket PC is to visit your Pocket PC manufacturer's Web site. You may even find that the manufacturer offers special deals for owners of their brand of Pocket PC.

All Pocket PCs can be expanded, but depending on the brand and model you own, your options may be limited. The following list shows the type of expansion available on some common Pocket PC models:

✔ Audiovox, Casio, and Toshiba Pocket PC 2002 systems include a CF Type 2 expansion slot. These models can use any CF expansion device compatible with Pocket PCs.

✔ The Audiovox, Casio, and Toshiba Pocket PC 2002 systems also include an SD expansion slot. This smaller size slot generally is only useful for an SD memory card.

✔ HP Pocket PCs include a CF Type 1 expansion slot. Because the Type 1 slot is thinner than the Type 2 slot, HP Pocket PCs can't use a few CF expansion devices that require Type 2 slots.

✔ HP Pocket PCs don't have an SD memory slot. This limits your ability to use a CF device at the same time as a memory card.

✔ HP, Casio, and Compaq offer expansion sleeves that enable you to add one or two extra devices to your Pocket PC. One problem with these sleeves is that they tend to add extra weight and size, thus stretching the definition of "pocket" in Pocket PC.

✔ Compaq iPAQ Pocket PCs don't include any expansion slots. If you want to add on to your iPAQ Pocket PC, you need to buy an expansion sleeve.

Adding Storage

Without any question, my favorite Pocket PC accessory is additional storage. Because Pocket PCs store everything in memory, it's easy to use up the available memory when you get carried away with adding new programs, eBooks, music, or whatever to your Pocket PC. In fact, that's one of the main hazards of being as versatile as the Pocket PC is — users tend to dream up all sorts of great things they can do with them.

As with all Pocket PC expansion options, make sure you know what type of memory card fits your Pocket PC before you buy.

Table 21-1 shows several manufacturers of memory cards for Pocket PCs.

Table 21-1	Pocket PC Memory Card Manufacturers
Manufacturer	*Web Site*
Kingston Technology Company, Inc.	`www.kingston.com/flash/compfl.asp`
PreTec Electronics Corp.	`www.pretec.com/`
SanDisk	`www.sandisk.com/cons/product.htm`

You may also want to check out the IBM Microdrive — a miniature hard drive that fits into a Type 2 CF slot. These are available in several different capacities, but only the 1GB model is really well suited for use in a Pocket PC because it was specially designed to draw less power than the lower-capacity drives.

Communications Accessories

After you add some memory to your Pocket PC, you'll probably want to add some accessories that help your Pocket PC communicate with the outside world. These accessories cover a broad range of capabilities, so I break them down into some general categories.

Adding a modem

Modems connect your Pocket PC to the Internet so you can use e-mail and browse your favorite Web sites. There are two types of modems available for the Pocket PC: wired and wireless.

Wireless modems may be cool, but they're also slow and expensive compared to wired modems. But if you just can't live without a wireless modem, you may end up wanting a wired modem, too, just so you can get stuff done faster.

Wired modems

Wired modems for the Pocket PC can be external ones that connect through the serial connector, or they can be internal ones that pop into the CF expansion slot. Each has its advantages:

- ✔ CF modems slip right into your Pocket PC so you don't have to use the serial connector. This makes for a smaller package and also allows you to use the CF modem while your Pocket PC is connected to an external keyboard.

- ✔ External modems either include a cable that plugs into your Pocket PC's serial connector or they connect directly to a serial cable that came with your Pocket PC. If you get an external modem that plugs into the serial connector, it will likely be one that you buy directly from the Pocket PC's manufacturer. If the modem uses your Pocket PC's serial cable, you may have to buy the cable separately.

- ✔ If you want to use a memory card or other device that fits into the CF expansion slot, you won't be able to use it at the same time as a CF modem.

Table 21-2 shows two manufacturers of wired modems for Pocket PCs.

Table 21-2	Pocket PC Wired Modem Manufacturers
Manufacturer	*Web Site*
PreTec Electronics Corp.	www.pretec.com/
Socket	www.socketcom.com/

If you have a serial cable for your Pocket PC, you can use almost any external modem — you don't need a special Pocket PC–compatible external modem.

Wireless modems

Wireless modems let your Pocket PC connect anywhere — sort of. You can connect anywhere as long as that "anywhere" is within the coverage area of your wireless service provider and you can get a strong enough signal.

Getting a wireless modem that actually works with a Pocket PC can be a real adventure. One reason is that so far, few wireless modems fit CF expansion slots. Most wireless modems fit PC Card slots, but these can be used only with a PC Card expansion sleeve. There is a wireless modem that fits onto the back of an HP Jornada series Pocket PC.

In reality, your best bet on getting a wireless modem that works with your Pocket PC may be to get the modem from the wireless service provider — that way you can be sure of getting a unit that is supported by the service provider.

Table 21-3 shows several sources of wireless modems for Pocket PCs.

Table 21-3	Pocket PC Wireless Modem Sources
Manufacturer	*Web Site*
GoAmerica	www.goamerica.com
Sierra Wireless	www.sierrawireless.com/
Verizon Wireless	www.verizonwireless.com
Novatel	www.novatelwireless.com

Another way to get high-speed wireless Internet access (as well as cell phone service in the same package) is to buy one of the new Audiovox Maestro Pocket PC models that has the wireless modem and cell-phone circuitry built in. Both Verizon Wireless and Sprint PCS will be selling these units at special prices when you order a service plan.

Adding a digital phone card

If you already have a digital cell phone, you probably have most of what you need to connect your Pocket PC to the Internet wirelessly. Using your cell phone as your Pocket PC's wireless Internet connection makes a lot of sense for several reasons:

✔ If you use a wireless modem to connect your Pocket PC to the Internet, you need to pay for a separate (and expensive) connection.

✔ If you use a digital phone card to connect your Pocket PC to the Internet through your cell phone, you can use the unused airtime from your cell phone for your connection, and you probably won't have to pay extra to access the Internet. This can save you tons of money each month.

✔ Digital phone cards are typically far less expensive than wireless modems, but provide connections that are just as fast as those of wireless modems.

✔ Digital phone cards generally use the CF slot, which makes them compatible with most Pocket PCs. Wireless modems are either built-in, designed for a specific Pocket PC, or too big for most Pocket PCs.

Table 21-4 shows some sources of digital phone cards for Pocket PCs.

Table 21-4	Pocket PC Digital Phone Card Sources
Manufacturer	*Web Site*
Socket Communications	www.socketcom.com/
Mobile Planet	www.mobileplanet.com/

You may also want to look in the accessory catalog from your Pocket PC's manufacturer to see whether they offer something similar to a digital phone card. The Casio Pocket PC accessory catalog, for example, offers a cable that connects the Casio Pocket PCs to the same types of cell phones that a digital phone card would.

If you have an Audiovox Maestro Pocket PC and an Audiovox CDM-9000 cell phone, look no further than the box that held your Pocket PC — the necessary cable is right in the box.

Connecting to your network

Your Pocket PC normally connects to your desktop PC using a USB connection, or in some cases using a standard serial connection. You may find that these types of connections simply aren't convenient in your case. If so, you can also connect using an Ethernet adapter in your Pocket PC to make a network connection. In fact, you can use ActiveSync to synchronize your Pocket PC over your network.

If all you need to do is connect your Pocket PC and your desktop PC, you need a crossover cable or a crossover coupling between the two. If you want to use a standard network cable, you need to connect your Pocket PC to the network hub or switch rather than directly to your desktop PC.

A network connection is probably faster than either a USB or standard serial connection when you're transferring files. But unless you've added a very large capacity memory card to your Pocket PC and are moving a huge amount of data, this won't make much of a difference.

Table 21-5 shows two manufacturers of network cards for Pocket PCs.

Table 21-5	Pocket PC Network Card Manufacturers
Manufacturer	*Web Site*
PreTec Electronics Corp.	www.pretec.com/
Socket Communications	www.socketcom.com/

Don't forget that network connections can be wireless, too. Proxim (www.proxim.com), for example, makes the excellent Harmony line of 802.11b wireless networking products, which can enable you to roam up to 1,000 feet from the wireless access point and still connect to your network and the Internet.

Getting Directions via Satellite

One of the most interesting accessories you can add to your Pocket PC is a GPS receiver. This accessory lets you know exactly where you are and makes sure that you can go virtually anywhere without getting lost. Originally designed for military use, the GPS system has proven to be a great tool for anyone who hates to rely on someone else's terrible directions.

Stand-alone GPS receivers have been around for several years, but using one to find your way required you to learn to navigate using latitude and longitude. Sure, some of the more expensive models have included crude maps, but they certainly weren't very complete and useful.

By connecting a GPS receiver to your Pocket PC, you suddenly have a very useful tool. Not only do you have the precision of knowing your exact location, but you've also got the detailed maps that your Pocket PC can display in color. Throw in voice prompts to tell you when to turn and you've got a real winner.

If you're going to use a GPS receiver with your Pocket PC, buy the largest capacity memory card you can. That way you're able to store several maps to cover your entire trip and still have room to store additional files on your Pocket PC.

Table 21-6 lists several manufacturers of Pocket PC–compatible GPS receivers and associated navigation software.

Table 21-6	Pocket PC GPS Receivers
Manufacturer	*Web Site*
Pharos	www.pharosgps.com
PreTec Electronics Corp.	www.pretec.com/
Teletype	www.teletype.com/

Adding a Keyboard

Any time you use a PC, you interact with it by inputting information. It doesn't really matter whether you're using a Pocket PC or a desktop PC — you still need a way to let the computer know what you want it to do.

The Pocket PC presents both unique challenges and unique opportunities with regards to input. As a result, some very interesting input accessories have appeared.

Your Pocket PC offers two primary means of inputting information. You can tap out words using the onscreen keyboard, or you can write on the screen. Both methods work, of course, but when you need to enter a lot of information, you'll soon be looking for another option. That option can be a real keyboard like the one on your desktop PC.

I've found several possible ways to add a keyboard to your Pocket PC. Each has features that may make it your favorite Pocket PC keyboard accessory:

✔ Several manufacturers have created tiny slip-on keyboards for the HP, Compaq, and Symbol Pocket PCs. These will really tax your patience, but you can find what's available at the Mobile Planet store (www.mobileplanet.com).

✔ The **KeySync** keyboard from **iBIZ** (www.ibizcorp.com) is a real keyboard that has been shrunk into just over half the space required by most desktop PC keyboards. This keyboard is quite convenient to take with you on a trip and easy to use because it has the feel of a desktop PC keyboard.

✔ **Targus** (www.targus.com) offers a folding keyboard for the Pocket PC. This is by far the smallest Pocket PC keyboard when it's folded, but that size makes the Targus keyboard a bit harder to use because you can't really type with it on your lap. Also, because the Targus keyboard connects directly to the connector on the bottom of your Pocket PC, each model is specific to one brand of Pocket PC.

Powering Your Way to Freedom

This next accessory isn't as cool or neat as some of the ones you've seen earlier in this chapter, but it's still something no Pocket PC user should be without. Pocket PCs all run on batteries, and they're automatically recharged whenever your Pocket PC is placed into the synchronization cradle. And because your Pocket PC uses very aggressive power management, in normal use, a Pocket PC runs a long time — anywhere from five to ten hours — on a single charge.

Okay, so your Pocket PC runs a long time on a charge, but that doesn't mean it can run forever. Eventually the batteries need to be recharged or your Pocket PC will die. And because you can't just pop in a fresh set of batteries from the drugstore, you have to bring your Pocket PC home and place it into the synchronization cradle for refueling.

Power from your car

So what does this have to do with a great Pocket PC accessory? Simple — you need a second power adapter for your Pocket PC so you can charge up the batteries no matter where you are. I recommend one that plugs into your car's cigarette lighter so you can use your Pocket PC while you're traveling. You may also want to buy a second AC adapter so you don't have to unplug the one on your desk.

The best source of power adapters for your Pocket PC is your Pocket PC's manufacturer. But if you'll be traveling in foreign countries, you'll also want to go to the iGo Web site (www.igo.com) to pick up the necessary plug adapters and transformers so you can use different voltages without harming your Pocket PC.

Power from the sun

Your Pocket PC could be a great camping and hiking companion. It's small, it can entertain you, and it can help you to know where you are so you don't get lost. There's just one problem — when the battery runs down in your Pocket PC everything stops working. And unless your idea of a great campsite is your own backyard, finding a place to plug in the Pocket PC's power brick can be a real adventure when you're out camping.

The solution is right there all around you — use the sun to power your Pocket PC. With the help of one of the really cool solar power units I found, you can sit out at a primitive campground for weeks and still be able to use your Pocket PC. Here are the details:

- The **Pocket Pal** solar charger (www.plastecs.com) is a small, inexpensive, folding unit that fits into a space even smaller than your Pocket PC. In full sunlight this unit can charge your Pocket PC in a couple of hours, and would be the perfect companion to a Pocket PC with a CF GPS receiver. For most models of Pocket PCs, the Pocket Pal simply plugs into the power jack on the Pocket PC, but some models require a special adapter. You'll find full details at the Web site.

✔ The **Sun Catcher Sport** (www.powerexperts.com) is a bit larger and more expensive than the Pocket Pal, but it also has some really nifty features that may make it a better choice — depending on your needs. The Sun Catcher Sport uses its solar cells to charge a 1250 ma, 12 volt battery, and it is this battery that powers your Pocket PC, cell phone, or whatever else you want to plug into its cigarette lighter jack. The rechargeable battery also means that the Sun Catcher Sport can do something few solar cells can do — it can power your equipment even when there is no sun! Remember, though, that you'll need the 12 volt power cord that powers your Pocket PC from the cigarette lighter to use the Sun Catcher Sport.

With one of these solar power units you can travel anywhere and never worry about finding the right electrical outlet to power your Pocket PC. Nor will you have to trail along several miles of extension cord when you go hiking or camping.

Emergency power packs

Have you ever considered that batteries must be made by Murphy and Company? How else could you possibly explain the fact that batteries will always pick the absolute worst time to go dead. For example, suppose you were using your Pocket PC to give that important presentation to some potentially very big customers — can you imagine a worse time for your Pocket PC's batteries to go dead? And, of course, that would be precisely the one time when you would forget to bring the Pocket PC's power brick, too, wouldn't it?

One excellent way around this potential mess is to bring along some emergency power in the form of an Instant Power Charger from Electric Fuel (www.electric-fuel.com). These ingenious devices contain a special type of battery — known as a *zinc-air battery* — which remains fresh and ready to use for years. Zinc-air batteries are activated by opening the package and allowing air to enter the battery pack. Until they are opened, the battery simply sits there without going flat.

Each Instant Power Charger has a SmartCord designed to fit a specific device, and a disposable PowerCartridge you can replace after it is used up. The PowerCartridge is good for about three complete recharges of your Pocket PC, and can be resealed to store any unused capacity for up to three months.

The entire Instant Power Charger is about half the size of your Pocket PC, so it's easy to slip into your pocket and bring along for those emergencies that can pop up at the worst possible time. And these batteries aren't made by Murphy and Company.

Cases for Your Pocket PC

Your Pocket PC probably came with a simple little leather or vinyl case — or maybe a flip-up panel — to protect its screen when you slip it into your pocket. You've probably noticed, however, that while the solution the manufacturer provided does protect your Pocket PC, it really leaves something to be desired in terms of utility and convenience. If so, you may want to consider getting something that was designed with your needs in mind.

Cases for protection

Cases to fit your Pocket PC come in all sorts of different styles. There are the minimalist cases provided by the Pocket PC's manufacturer; there are hard shell metal cases designed to protect your Pocket PC from extreme conditions; and there are large, more elaborate cases that can hold your Pocket PC, a cell phone, and even a quick change of clothes (if you pack light).

One thing you may want to watch for when buying a case for your Pocket PC is a belt loop so you don't always have to try stuffing everything into your pocket. For some reason, none of the Pocket PC manufacturers seem to include this highly useful feature in the cases they supply with their Pocket PCs.

I've found a couple of great sources for cases to fit your Pocket PC:

✔ **RhinoSkin** (www.rhinoskin.com) makes a number of styles of cases. Their cases tend to take a minimalist approach to pack the best protection into the smallest size. One of their more popular styles is the aluminum and titanium Slider case, which should protect your Pocket PC from just about any reasonable threat.

✔ **RoadWired** (www.roadwired.com) has a broad range of different cases to suit many different needs. You can get a simple case that clips onto your belt, or one that has 20 different pockets and compartments so you can bring along your Pocket PC, your cell phone, and any other assorted gadgets you may need. If you can't find a case at RoadWired to fit all of your gear, maybe you need to pack a little lighter!

Digital input with the SmartPad

The Seiko SmartPad (www.seikosmart.com) is a Pocket PC case but with a unique twist that no one else can match. The SmartPad (which I mentioned earlier in Chapter 3) includes a digital pen that you can use to draw on an ordinary pad of paper. Almost magically, whatever you draw on the paper instantly appears on your Pocket PC's screen. If this isn't the coolest way to create notes and draw on your Pocket PC, I don't know what is.

The SmartPad comes in two different models to fit different types of Pocket PCs. The original — simply known as the SmartPad — works with Pocket PCs that have their infrared port on the top. This model also includes a pocket along the side for your cell phone. The newer model — cleverly called the SmartPad II — gives up the cell phone pocket but allows you to move the infrared emitter so it can work with a Pocket PC no matter where its infrared port may be.

The SmartPad also includes an overlay that you can place under the pad of paper. This overlay includes a small keyboard that you'll find much easier to use than the Pocket PC's onscreen keyboard.

Mobile Mounts for More Convenience

If you've ever tried to use your Pocket PC to help navigate while you were driving, you no doubt realize that holding your Pocket PC in one hand while you drive with the other hand is not the best idea ever. Not only is it pretty difficult to do, but it's also pretty hard to explain when you run into the back end of a patrol car.

The manufacturers of GPS receivers and navigation software always warn you about the dangers of trying to use your Pocket PC while you're driving. These warnings aren't something to ignore — driving does require your full concentration. I'm telling you about these mobile Pocket PC mounts only because I know that you will heed the warnings and act sensibly when using your Pocket PC — otherwise you wouldn't be reading this book!

I've found two sources of mobile mounts for your Pocket PC:

- The **MagnaHolder** from **Pharos** (www.pharosgps.com) is a clever little holder that clips to the air conditioning vent on your car's dashboard. This holder has two powerful magnets in the mount, and a small metal plate that sticks onto the back of your Pocket PC. All of your Pocket PC's ports remain usable when it is sitting on the MagnaHolder, and the magnet holds your Pocket PC securely while allowing you to easily remove your Pocket PC when you park your car.

- **Arkon Resources** (www.arkon.com) makes a number of different mounts that can clip to your dash or stick to your windshield using suction cups. The various Arkon mobile mounts use a unique system of spring-loaded, movable padded jaws to hold your Pocket PC, and they even include a handy stylus so you don't have to try getting the one out of your Pocket PC. If Arkon doesn't have a mobile mount that works in your vehicle, maybe it's finally time to replace that horse-drawn cart.

Sending Pocket PC Sound to Your Radio

Your Pocket PC can produce really great sound, but you would never know it by listening to the tiny little speaker that is built into it. Listening to head-phones plugged into your Pocket PC can easily prove that to you. One way to take advantage of the great sound that's just waiting to get out of your Pocket PC is to play the output through an FM radio. This could be the radio in your car, a boombox at the beach, or any other sound system that has a radio receiver attached.

Your Pocket PC is capable of producing stereo sound, but the built-in speaker is monaural only. Anything you connect to the earphone jack on your Pocket PC gets a stereo signal.

In addition to the obvious benefit of sending music from your Pocket PC to a radio, remember that if you use a GPS receiver and navigation software, you can send the voice prompts to your radio, too. This would also work well for audio books.

The SoundFeeder from Arkon (www.arkon.com) provides a simple and inex-pensive means of sending the sound from your Pocket PC to a nearby FM radio. In addition to the SoundFeeder, Arkon also makes several mobile mounts that have the SoundFeeder built in.

Connecting Your Pocket PC to a Big-Screen Display

Let's face it. Your Pocket PC's screen is simply too small to use when you want to give a presentation to a group of people. Not even the people in the front row would be able to read your PowerPoint slide show (although for some of the PowerPoint shows I've seen that might be considered a blessing). If you're going to show what's on your Pocket PC's screen to a crowd, you really need a bigger display.

Well, you *could* pass your Pocket PC around the room, but that doesn't make for a very lively show, does it? Besides, what happens when the guy in the fifth row decides he wants to see what else this neat little gadget can do? There goes your show.

A much better idea than trying to make everyone crowd around your Pocket PC is simply to send the show to something quite a bit larger. The problem, of course, is that your Pocket PC doesn't seem to have any way to connect to a bigger display. But as you have no doubt guessed, I have found ways to cor-rect this little problem.

There are two different manufacturers who make cards that fit your Pocket PC's CF slot and allow it to output to a large display:

✔ The **Presenter-to-Go** from **Margi** (www.margi.com) is a handy little unit that can display output from your Pocket PC on a large-screen monitor or through a digital projector. The Presenter-to-Go comes with a business card–sized infrared remote so you can control the display from several feet away.

✔ The **Voyager VGA CF** from **Colorgraphic** (www.colorgraphic.net) works very much like the Presenter-to-Go, although the Voyager VGA CF can also be connected to a TV set for those times when a large monitor or digital projector is unavailable.

Chapter 17 covers both of these options in more detail.

If you want to display content from your Pocket PC on your monitor, but don't want to spend a bunch of money on a piece of hardware, you might want to consider downloading a copy of Remote Display Control for Pocket PC. This free download (www.microsoft.com/mobile/pocketpc/downloads/powertoys.asp) is one of the Microsoft Powertoys for the Pocket PC. With the Remote Display Control you can zoom the Pocket PC display on your monitor up to three times normal size — although zooming doesn't increase the resolution of the display. Since Remote Display Control works through your ActiveSync connection, you don't need to buy any special hardware, either.

Getting the Most from Your Pocket PC

The final item on my list of the best Pocket PC accessories is *Pocket PC For Dummies,* 2nd Edition. If you want to get the most value and fun from your Pocket PC, this book is simply the best accessory of all. Where else are you going to find out about all of the neat things your Pocket PC can do? Who else is going to show you all the great little tricks that make your Pocket PC easier to use? Where else are you going to find all those great *The 5th Wave* cartoons?

Chapter 22

Ten Great Pocket PC Business Programs

*O*ne of the most exciting things about a Pocket PC is its ability to be expanded by adding new programs. In writing this book I've encountered a lot of really neat business-related programs that can make your Pocket PC do even more for you. In this chapter I show you a quick sampling of some of those programs. Remember, though, that this is just a sampling rather than a comprehensive listing. With the Pocket PC growing in popularity every day, it just isn't possible to cover everything.

PrintBoy CE

Your Pocket PC lacks a very important function that you almost certainly take for granted on your desktop PC: printing. Your Pocket PC has to rely on your desktop PC when you want to print out a document.

PrintBoy CE from Bachmann Software (www.bachmannsoftware.com) enables you to print directly from your Pocket PC. Figure 22-1 shows the opening screen for PrintBoy CE when I'm about to print from my Pocket PC.

PrintBoy CE automatically finds any Pocket Word, Pocket Excel, or e-mail files on your Pocket PC. You can then select the files you want to print.

Figure 22-1:
With
PrintBoy CE,
you can
print from
your Pocket
PC.

  If you have a connection to your network — either wired or wireless — select Network PC with shared printer or Network: IP printer in PrintBoy CE's Port list box to use that printer. You'll need to know the name of the computer as well as the name of the printer to make the connection. You can find the correct printer name in the desktop PC's Printers folder.

Surerange Pocket Database

Databases are very important tools for most businesses. Almost everyone needs to keep track of lists of related information, and a database program is the perfect way to keep a lot of information organized in an easy-to-use fashion.

Even though your Pocket PC comes loaded with pocket versions of the most common applications in Microsoft Office, it doesn't include Pocket Access. There is a version of Pocket Access available, but it's not intended for use on the Pocket PC.

Surerange (www.surerange.com) has stepped in with a program called Pocket Database, which fulfills your need for a database program that runs on your Pocket PC.

Surerange also produces CEQuery, a program that enables you to perform *SQL* (Structured Query Language) queries on databases. SQL is one of the most well-known and powerful database query languages. CEQuery brings the power of SQL to the Pocket PC, which puts incredible power in the palm of your hand.

Surerange Custom Convert

Life would be simpler if everyone always used the same units of measurement. They don't, of course, so it's often necessary to be able to convert from one unit to another. Surerange's Custom Convert (www.surerange.com) is a nifty little program that has hundreds of common and not-so-common conversion factors built right in. With this program you never have to remember the exact ratio of one unit to another; you simply select the two units, enter the quantity in the first unit, and you get your answer immediately.

Figure 22-2 shows an example where I'm using Custom Convert to calculate the beverages for my next party.

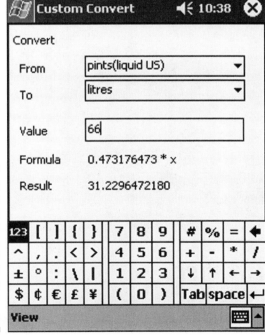

Figure 22-2: Custom Convert helps you make all sorts of useful conversions on your Pocket PC.

Developer One Agenda Fusion

If you use your Pocket PC to help you keep track of a busy schedule, you've probably wished you could see a bit more of your schedule at a quick glance. The Developer One Agenda Fusion (www.developerone.com/) makes this and a number of other scheduling tasks far easier.

Figure 22-3 shows just one example of how Agenda Fusion improves on your scheduling options. Here I'm able to view my agenda for today and also see what's on the schedule for the rest of the week. In addition to simply showing your schedule, Agenda Fusion can help you manage your contacts, set alarms, and generally make keeping track of a busy life a whole lot easier.

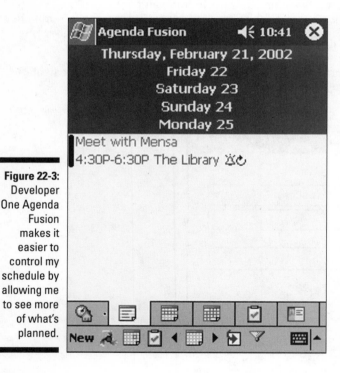

Figure 22-3: Developer One Agenda Fusion makes it easier to control my schedule by allowing me to see more of what's planned.

Conduits Pocket Artist

Conduits (www.conduits.com/) produces a number of very useful Pocket PC applications. Figure 22-4 shows one of these, Pocket Artist. With this program you can view and manipulate various types of image files right on your Pocket PC. The latest version can even read and write Photoshop PSD files and has support for multiple layers.

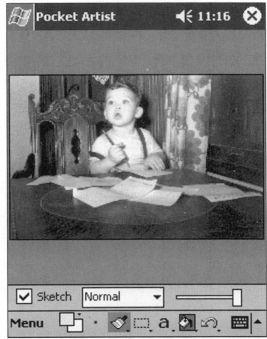

Figure 22-4: Pocket Artist makes it possible to work on graphic image files on your Pocket PC.

Arc Second PocketCAD Pro

Arc Second PocketCAD Pro (www.PocketCAD.com) is a fairly specialized program that shows just how versatile a Pocket PC really is. If you happen to be a builder, an engineer, an architect, an inspector, or anyone else who routinely depends on blueprints or other technical drawings, you know how cumbersome carrying around huge printouts can be. With PocketCAD Pro you can carry those drawings right inside your Pocket PC. Not only that, but with PocketCAD Pro you can create or edit those drawings on the spot and then share the drawings with any AutoCAD-compatible program on your desktop PC.

Figure 22-5 shows Arc Second PocketCAD Pro displaying a portion of a blueprint.

TIP

Use the Tools⇨Options command to automatically hide the PocketCAD Pro toolbars so that you have a much larger working area.

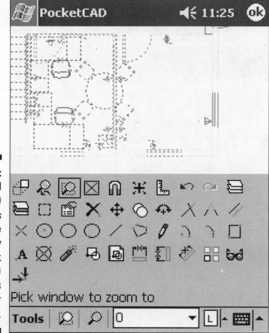

Figure 22-5: Arc Second PocketCAD Pro gives you the ability to work on CAD drawings on your Pocket PC.

CNetX Pocket SlideShow

CNetX Pocket SlideShow (www.cnetx.com) is another of those programs that can really demonstrate just how much power your Pocket PC holds. This program enables you to bring along PowerPoint presentations on your Pocket PC, and then show them on the Pocket PC's screen or on a large screen using a tool like the Colorgraphic Voyager VGA CF or the Margi Presenter-to-Go. You can create self-running slide shows and even use fancy transition effects between slides.

Figure 22-6 shows CNetX Pocket SlideShow displaying one of the slides in a presentation produced by the Nevada Film Office (www.nevadafilm.com) and used here by permission of the Deputy Director, Robin Holabird.

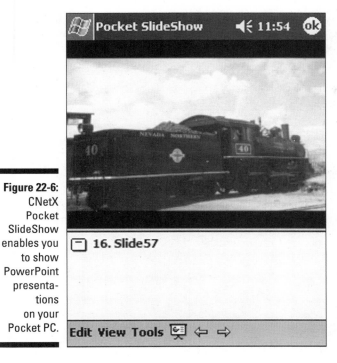

Figure 22-6:
CNetX
Pocket
SlideShow
enables you
to show
PowerPoint
presenta-
tions
on your
Pocket PC.

Handheld Speech Lookup

Lookup from Handheld Speech (www.handheldspeech.com) is one of those amazing Pocket PC programs that just makes so much sense, you wonder why it isn't a standard item on all Pocket PCs. This program uses voice recognition to listen to your commands and look up, call, or send an e-mail to anyone in your Contact list. This is also the program that will make your friends realize that they should have a Pocket PC rather than one of those other things.

Figure 22-7 shows Handheld Speech Lookup after I asked it to find the record for one of our employees.

Developer One CodeWallet Pro

CodeWallet Pro from Developer One (www.developerone.com) enables you to securely store all of the important information you need on a daily basis. This includes things like credit card numbers, user names, passwords, phone numbers you don't want anyone to know, and so on. Now you can feel safe about storing this type of information on your Pocket PC without worrying that someone else will be able to access it.

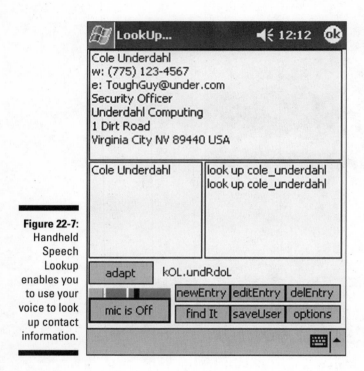

Figure 22-7:
Handheld
Speech
Lookup
enables you
to use your
voice to look
up contact
information.

Figure 22-8 shows CodeWallet Pro in action after I've unlocked the data by entering my password.

FieldSoftware PocketPixPrint

PocketPixPrint from FieldSoftware (www.fieldsoftware.com) makes it possible to print images from your Pocket PC using an infrared-equipped printer or by printing to a shared printer on your network. FieldSoftware also offers a program, PrintPocketCE, which is similar to the Bachmann PrintBoy CE I mentioned earlier in this chapter. However, both of those programs are intended for printing Pocket Word, Pocket Excel, and e-mail files. PocketPixPrint prints copies of any image files found on your Pocket PC.

Figure 22-9 shows PocketPixPrint as I'm getting ready to print an image file.

Figure 22-8:
CodeWallet
Pro makes
it possible
to keep
sensitive
information
on your
Pocket PC
away from
prying eyes.

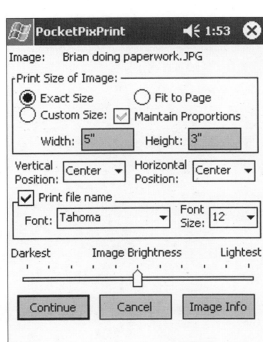

Figure 22-9:
PocketPix-
Print prints
image
files directly
from your
Pocket PC.

Chapter 23

Ten Great Pocket PC Games

In This Chapter

▶ Fun, new games

▶ Classic game favorites

Computers make great game machines, and your Pocket PC is certainly no exception. With super graphics, great sound, and small size, it's no wonder that so many people have been developing games for the Pocket PC.

When I was setting about to do this chapter, the biggest problem I had was simply in deciding which games to leave out. It's just a fact that there are hundreds of really neat and fun games that run on the Pocket PC. As a result, I had to be somewhat arbitrary and I may have left out your favorite. Well, the truth is that authors simply don't have a lot of time to play, and I couldn't test every game. Even so, I think you'll have to agree that I've found some pretty cool stuff.

Oh, and remember that I'm not ranking the games. Their relative position within the chapter is simply random. It's up to you to decide which of these seems interesting to you. So let's play!

Sim City 2000

Sim City 2000 from Zio (www.ziosoft.com) is a very addictive game. In this game you are in charge of building and running a city. You control what is built, the local amenities, taxes, and even disasters such as floods and tornados. Along the way, citizens move in or out, industries thrive or fail, and you get to be the hero or the goat.

Figure 23-1 shows the beginning of a city I created (which was later destroyed when several natural disasters struck). I don't think I'm going to run for mayor any time soon.

Figure 23-1:
In Sim City
2000 you
build and
control
virtual cities
on your
Pocket PC.

Arcade Park

If you still long for the old classics like Arkanoid, Asteroids, Black Shark, and Pacman, you'll want to check out Arcade Park from C-eon (www.c-eon.com). These games are about as different from Sim City 2000 as possible. The games in Arcade Park are all about frantic, fast reactions and trying to beat the computer. Believe me, once you start playing these games, you'll be glad that your Pocket PC doesn't have a slot for quarters!

Figure 23-2 shows me in the middle of losing another game of Arkanoid.

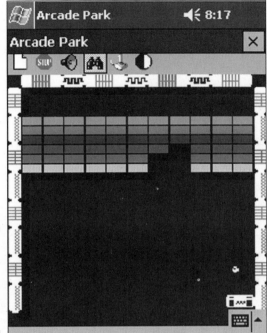

Strategic Assault

Strategic Assault (www.strategicassault.com) could be described as Sim City gone military. In Strategic Assault, you are responsible for gathering resources, building an army and bases, and defeating your enemy. This is one of those games where you really need to keep track of the details or you'll soon find your base is being destroyed and you have nothing left to defend it.

Figure 23-3 shows how Strategic Assault looks as I'm about to start another round (and end up getting pounded again).

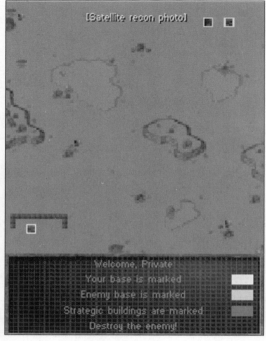

Figure 23-3:
Strategic
Assault
makes you
plan your
moves
carefully so
you don't
lose
everything.

Pocket Gambler

Pocket Gambler from Zio (www.ziosoft.com) is a totally different genre from the games I've mentioned so far. Pocket Gambler includes seven different casino games including Caribbean Poker, Blackjack, Baccarat, Video Poker, Slot Machine, Roulette, and Craps. Whether you want to play any of these games just for fun or to become a better player for when you visit a real casino, Pocket Gambler will certainly keep you playing. It's also a lot less expensive than playing the games in a casino, too.

Figure 23-4 shows the Caribbean Poker game as the dealer is just starting to hand out the cards.

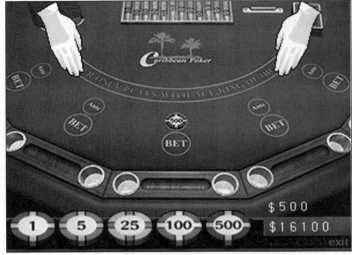

Figure 23-4:
Pocket Gambler is almost as much fun as visiting a casino in person.

Turjah

Turjah from Jimmy Software (www.jimmysoftware.com) is a space battle game where you must defend the Earth from the Turjah invaders. In this game, you are faced with a whole fleet of enemy fighters and you must maneuver your spacecraft and shoot them down. It sounds easy until you try it, and then you're hooked.

Figure 23-5 shows a game of Turjah where my fighter is about to be wiped out by a pack of approaching craft.

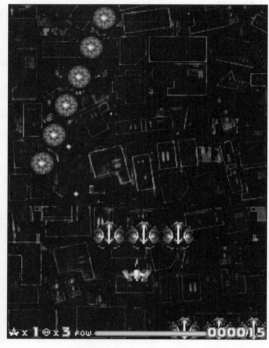

Figure 23-5:
You must defend the Earth from the invading Turjah fighters.

Tennis Addict

Tennis Addict from Hexacto (www.hexacto.com) engages you in a totally different and non-violent type of competition. In this game you play tennis against a very realistic opponent, and you can choose all sorts of game details down to the responsiveness of your racket and the type of court where the match will be held. And you don't have to worry about an angry player throwing his racket at you when you play Tennis Addict.

Figure 23-6 shows the early stages of a Tennis Addict match before I'm completely swamped.

Figure 23-6: Tennis Addict places you in a very realistic competition on a variety of different tennis courts.

Infectious Ground

Infectious Ground from Ludigames (`www.infectiousground.com`) is a futuristic shoot-em-up full of monsters, chain guns, rockets, and other fun stuff. If you're just dying to blast some ugly beasts into a million pieces, Infectious Ground is definitely right up your alley!

Figure 23-7 shows a scene from Infectious Ground where I'm just about to blast a roach.

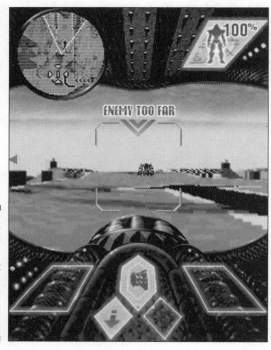

Figure 23-7:
In Infectious
Ground you
get to blast
away and
never have
to clean up
your mess.

Rayman

Rayman from Ludigames (`www.raymanpocket.com`) is a fun game that you won't feel bad about allowing your kids to play — although I wish you good luck at getting your Pocket PC back from them! In this game, you are Rayman and you must find your way through a series of different scenes by running, jumping, climbing, and riding on magic plums. This is an excellent adaptation of one of the classic game-console favorites and will keep you playing for hours.

Figure 23-8 shows a scene from Rayman where I'm about to start looking for the treasures that are to be found along the way.

Figure 23-8:
Rayman is a
fun game
that is
suitable for
all ages.

Full Hand Casino

Full Hand Casino from Hexacto (www.hexacto.com) is another example of a game that works very well on the Pocket PC. Full Hand Casino includes Blackjack, Roulette, Slot Machine, and Video Poker. If you're anything like me, you'll end up spending far too much time in the Full Hand Casino (but at least you don't have to put up real money for your bankroll).

Figure 23-9 shows one of the reasons why I really enjoy Full Hand Casino.

Crossword

Crossword from Jimmy Software (www.jimmysoftware.com) is a game for people who would rather sit and exercise their minds. It's not an exciting adventure game, but it's perfect if you want a stimulating challenge.

Figure 23-10 shows Crossword after I've managed to figure out a few words.

Okay, so in this chapter I've only been able to show you a small sampling of the great games you can play on your Pocket PC. Even after seeing so few of the games you should still be able to tell that the Pocket PC has a lot of potential as a great game platform.

Most Pocket PC games are available in a try-before-you-buy option. Some have demo versions while others are shareware. Go ahead and check them out — you'll end up having a lot more fun with your Pocket PC than you thought possible.

Figure 23-10:
Crossword may not have high adventure, but it's quite a challenge.

Index

• F •

• *U* •

• *V* •